Francisco Valdés-Ugalde
Democracy in Latin America

Latin America in Perspective

Society, Culture and Politics

Edited by
Rebecca Lemos Igreja and Camilo Negri

Volume 2

Francisco Valdés-Ugalde

Democracy in Latin America

The Failure of Inclusion and the
Emergence of Autocratization

DE GRUYTER

Colégio Latino-Americano
de Estudos Mundiais

FLACSO
BRASIL

ISBN 978-3-11-163129-5
e-ISBN (PDF) 978-3-11-077367-5
e-ISBN (EPUB) 978-3-11-077379-8
ISSN 2749-9367

Library of Congress Control Number: 2023941016

Bibliographic information published by the Deutsche Nationalbibliothek
The Deutsche Nationalbibliothek lists this publication in the Deutsche Nationalbibliografie;
detailed bibliographic data are available on the internet at http://dnb.dnb.de.

© 2024 Walter de Gruyter GmbH, Berlin/Boston
This volume is text- and page-identical with the hardback published in 2023.
Cover image: TA/iStock/Getty Images Plus
Typesetting: Integra Software Services Pvt. Ltd.

www.degruyter.com

Contents

List of figures

https://doi.org/10.1515/9783110773675-203

List of tables

https://doi.org/10.1515/9783110773675-204

Introduction

> It is not true that men are born free and everywhere they are in chains. Men are
> born infants, dependent and therefore unfree.
> Kalman H. Silvert

The reader has before him a book that lies halfway between specialized analysis and political theory. The reason for having written it this way is quite straightforward: Understanding the reality of a region of the world is not only a task of scrupulously collecting and measuring "hard" data under a certain scientific approach; it also involves capturing the mood of an era. Democracy in the world is suffering from fatigue that comes from the exhaustion of its forces and engines to carry out the task that is ever present and not always recognized by its actors: the inclusion of all citizens in political decisions through suitable mechanisms. The duo *doxa* and *episteme* are always present in the scientific knowledge of political reality. They are inseparable and, at the same time, distinct. Showing the relationship and differentiation between them depends on the intellectual rigor of those who offer explanations of the human world, but their convergence is inevitable whatever the methodology and honesty of the approach.

This book arises from the conviction that the democratic agenda is far from being exhausted or resolved in scientific and political debates. In fact, this agenda is being updated today in multiple new conflicts that political regimes, democratic and non-democratic, must face, both because of the pluralization of identities and social groupings and because of the international arrangement of forces that is taking place *as we speak*. The shaping of the contemporary political order is occurring within a world very different from the one that was forged after World War II and during the Cold War and its aftermath. Deprived of the safeguards and sentinels that sustained the world in the now-extinct balance between geopolitical blocs and increasingly on the defensive, democratic political systems today face their nemesis: autocracies that sprout like grafts that have taken root in the seedbeds of resentment and encouraged by an anger that resorts to old and decadent doctrines to challenge democratic canons as the culprit of its ills. Likewise, great authoritarian systems, such as China and Russia, almost all of Africa -which has surprised the world with a considerable democratic evolution- and not a few Asian countries are experiencing social mobilizations in favor of freedom and political openness that come up against resistance and repression from the beneficiaries of autocracies. Everywhere we see crises and worrying symptoms of decadence in the old democracies born of the French and American revolutions, and in Latin America we observe their late flowering and early decadence, the latter in parallel with the former. We should ask ourselves – not without cautious optimism – whether this

https://doi.org/10.1515/9783110773675-001

decline is of democracy or the particular institutional forms on which it was based in the 19th and 20th centuries. For the reasons given and the evidence found, this book embraces an idea that dares to suggest that, in the midst of a chaotic, polysemic, and dissonant present, paths are opening for a transformation of democracy as an institutional system and that many of the crises it is experiencing are the result of Demos -also touched by the evils of time- trying to move away from the exhausted forms of a Kratia that has become toxic. In this journey of no return, this infant sovereign, polymorphous and perverse (as Freud said about childhood), plays with destructive and constructive forms, and will have to choose the materials that will build the systems of (self-) government that each idea of himself provides. Nothing now can foretell a better future, but the materials to make it happen are at hand, as are the weapons of self-destruction.

In addition to these symptoms of internal crisis, we should mention the international challenge that democracy is facing from forces located in the South and the East that claim to hold the key to the "true path": autocratic, one-party systems or redeeming despots who claim to place the most cherished values of societies above aspirations considered elitist, bourgeois, or stateless because they identify with the struggle in favor of personal autonomy and political freedom, as if these were the cause of the disease. The resentment of the universal -to which post-imperial and post-national globalization has brought us closer- has activated the primitive triggers of fear of the unknown and the return to the womb of ancient religious and secular pastoralism. We are a far cry from the creative and exemplary impulses of democracy's constitutive moments, such as freedom and individual or collective autonomy, as we face patrimonial despotism and theocratic and ideocratic doctrines. Formulating this concern as a question, "Are we not at the edge of a historical form that has been spent, that needs to reinvent itself applying an imagination that eludes the muses of democracy?"

It is paradoxical that this international factor should be so highly internalized in public spheres. On a scale perhaps never before experienced, even if it has its equivalents in the mutations of the great empires of the past, every "anomalous" political event -if there is such a thing as "normality"- in one fabric of the globe affects other distant cells belonging to bodies that are only apparently alien. How else can we understand the general commotion over Viet Nam, the Tiananmen massacre, the attack on the Twin Towers, the globalization of the Sars-Cov-2 pandemic, the invasion of Ukraine, the dismal violence in Latin America, or climatic disasters? The aversion we feel when faced with autocrats who ooze from corrupt political bodies, or the jubilation over freedoms won, or great scientific discoveries have become shared feelings beyond where they occur, because they represent signs of what may happen in other places with which they share their being and their time and that by their effects are added to our existence. Perhaps this has always been the history of places isolated by geographical boundaries, but today there is no corner of the planet that is radically cut off from the rest of the world. The political and communicative sphere is a cosmopolitan fact marked by virtues and defects that provide difficult dilemmas for political decisions. When Max Weber contrasted the ethics of conviction from the ethics of responsibility (Weber, 2004) -a distinction that Machiavelli had previously noticed when he re-interpreted the classical world- he made it clear that this separation could reach intolerable levels. What was thought of as exceptional decisions of dubious moral-ity when polities and societies face impossible crossroads has been routinized to the point of becoming widespread, institutionalized cynicism that permeates all the pores of beings that can no longer stand themselves. This seems to be the major ailment of democracy and democrats in the theater of politics.

In its origin the thesis of this book is straightforward and recalls a book on Mexico that I published in 2010 (Valdés-Ugalde, 2010). In that book, I discussed the end of Mexico's second government following the transition to democracy that marked in 2000 a significant milestone with the first alternation of a party in power. A worrying phenomenon had occurred. The legal bases for pluralism, po-litical competition, and alternation between governing parties had been estab-lished, but the rules of the game for the exercise of state power had not been changed. Competitive access to power by guaranteeing citizens' suffrage had un-questionably been achieved with a change of the political regime. Yet, basic com-ponents of a state that were shaped and governed for over seventy years by a single political party under the "hegemonic party presidential system," as defined by Giovanni Sartori (2005, p. 204 and *passim*), were preserved (and are still cur-rently in force). Back then I became convinced that the divorce between the rules of access and the rules of exercise of power would produce a certain schizophre-nia. Growing political freedom would clash with the freedom of rulers to govern arbitrarily by appealing to an arbitral system (the law) that itself had been marked by schizophrenia and that nourished its two personalities, alternating be-tween democratic advance or retreat. This would be a very different dialectic from the mission of establishing democratic control of power. With time I real-ized that this was not an isolated situation; in a large number of recent democra-cies, most of which developed during what is known in political science as the "third wave of democratization," there were symptoms of a similar problem that merited study in spite of the prevailing triumphalism in political and academic circles over the almost simultaneous arrival of democracy in a large number of countries in the last two decades of the twentieth century.

The question warranted a review of much of the literature that emerged dur-ing the democratic transitions in order to find answers to this problem. As well as resorting to the political science and sociological literature, it seemed essential to me to examine normative political theory. Without theory there is no knowledge, only data piling up, and without normative theory there is no direction, only meanderings. Battles are fought in all fields. There are no purely "empirical theories". Every theory is based on facts of reality but cannot be reduced to those facts. Theory comes before facts, and organizes observable facts in the most coherent way possible (causal or not) and, once developed, its argumentative organization is subject to the continuous test of debate. In so doing, specialized knowledge enters the torrent of doxa and amalgamates with it, and the latter returns the subject matter fashioned with its own language for new works of Hercules. At the end of the day, politics is, *par excellence*, the future factory of collective life and has indissolubly linked a being with a duty to be. Both need to be understood and confronted side by side.

The argument of this book is as follows. Most Latin American and Spanish-speaking Caribbean[1] countries became fully incorporated into the democratic community around the last quarter of the twentieth century. Some were previously democracies, such as Venezuela and Costa Rica. Others suffered dictatorial coup d'états, mainly the four countries of the Southern Cone (Argentina, Brazil, Chile, Uruguay), and others suffered from various forms of authoritarianism that lasted decades or alternated accidentally with democratic governments. Due to its historical background and the global moment in which this incorporation took place, the two major restrictions that frame this Latin American democratic era are, in addition to geography, social inequalities and economies largely open to the outside world. Inequalities have endogenous origins, while economic openness has the double meaning of acquiesced global integration and numerous internal adjustments. Most Latin American societies are, with few exceptions such as Uruguay and to a lesser degree Argentina, socially and politically heterogeneous, with large ethnic, cultural, regional, and political differences.

While people are now enjoying greater political freedoms, societies conduct politics in conditions in which democratic regimes and states are still undergoing formation. They are not mature regimes with long traditions involving political parties and procedural forms. To a large extent, this stage is one of experimentation and change, sometimes too intense and too frequent to test the adequacy of diverse varieties of political organization and governance. The elites benefiting from economies that carry social and political despotism in their DNA continue to play an active or passive role, depending on the circumstances, in order to preserve this despotism of their way of being. Inequality continues to be a fundamental driver of politics that throws excluded or disadvantaged groups into

---

1 Except for Cuba, which is the oldest dictatorship in the hemisphere.

social protest and, apparently to a lesser extent, organized political action. Political regimes are overwhelmed, if not swamped, by demands for social inclusion, many of which represent centuries-old debts to "original peoples", to workers, to the poor. And they are also injected by their opposites: the resistance of the elites, the closing of avenues for consensus building, and not infrequently repression. In this environment, resentment, always sterile and destructive, is often one of the motivations for venting. However, either because of how coordination occurs between societies and democratic regimes, or because of their short democratic life (barely two generations of continuity in most cases), the general political order, i.e. the state, has not yet undergone sufficient transformations to produce stable balances, based on broad social consensus that can give rise to a "legitimate order", to use Weber's words, of a new type. Let us say that an extremely heterogeneous citizenry and specific historical circumstances have favored building incipient democratic political regimes whose impact on the state is far from having made the necessary progress to achieve basic criteria required by a democratic state based on the rule of law. In the words of Norberto Bobbio, a liberal state that is also a social state.

The term "functional democracy" has been used for two centuries. It was common at the founding of the American republics and has continued to be used whenever things get complicated and doubts arise about the capacity of democracy "to solve problems". Democracy is or is not functional if it "solves" problems. Not infrequently, and this is still the case today, when the inability to govern arises, whether in terms of preserving order and stability, or applying the law impartially, or legislating and developing public policy, the lack of "functionality" of democracy has been invoked to question whether it is an ideal form of government in such situations. Dispensing with democracy has often been justified in order to "solve problems", only to later revisit situations in which what was sought was not "resolved" and the possibility of making collective decisions under conditions of freedom and the rule of law was lost. An oft-cited axiom is that the only perfect rationality is dictatorship. Once there is more than one decision-maker, rationality becomes imperfect. In Latin American states, poorly performing institutions constantly fail to produce public goods. This deficiency leads to a vicious circle of generalized political dissatisfaction, which opportunistic authoritarians then exploit to concentrate power and suppress freedoms and rights. And this feeling becomes more acute the closer one is to the myth that all times past were better. In this recurrent pattern we can cite evidence that representative democracy achieves a relevant outcome at the level of the political regime, where conflict is processed, but when politics gets stuck in the regime in a kind of acceleration without movement, without generating satisfactory medium- and long-term agreements for the parties, the engines of public decision-making begin to throw off sparks and grind to a halt. Although the space to process these agreements is the regime, they can only find lasting life when they are institutionalized in the state and in its constitutionality, a sphere in which it is not possible to reach far-reaching agreements with a time horizon required for long-term building projects.

The first chapter is a general overview of the problem of political democratization; of the relations between citizenship, political regime, and state in this democratization process and focuses on the empirical dimensions of developing representative democracy in Latin America. Based on central elements of Latin American history and its recent experience that, for the first time and in a sustained manner for almost half a century, has undergone sustained democratization processes, we must view the problem of persistent and acute inequality of power as a symptom of the inability of regimes to include demands and rights in the state, which the government would be obliged to respond to. The circularity of this process undermines the regime's capacity to process political conflict and fuels environments hostile to representative democracy that channel democratization towards forms of de-democratization, as Charles Tilly (2007) called them. In discussing with the literature whether or not it is worthwhile to distinguish democratic dimensions in the state, we say it is, but assuming that the political regime and the state are not democratic or authoritarian for the same reasons, but for different specificities.

The following chapters are devoted to discussing this argument and exploring its heuristic possibilities. The second chapter addresses the performance of the state in Latin America and its (in)capacity to widen inclusion, based on two systems of indicators, i.e., the World Bank's World Governance Indicators (WGI) database and those of the Varieties of Democracy Institute of the University of Gothenburg. The third chapter is mainly theoretical-methodological, reviewing the measurement of democracy and a reworking -based on contemporary political theory- of the concept of *representative democracy* with the aim of measuring its quality by means of an exploratory factor analysis based on the indexes and indicators compiled in the extraordinarily rich database of the V-Dem Project. Chapter 4 discusses the results of the measurement of the quality of representative democracy in a sample of 15 Latin American countries and a similar group of European countries selected for this study. Chapter 5 returns to the problem of obstacles to democratization in Latin America that explain the poor quality of representation and, based on the results of Chapters 2, 3, and 4, delves into the rules of the political game as contradictory networks of actors and institutions with a low capacity to channel political conflict towards building a properly democratic statehood. Finally, Chapter 6 deepens our reflections and draws conclusions on the current state and uncertain prospects for democratic development in Latin America in the global context.

If I had to summarize the book in one central point, it would be as follows: representative democracy is so weak that it is difficult to find in Latin America. That is the problem. The multiple dynamics that are required between citizenry, political regime, and state are poor and underdeveloped. Hence the need for a paradigm shift: from the transformation of access to power to the reconfiguration of its exercise-and then back to access.

In the course of writing this book, I acquired priceless debts with people and institutions to whom I am eternally grateful for their help, suggestions, inspiration, debates, discussions -sometimes harsh, as should be in scientific work. First, I owe special thanks to my student and colleague Georgina Flores-Ivich with whom, in a first attempt to test the empirical analysis of representative democracy, we wrote a rough version of Chapter 3. It was she who stoically aided me in building approximations to the problem of exercising power and implementing representative democracy. Gloria Cristina Chávez Valdez assisted and accompanied me in writing this book, particularly in pulling together data, tables, graphs and their interpretation, reading and re-reading the manuscript and other notes, and in periodic planning and revision meetings. To Rodrigo Salazar Elena and Raúl Pacheco-Vega, I am indebted for their generosity in reading and rereading several versions of the original draft of parts of this book. To Karina Ansolabehere, Gisela Zaremberg, and Marcela Torres Wong I owe countless discussions and exchanges in seminars and study groups devoted to the problems of democracy, human rights, and the state that we conducted at Flacso[2] Mexico between 2010 and 2018. I am grateful to Flacso Chile for hosting me during an initial stage of this research project in 2018–2019 and to the Institute of Latin American Studies at Columbia University and its then director, Claudio Lomnitz, who for a few months allowed me to enjoy a fabulous library, thanks to the Edmundo O'Gorman scholarship. My gratitude also goes to the editorial committee of De Gruyter´s Latin America in Perspective collection that selected the original project and to the anonymous readers who reviewed it. To the Instituto de Investigaciones Sociales of the National Autonomous University of Mexico, my home for more than thirty years, I am grateful for the hospitality and the environment it has always offered me to carry out my research work.

The intellectual debts that I must honor can be seen in the pages of this book where they are amply referred to. However, there is one that I must mention in particular, the great source of inspiration that I found -and find- in the work of Guillermo O'Donnell. I was never his student but, without his knowing it, he was one of my mentors. I had the opportunity to meet him in the 1980s in Buenos

---

2 Facultad Latinoamericana de Ciencias Sociales.

Aires and since then I had contact with him on several occasions at congresses, seminars, and conferences. I was once fortunate and honored to meet him in the audience during a talk I gave at the Kellogg Institute for International Relations at the University of Notre Dame. In following his fruitful intellectual trajectory, I always identified with his "voracious interest in politics" and with his central concern about what kind of state democracies need to survive, consolidate, and ensure the future of individual and collective freedom.

Finally, I must thank my friends Roger Bartra, Cristopher Domínguez Michael, and Héctor Manjarrez for the conversation on politics that we have had over three or four decades. To Claudia Schatan, my partner, I owe a lifetime of dialogue on the political economy in which we live, and to our daughter Natalia Valdés-Schatan to whom I owe endless discussions in which she brilliantly served as *advocatus diabolis* to my arguments and counterarguments. This book is dedicated to my devil's advocate. Of course, what is stated herein is entirely my own responsibility.

Mexico City, April 2023

Chapter 1
Democratic transitions and the institutionalization of representative democracy. An overview

> political democracy and its universalistic and equalizing dimensions seem to be left floating in
> a fragmented and unequal society that is loosely linked to a state that performs poorly . . .
> This tends to deprive social life of a sense of collective orientation, of the feeling that the state
> is a rudder that can give it direction. By the same token, as the state at times seems to
> disintegrate in the banality of its incapacities and in the frequent scandals of its corrupt
> colonization, politics itself tends to share in that banality.
> Guillermo O'Donnell

Never since the transition to democracy have so many Latin American citizens had the freedom to elect their governments over such a long period of time. Beginning in the last quarter of the 20th century, Latin American states began to return to the republican, representative, and democratic character they adopted *de jure* but not *de facto* at the time of their independence from Iberian rule. However, a new wave of "autocratization" is knocking at the door and, with it, the ghost that haunts our history: the appropriation of democracy by old and new oligarchies, which historically has had the effect of excluding large groups from political representation. We should add yet another phantom: the anti-systemic leftist sectors willing to impose regressive utopias that include the disappearance of "bourgeois" democracy. Here, as in other latitudes, authoritarian actors have learned to survive through democratic procedures in order to preserve and advance their particular interests over the public interest. This book addresses the ways in which democratic and authoritarian forces are intertwined in the political processes and institutional design of representative democracy and how they affect the inclusion of the citizenry in shaping policies and making political decisions.

The "third wave of democracy" reached Latin America's shores in the last quarter of the 20th century and, in a surprising synchrony, most countries in the subcontinent embraced democratic regimes simultaneously for the first time since their independence from colonial rule, honoring their original longstanding adherence to the republican ideals set down in most of their early constitutions. From Tierra del Fuego to the Rio Grande, governments were established through more or less free elections in most of the continental and Caribbean lands with the sole exception of Cuba. Whether from revolutions, as in the cases of Nicaragua and El Salvador, or from military regimes, as in Brazil, Chile, Argentina and Uruguay, or from previous authoritarian regimes, as in Mexico, Bolivia or Peru, between 1978 and 2006 a wave

https://doi.org/10.1515/9783110773675-002

of democracy swept the region, ushering in a new era of freer and more complex relations between citizens and elected governments.

However, authoritarian actors subsist and often overshadow democratic procedures as they attempt to preserve authoritarian institutions and practices that are inherent to their way of being in power. Authoritarian practices and institutions remain active and create spaces or enclaves where they insulate and protect themselves from democratic accountability, albeit often in collision with democratic groups demanding their transformation. From Chile's senators-for-life or appointed senators to Mexico's executive and judicial branches, the ability to impose decisions and policies impervious to democratically elected representatives speak to the power of oligarchies to invade the institutional structures of a regime, a government, or a state. There is no democracy in the world completely impervious to these regressions. Moreover, their presence and action in all democratic political systems is a sign of the times. Yet, following the establishment of democratic regimes in most Latin American states, there is an experiment underway involving the transformation of oligarchic structures into democratic institutions on a regional scale similar in scope only to post-Napoleonic Europe in the 19th century and the decolonization of Africa and Asia in the 20th. However, unlike what happened in other experiences, by virtue of the different and even irreconcilable practices that are bundled together in state agreements of mutual convenience of the approving parties, democratic institutions are shaped by actors interested in preserving power under patrimonial formulas and in protecting their power from the democratic exposure that would abolish it. *Mutatis mutandis*, such actors condition the principal strategies of the actors of change, who often give in to preserving these practices in exchange for allotments in the distribution of power in pluralist regimes.

Cases and examples abound of the prevalence of authoritarian institutions and practices that remain active in democratic regimes and states: suppression of alternation in power, electoral fraud and manipulation, clientelism fostered with public resources, quasi one-party systems or parties with a penchant for becoming the only option, systematic violations of fundamental rights and freedoms, protection of criminal organizations and illegitimate powers by governments, institutional structures that make access to justice impossible for ordinary citizens, etc. A nuanced list of the forms of despotic exercise of state power would be much longer, but this summary illustrates the problem. Thus, democratic influences have collided with autocratic actors and interests, creating a recurrent tension between democracy and authoritarianism within the constitutional structures of representative democracy. Latin America has been proverbially seen as a realm of caudillo rule, a region of the world that, with very few exceptions, has been averse to liberal democratic progress and its benefits: equality among people and their inclusion in political decision-making. This collision leads us to ask to what extent and in what ways democratic and authoritarian forces are intertwined in political processes and institutions, and what effects they have on the different dimensions of representative democracy.

The main objective of the book focuses on the following question: Have democracies contributed to inclusive representation of citizens and, consequently, to better performance of the state at their service? The question can be broken down into three main dimensions: 1) To what degree have democracies represented citizens' demands and have citizens' representatives sought, through the exercise of power, to convert demands into effective rules and rights? 2) What political institutions have been significant in achieving that representation and translating it into rights and social welfare through political decisions, public policies and public goods? 3) Who are the actors and institutions driving or hindering these processes of representation and shaping the exercise of state power? The answers to these questions constitute the core of the book.

The questions are part of the challenge posed by democracy throughout history, as elegantly defined by one of the great thinkers of our time when referring to the challenge implied in the impossibility theorem formulated by Arrow in the mid-20th century (Arrow, 1970):

> coming to grips with the need to include all the people in the process of social decision-making [. . .] an implicit pledge that would be deeply offended by accepting a dictatorial outcome, even when it is entailed by axiomatic requirements that individually seem reasonable enough. (Sen, 2017, pp. 269–270).

The general hypothesis of this book is that representative democracy has contributed considerably to the recognition of rights of the population and duties of the state that are different from those that had been accepted in previous stages in fundamental political pacts. Representative democracy has also contributed to mobilizing structures of the political regime that favor those rights and duties, such as party structures that allow actors previously excluded by authoritarianisms -such as leftist parties and a great diversity of popular movements- to compete. This regime mobilization has increased political pressures on the state towards overcoming resistance aimed at fully accommodating constitutionally recognized rights and duties, in the form of compliance with commitments to those rights and duties through public action. However, from civil society to the state, navigating through the political regime, there are factors that hinder the full validity of what some authors call the "new Latin American constitutionalism" (Gargarella, 2013). At the intersections between these three political dimensions of citizenship, the political regime, and the state lie these obstacles whose effect is to constrain the formation of political decision-making structures that modify the core, the "engine room" of the state as producer of the necessary and specific public goods that are the key to this change. However, in this respect we can distinguish important differences between countries that denote different degrees of advancement of the aforementioned rights and duties which, in turn, depend on the type of democratic representation generated by political regimes. Distinguishing them requires a comparative analysis based on evidence that allows us to get to the heart of this problem.

1.1 Translating at Babel

Democracy is a Tower of Babel. Many languages and dialects invoke it and give it different meanings. It is impossible to enumerate the definitions that have been given to democracy and the fate they have had. Nor is it feasible to ignore the polysemy of the word, which is a phenomenon of study in itself, a word loaded with a universal aspiration. Undoubtedly the object of legitimate knowledge, this vast chorus is not our fundamental interest, nor is it altogether alien either. The idea of democracy developed in this book is both broad and restricted. Or, rather, it is a narrow and regulated idea in order to understand specific processes that occur within a broader perspective of the general development of the relationship between people and power, between the "demos" and the "kratos" and, even more broadly, of the emergence of the *demoi* or democracy of nations. This is a broad view because the forms and methods of self-government, of appropriation of power, are so vast throughout history (Keane, 2009) that their description can cover endless volumes, and their meaning and raison d'être many additional volumes. The most important aspect to retain about the broad idea of democracy is that it is an open-ended process, an invention that is continually changing and adapting. Each national experience is part of broader trends that shape the overall process of democratic development. The central aspect that this phenomenon as a whole can have is the never-ending human quest to control the power that some have over others, and to give that power the sense of self-government free of domination, of control over domination ("the rule that nobody should rule", Keane, 2009, p. 864). In this sense, this book offers a grain of sand from the enormous quarry of the human quest to use and control power. The text reviews the Latin American struggle to achieve democracy based on the recent experience of a group of countries and under the assumption that their democracy is incomplete and evolving.

However, just as democracy encourages a perspective as broad as the historical phenomena and events that it describes, its conceptualization should be circumscribed in order to make it feasible to scrutinize the processes that compose it in specific time periods and geo-demographic spaces. In this case, we are dealing with Latin America in the period known as "transition", "consolidation" and, recently, regression and autocratization, which, in general terms – except for specific clarifications – occurred between 1980 and the first three decades of the 21st century. This analysis begins based on the idea that

> The proper object of inquiry, as well as of political practice, lies more in democratization than in democracy. *It consists, beyond the core provided by the regime and its own eventual further democratization, of the acquisition and legal backing of wider and more solidly supported rights and freedoms that pertain to the civil, social, and cultural aspects of citizenship* and, more broadly, of the agency of everyone irrespective of his/her positions as a citizen. (O'Donnell, 2010, p. 213) (emphasis added).

Our purpose then is to explore the interaction between representatives and constituents, between elected rulers and citizens at the level of the regime, the government, and the state, and to answer the question of whether the rules and institutions of the regime include all citizens, and allow and encourage their demands to be translated into rights embodied in the state, and whether the state makes them effective through the government in accordance with the requirements of the concept of democracy. The distinction between regime, government, and state is relevant here. Following O'Donnell (2010, pp. 20–28), by regime I consider the factors that determine the channels of access to government decision-making positions, the actors included or excluded, the resources used for such access and the identification of the main state institutions that link the state to the regime. The government is made up by the entities of the administrative apparatus in which "the incumbents . . . make . . . decisions which are normally issued as legal rules binding over the population and the territory delimited by the state" (O'Donnell 2010, p. 56). The state is a political community located in a territorial entity that has a legal system that assigns "rights, freedoms, and obligations" and has bureaucracies that implement these rights, freedoms and obligations.[3] The distinction allows us to separate political processing from agency, from the administration of public goods, and from the sphere in which the meaning and rights of the political community and its members are embodied.

---

3 The famous Weberian formula for defining the state, "a form of human community that successfully claims for itself the monopoly of legitimate physical violence" does not exhaust the meaning of the state. To this community we add several intrinsic dimensions, that are invisible in the mere definition: 1. a division between rulers and ruled; 2. a relationship of acquiescence or acceptance between both groups about the legitimacy of the authority of both groups, citizens and rulers; and 3. an administration that organizes resources to govern by assigning freedoms, rights, and responsibilities (Weber, 2004 [1919]). This definition of the state presupposes components of a social climate that make it possible to lend structure to these dimensions (Valdés-Ugalde, 2023). In addition, we should recognize that every *political community* has a personality that characterizes it and is composed of mentalities, ideas, beliefs, and values. This ideological and psychological component is decisive for understanding its ways of acting.

Similarly, it allows us to identify the sphere of interaction between regime and state, or rather, the space in which political forces interact to shape the political regime and the state. The most relevant effect of this interaction is to legitimize within the state the practices authorized in the regime, and which make it possible to distinguish accepted practices from those that are proscribed. Likewise, legitimization is transformed by interactions within the regime, but activities and *procedures* that are legitimate need to be elevated to the level of the state in order to be considered, administered, and practiced as such.

Among the demands that the regime processes and that the democratic state fosters and protects as part of the constitutional agreement, there is one of special importance: citizens' participation in public decisions and in the control of political power, in which they project their notions of power, their aspirations to exercise it, and their idea of the society in which they live or want to live. This intervention is the central engine of politics, the origin of the dynamics of power distribution, and state priorities. In representative democracies, such participation is carried out jointly with institutional intermediation in which representatives play a central role. This book, therefore, focuses on the nature and quality of this interaction between rulers and ruled, which is processed, modeled, and regulated by the political regime, and defined and safeguarded by the state as meaning and law.

1.1.1 Not *from* or *towards* democracy, but *in* democratization

When the studies of transitions to democracy in Latin America were exhausted, a new literature emerged that queried the possibilities and forms of consolidation of the new or reformed political systems. This second stage has been followed by a third in which new questions have been asked about the character of these democracies, mainly in relation to the degree and diversity of forms of inclusion of citizens and population groups in political decisions and in the modulating of public policies. Since their birth as independent Latin America republics, their political systems are, for the most part, democratic systems constitutionally defined as representative republics, i.e., systems whose actors decide on a republican form of government and establish such governments through popular vote. This origin has indelibly marked the Latin American political process. For two centuries or more, elections have been held periodically, often interrupted by "uprisings", coups d'état, or political crises that lead to disorder or revolts; or elections are carried out as a ritual of legitimization of authoritarian systems with hegemonic capacity, although elections are always a recourse as a form of government legitimization. Nevertheless, the history of Latin America is the history of a representative democracy deliberately captured by the political and economic elites and generally armored against the penetration by popular sectors seeking political representation in decisions regarding state affairs. Of course, it is also the history of dictatorships that have temporarily but recurrently suppressed republican life. Hence, two hundred years after the separation of the Latin American colonies from their colonizers, there is a consensus in history and the social sciences about the persistence and very wide dissemination of a closed or obturated republicanism that remains stable as long as the social groups from the lower strata of the social pyramid do not demand their active entry into politics.

1.1.1.1 The surrealism of the oligarchic republic

In what way has history influenced contemporary political developments that ultimately have an impact on stopping or rolling back democracy in Latin America? This is a history of advances and setbacks. When they became independent republics during the 19th century (Cuba in 1902), Latin American countries adopted forms of representative democracy, but they did so to preserve fundamental aspects of the colonial order. They had the trappings of republics but maintained the old system of privileges and, unlike what happened in other regions, they were not founded giving centrality to a nucleus of citizens -which expands over time- but to the oligarchies that inherited feudal practices and institutions. Despite their separation from Spain and Portugal, the imprint of the political structures of the monarchic and feudal colonial order remained in the new republics, forging their historical personality, and has characterized the political systems of the subcontinent. Against the background of feudal legacies, the idea of citizenship made up of autonomous, educated, and thinking individuals, capable of forming their own criteria on public affairs, has made discreet and sometimes significant advances; yet, at the same time, Latin America retains the enormous weight of "path dependence" of pre-existing patrimonial structures and practices.[4] In the case of Latin American states, this is the path determined by colonial heritage which, in politics, imprints its mark through the multiple forms of oligarchy that are the elites' political preference. Keane (2009) refers to this peculiar process as the "amusing dialectics" of "the ruptures (. . .) inspired by the bizarre revolutionary events triggered by the 1807 advance of the troops of Napoleon Bonaparte towards mainland Spain" (Keane 2009, p. 381), the Ibero-American independences being one of those "bizarre events."

---

4 The mainly economic literature that uses this concept to approach history is vast. A pioneering example is that of Coatsworth (1978), applied to 19th-century Mexico.

Political equality vis-à-vis the Iberian ruling classes was a cherished value and pursued politically by the Ibero-American elites, but which excluded popular groups. This equality was an essential claim made by Ibero-Americans to the Spanish and Portuguese crown and courts.[5] However, viceregal history rested on the establishment of a class and caste structure in which ethnic origin and social status were the motive for a rigid stratification that consecrated as unequal the groups above and below them in the social hierarchy. The equality sought by the elites was, therefore, an equality at the top of a pyramid, while determining that the remaining overwhelming majority of society was unequal. During the colonial period and even after, the cultural and legal consecration of social inequalities was typical of Latin America, as seen in the civil codes of the 17th to 19th centuries and in the persistence of dominant mentalities that ritualize inequality. Contrary to what happened in the liberal revolutions, the Latin American independence movements were consummated when, with Ferdinand VII restored to the throne, the Constitution of 1812 was ephemerally adopted and the Creole elites prevented its application in their lands. Unlike Spain at that time, the preservation of the colonial order and not its liberal transformation was the priority of the groups that triumphed against the royalist armies and subjugated those who had fought for independence from below, such as Hidalgo and Morelos in Mexico. In their political significance, the Latin American independence movements were an "inverted version" of the American Revolution of 1776–1789. If the latter represented the detachment from a colonial and monarchical order led by an avant-garde bourgeoisie, the former represented the separation of the oligarchies from a colonial ruler that was taking steps towards modernity with the aim of preserving in the "new world" the old colonial order that ensured its domination (Keane 2009, p. 381).

Paraphrasing Guillermo O'Donnell on the character of citizenship in the region (O'Donnell, 1993), Latin American states are "low-intensity" states.[6] They are states with a low capacity to collect taxes, control elites, defend their territory, or ensure their legitimacy in society. Fukuyama describes a sobering feature when referring to one of the causes of this weakness: the absence of wars between states (Fukuyama, 2014, pp. 240, figs. 13 and 14). The relative absence of warlike conflicts had two relevant consequences: a low need to build solid institutions for defense, otherwise fundamental to civilian life, and a weak appeal to the people for military defense because of the elites' fear of facilitating revolts and internal

---

5 The transfer of the capital of the Portuguese empire to America in 1822 gave Brazil a different nuance by establishing in Rio de Janeiro the seat of the Crown and a space for the protection of the elites in the face of the 1820 liberal revolution in Portugal, which was more radical than in Spain.
6 This statement is echoed in other views: "What is interesting about Latin America in the 19th and 20th centuries [. . .] is the dogs that didn't bark" (Fukuyama, 2014, p. 237).

conflicts. The solid institutions that the major European countries built derived from both complementary factors: strong institutions and inclusion of the people in national defense. This second factor was a motive behind the prolonged internal struggles by which the subordinate classes, in exchange for their loyalty to the elites, demanded and obtained distributive concessions that reduced inequality (Tilly, 1992). These concessions were not present in Latin America or, in any event, took on a different form (Collier and Collier, 1991; Kapiszewski et al., 2021).

Given these characteristics of Latin American states, it is not surprising that one of the most outstanding features of Latin American political systems, which refuses to disappear, is the imprint of "caudillo democracy" (Keane, 2009, pp. 374–454): the tendency of charismatic leaders to emerge that was dominant in the 19th century. Until well into the 20th century, these leaders were, with sporadic exceptions, military figures. Control of the militia was solidly linked to the ability to control the government. However, the need for elections never disappeared, making Latin America a region in which asserting power required the control of armed forces and, at the same time, the legitimacy of the ballot box. The United States under the Monroe Doctrine played a relevant role in this dynamic by supporting governments that protected its interests regardless of their democratic or dictatorial nature (Keane, 2009, p. 379). Of course, the United States destabilized or openly fought governments opposed to its interests. Thus, an external factor reinforced endogenous authoritarianism. This trend did not abate until the end of the 20th century, when the international climate gave greater importance to democratic legitimacy.

In spite of the advances made in the 20th century in the expansion of Latin American political systems to incorporate organized workers into political participation (Collier and Collier, 1991), authoritarian forms continued to persist and alternate with others of a democratic nature. Except for Costa Rica since 1950, all other countries in the continent have had authoritarian governments or dictatorships, until the 1980s, when Latin America returned to a democratic path buttressed by the winds brought by the third democratic wave. Despite this significant progress, state capacities and the low quality of citizenship have continued to affect democratic development, leading to significant deformations. Two of these were noted by Guillermo O'Donnell under the label of "delegative democracies" and "low-intensity citizenships", in which a combination of authoritarianism and democracy persists in political regimes (O'Donnell, 1993, 2010).[7] The unique structure of Latin

---

7 Other modalities of deformation of democracy, partially coinciding with those described by O'Donnell have been conceptualized as "oligarchic disfigurement" and "populist disfigurement" (Urbinati, 2014).

American political regimes is manifested by low bureaucratic capacities, heterogeneous societies with low citizen "intensity," and poorly enforced legal systems -in
Latin America "nowhere is the law applied equally" (O'Donnell, 2010, p. 205). The
background of social inequality inherited from the colonial past persists in a bas-
tardized modernization.[8] Social inequality, expressed in class, group, ethnic, and
gender differences in the distribution of material, political, and cultural resources
exists alongside the state's weak capacity to guarantee legal equality. This means
that social conflicts, as processed by the political regime, do not necessarily guarantee an effective implementation of rights. It is well known that there is a widespread
tendency for constitutions and laws to "incorporate" *de jure* rights, but lack the tools
and institutions capable of effectively applying the law. Data provided over the recent period by the World Justice Project confirms the disparity in law enforcement
in Latin America. Most countries rank below the median registered by the rule of
law index, hovering around the lower half of the measurement scale.[9]

The perspective from which we observe the "new" democracies, i.e., a
label of sorts for those that have predominated in Latin America since the
third wave -notwithstanding their bicentennial histories- may vary if, instead of
thinking that they have reached a "saddle point", they are viewed in a broader process of global transformation of democracy. Keane (2009) holds that this path leads
to "monitory democracy," a new type of regime, while other authors observe a
transformation of representative democracy in which it absorbs forms of direct
and deliberative democracy (Alonso, Keane, and Merkel, 2011; O'Donnell, 2010; Saward 2006; Sen, 2017; Urbinati, 2006). The mixture of democratic forms with authoritarian remnants has not received sufficient attention. The form they take and the
effects they produce within political systems that combine republican institutions
with representative -and even participatory- democracy, and authoritarian forms
of exercising power, deserve more attention than they have received so far. How to
do so? In what way can we situate ourselves to best observe the plot between democratization and de-democratization, to use Tilly's expression? (Tilly, 2007)

---

8 This characteristic of Latin American societies has been conceptualized under the category of
"internal colonialism", although the parallelism between the colonial order and contemporary
inequality does not go beyond the figurative. This idea has been insufficient to identify the complexity of Latin American "modernization".
9 With the exceptions of Chile, Costa Rica, and Uruguay, which are above this line (World Justice
Project [WJP], 2021).

1.2 Democracy and democratization: Access to power and its exercise

Democracy does not only include access to power, but also its exercise. There are democratic forms of access to power and democratic forms to exercise it, just as, on the contrary, there are authoritarian forms of doing both. In the same way that one cannot pass off as democratic an authoritarian exercise of power from a government or an inscription in the state of principles, values, and norms that authorize oppression, just because it has been the result of a valid electoral act, it is also unacceptable to justify a "democratic" regime if the governments and the state that regulate it are kind and upright when they exercise power, but are not the result of democratic collective decisions. There is no democracy without a democratic regime, government, and state at the same time. In other words, the process of inclusion-exclusion of the citizenry in political decisions takes place at the three institutional levels and may have different characteristics within each one.

The global framework in which the late democratization of Latin America is taking place is perfectly described by Jürgen Habermas when he situates the political systems between the fall of the Soviet bloc and the unfinished "triumph" of a capitalism that does not commit itself to equality and justice despite having the capacity and the means to do so.

> After the collapse of state socialism and the end of the "global civil war," the theoretical error of the defeated party is there for all to see: it mistook the socialist project for the design -and violent implementation- of a concrete form of life. If, however, one conceives "socialism" as the set of necessary conditions for emancipated forms of life about which the participants themselves must first reach an understanding, then one will recognize that the democratic self-organization of a legal community constitutes the normative core of this project as well. On the other hand, the party that now considers itself victorious does not rejoice at its triumph. Just when it could emerge as the sole heir of the moral-practical self-understanding of modernity, it lacks the energy to drive ahead with the task of imposing social and ecological restraints on capitalism at the breathtaking level of global society. It zealously respects the systemic logic of an economy steered through markets; and it is at least on guard against overloading the power medium of state bureaucracies. Nevertheless, we do not even begin to display a similar sensibility for the resource that is actually endangered-a social solidarity preserved in legal structures and in need of continual regeneration. (Habermas, 1998, p. xli–xlii)

In this global context, the importance of democracy becomes even clearer in a region that, for the first time in its history, must fend for itself without the imperial tutelage of yesteryear and make its way into the empty space strewn with the rubble of the fallen blocs of the Cold War and, at the same time, settle accounts with its historical legacies. Thus, looking at the phenomenon of democratization implies observing different dimensions of the public space in which the characteristic feature of this system of government takes place: the political representation of the values and aspirations for a "good society" that have been frustrated so many times.

1.2.1 The only game in town?

When can it be said that democracy is here to stay, that it has been institutionalized, that it has become the undisputed magnetic pole of organization of the institutions of the political regime and of the state? It is a commonplace to affirm that this is the case when democracy is "the only game in town". However, most studies on the democratic transformations of political regimes in the so-called "third wave" of democratization recognize that in new democracies, as well as in long-established ones, new and old institutions and actors remain, are recycled, or are formed; that the institutions resulting from democratic innovations interact with the old ones and that very complex and often opaque relationships are created between both and the actors that undertake their action in them, which must be unpacked and clarified to understand the consequences they have for the democratizing process. Some have called them "authoritarian enclaves" that hinder, undermine, or neutralize the adequate flow of communication and permanent and uninterrupted deliberation between the represented and the elected representatives in order to elevate the rights, preferences, judgments, and opinions of the former to the political decision of the government or the state and the public policies they generate.

There are, then, ample reasons to consider that in democratic regimes there is a continuous struggle to convey the interests of constituencies through the action of representatives and that this mechanism, or series of mechanisms, does not operate in a transparent and fluid way; rather, it faces all manner of interference and obstacles that originate in the space of intermediations that we call politics. The "crises" of democracy are part of its very existence and are often constituted by this dynamic of conflict that emerges from the struggle to establish alternative forms of political order (Przeworski, 2019). The predominance of the democratic game over the authoritarian one depends not only on the verification of regular elections, but also on the procedural framework of the regime offering the tools to favor the balance of power between citizens and the State under conditions of political equity. There are recent situations that exemplify the problem. The 2020 elections in the United States have been disqualified by the losers of the presidential race. As the electoral organization depends on the state legislatures, in which the GOP majority predominates (30 out of 50 in 2022), a process of restricting the citizen vote and redistricting -gerrymandering- was undertaken to tilt the balance of the system in favor of the Republican Party and to the detriment of the electoral rights of disadvantaged social groups. In Russia, after the collapse of the Soviet regime, a fragile democracy was established, which did not resist the onslaught of the oligarchy that took over state enterprises and, despite maintaining electoral rituals, quickly moved towards the formation of an autocracy that limits political rights and closes the political system under the hegemony of a single party. In both cases, changes were made in the state (sphere of legitimacy) to legitimize and legalize nondemocratic practices that are inscribed in the political regime as procedures to obtain results that ensure the dominance of a party or group. All this was done in the presence of a disarmed citizenry.

In Latin America, this conflict has been central to democratic processes. In all Latin American states without exception, since the establishment of uninterrupted electoral democracies, there has been a continuous dispute between forces that seek to establish permanent democratic conditions in the regime and the state, and others that seek to preserve exclusive and excluding plots of power or resources. In this way, dictatorships and oligarchies extend their dominance beyond the governments they control and, at the same time, social groups that strive for democracy remain in dispute over the political procedures that allow or hinder the advancement of their respective agendas (Lührmann and Lindberg, 2019). Hence the value of approaching democratization (as well as autocratization) as a process involving the different components of the polity. Many games are played in this process, and even if democracy holds sway as the main game, there are often non-democratic players waiting for a chance to replace it. At the end of the day, democracy is vulnerable because its strength lies, ultimately, in the freedom of all and in the respect for the freedom of each one. In the analysis of each political system, one can see a more or less varied scale of traits that contain elements belonging to democracy and authoritarianism respectively. Restrictive definitions of democracy that, for example, circumscribe it to fair elections are very useful for viewing electoral dynamics, but they are only one feature of democracy that coexists with others.[10]

In Latin America, some countries have retained features of previous authoritarianisms (the Chilean constitution, the party system in Argentina, the power of the military in Uruguay, Brazil, and Guatemala, the hegemonic political regime in Mexico); in others, new types of authoritarian groups and currents have emerged, such as some religious denominations that oppose fundamental rights and seek

---

[10] Each available index for measuring democracy captures different traits for assessing a regime as democratic, but the variety of indices reflects a multiplicity of conceptualizations that vary according to the approach (see Chapter 3).

to exercise power to prevent them, or political movements that seek to concentrate all power in a single bloc, limiting the ability of other actors to participate on equal terms.[11] Despite the variety of anti-democratic factors, the vast majority have made use of electoral systems in one way or another. Some have used it to build majorities that seek within the government to prevent the growth of minorities, and some have gone to the extreme of controlling elections to prevent opposition participation. Thus, "the only game in town" is almost never the only one, and so it behooves us to observe how the currents that undermine it behave.

1.3 Democracy is a matter of concern for the regime, the government, and the state

The polysemy of the term democracy requires clarification. Since the publication of the influential *Transitions from Authoritarian Rule* (O'Donnell et al., 1986), challenges have arisen to theories put forward in this pioneering study of third wave democracies. As we said above, there has been a great deal of analysis on "quality of democracy", "democratic consolidation", democratic culture, etc. Little has been done, however, to develop a political science of the democratic state. Adam Przeworski recently warned that

> the issue of the state apparatus is something that is almost overlooked by political thought. There are studies of state capacity, of course, but we study elections a hundred times more often than we study the functioning of *state democracy*.[12] (Emphasis added)

Many of these studies are based on the binomial political regime-state as interrelated components of democracy. Certain scholars have criticized studies of the quality of democracy in that they tend to extend the concept of "democracy" to the point where it loses its explanatory capacity (saying everything and nothing) by falling into research strategies that confuse different types of elements by placing them within the same category, leading to tautological reasoning. Instead, they propose introducing a distinction between access to power and exercise of power (Mazzuca, 2010; Valdés-Ugalde, 2010, Munck, 2016) and, symmetrically, the separation between democracy and state with the aim of distinguishing them as domains that should be kept conceptually separate, so that research on the relationship between the two is possible (Mazzuca and Munck, 2020). According to

---

11 This group is joined by numerous radical left sectors that continue to maintain a contradiction, i.e., the "popular" dictatorship as a synonym of superior democratization.
12 *La Nación*, Argentina. Interview by Astrid Pikienski, June 18, 2022.

this proposal, the democratic component would be limited to the political regime, while the monopoly of force and the bureaucratic functions of government would be properly observed within the state. The argument on which this theoretical strategy is based posits that the literature interested in assessing the quality of democracy has expanded this concept beyond what it can contain, and encompassed aspects of the state, such as public administration, law, and order, which do not belong in its purview. Such scholars point out that the regime is in reality the space in which the essence of democracy can be identified (elections, electoral competition, and party system), while the area of responsibility of the authority granted as a result of suffrage corresponds to the state and should not be confused with democracy. There are many reasons and much historical evidence that make this strategy viable for certain research purposes. An example would be to answer the historiographical question of whether the state is necessary to produce a democratic regime, or whether a regime can be the origin of a state, or whether both cases are possible (Mazzuca and Munck, 2020). However, by identifying democracy with the access to power (regime) but not with its exercise (state), this distinction has the disadvantage of excluding the *exercise* of power by the state from an analysis of democracy. If one cannot speak of the democratic or non-democratic character of the exercise of power, then one cannot think of the state as part of democratic theory or of the empirical study of its features. Yet the evidence shows that the unrestricted exercise of power in authoritarianism is clearly distinguishable from that practiced in democracy, and thus how we view the state cannot be indifferent to that distinction. In other words, a state cannot be the same in a democratic situation as in an authoritarian one, and the organization of the functions of the state, i.e. the production of public goods -including the monopoly of violence and public administration-, can be differentiated in both situations. For example, the use of public resources in a state that has the necessary restrictions to favor the public interest and prevent private individuals from taking advantage of them is not the same as in a state that does not have such restrictions. However, both types of exercises of power can come about through fair elections. Controls on the exercise of power are different by virtue of internal peculiarities of the state that are not unique to the regime.

Limiting democracy to the space of the political regime and separating the state from its conceptual domain is a research strategy that has advantages. The major one is to note that the state's territorial, national, and administrative dimensions (Mazzuca and Munck, 2014) may have relative independence from the regime's democratic or authoritarian character. However, this distinction is insufficient to capture the way in which the interaction between democratic and non-democratic forces in the regime accentuates or diminishes the impact of those forces on the state. On the other hand, there is a growing consensus that "parliamentary democracies" tend to be the most compliant with the constitutional provisions binding the state and the government under whose umbrella they operate, while the opposite is true as a regime moves away from this category (Gutmann et al., 2022a). The evidence gathered through different measures of the quality of democracy tends to underscore this affinity between the plasticity of parliamentarism and constitutional compliance, as well as the greater closeness between citizens, regime, and state in parliamentary systems -more horizontal-, as opposed to rigid and hierarchical presidential systems.

Despite its virtues, the access/exercise, regime/state distinction does not adequately depict two elements that are crucial for the analysis of representative democracy: the "surplus of politics" (Urbinati, 2006) and the evaluation of the political system (regime-government-state) from the perspective of the substantive principles of democracy -equality and majority- (Beetham, 1999, pp. 89–114). Whatever the institutional arrangement of democracy is at a given moment, what confers its democratic nature is the presence of both principles within it. The "surplus of politics" can only be understood beyond elections, in the inter-electoral relationship between *demos* and *kratos*, between the people and their representatives or, in other words, between the citizenry and the bureaucracy of government in all its branches. This means that representative democracy conceptually encompasses the relationship between representatives and constituents during periods of government, and not just when elections are held. This relationship involves processes that are reflected in the state, for example, in legislative processes, constitutional changes, or public policies and their interaction with public opinion.

When contemplating such a vast literature, doubt arises about the distinction between democracy-regime, on the one hand, and efficiency-state, on the other. Why call "high-capacity democracies" those that combine political regimes that meet the best democratic conditions and highly efficient states, and conversely "low-capacity democracies" those that have regimes of low democratic quality and inefficient states, as Mazzuca and Munck do? (2020) Is there not a conceptual overlap in reducing democracy to the regime and yet conceiving as "high-capacity democracies" states that link the administrative "efficiency" of the state with the satisfaction of democratic principles by the regime? This overlap surfaces suspicion that the state, and not just the regime, contains attributes that are essential to define it as democratic. If the state has certain properties, are not some of them necessary for democracy or for authoritarianism? For example, the use of legitimate violence is not the same in an authoritarian system as it is in a democracy. Does inscribing a bill of rights in the constitution and the precise description of the normative framework that protects it *de jure* and *de facto* distinguish a democratic state from an authoritarian one? Or do the type of procedures and norms that govern the actions of institutions in a democratic government not differentiate it from those that direct an authoritarian government? In response to these questions, we hypothesize that it is theoretically viable, valid, and not tautological to describe as democratic or authoritarian the regime, the government, and the state, according to the different attributes of democracy that correspond to each of them.

A negative consequence of the sharp distinction between democracy and the state is to exclude the impact of democratic representation -the political engine in democracy- on the evolution of state structures (territorial, national, and administrative), and the normative dimension of agency (judgment, opinion, and will), which the citizenry continually brings to bear on both the political regime and the state (Habermas, 1998 pp. 132–193). Admitting this exclusion may lead us to ignore the litany of failures that democracy is currently experiencing, and which are reflected in the autocratization projects that have emerged from within (Lührmann and Lindberg, 2019). If, as Guillermo O'Donnell warned, "going beyond the regime is a risky enterprise [. . . for . . .] it could lead to a slippery slope that ends with equating democracy with everything one happens to like" (O'Donnell et al., 2004), not taking that risk means not addressing the challenge that agency poses to the democratic enterprise itself: "the production and reproduction of a life worthy of human beings."[13] It would mean not wagering what Guillermo O'Donnell proposed, i.e., that democracy should be the vehicle of inclusion in political decision-making and sticking exclusively to its traditional forms, without acknowledging its capacity for transformation in order to channel the permanent disagreement of every society with its own image (Lefort, 1991), would mean, at the end of the day, shying away from the "dialectics between liberalism and radical democracy that [. . .] has exploded worldwide" (Habermas, 1998, p. 471).

For the purposes of understanding political action, agency must be understood beyond its simple sociological definition as "propositional action", since politics is the sphere of construction of the law and, more broadly, of the norms that support communicative interaction (Habermas). The notion of agency must fully incorporate the normative dimension in at least two senses: in terms of agents' autonomy with respect to their own ends and from the point of view of the deliberation that they must sustain in order to make life socially meaningful. That is, they must be receptive to the fundamental tension between individual autonomy and collective action. The first aspect leads us to "negative" freedoms, but the second leads us to the domain of positive freedoms that are undertaken through collective action. The regime, the government, and the state are "solutions" to collective-action problems

---

13 "Autonomy and self-realization are the key concepts for a practice with an immanent purpose, namely, the production and reproduction of a life worthy of human beings" (Habermas, 1998, p. 468).

that under democratic conditions must not only respect and protect individual autonomy, but be the space for "the active development of public engagement to address the neglected questions" (Sen, 2017, p. 404). Hence, democracy, or in other words, the democratic core of state institutions, is inevitably the subject of tensions whose observation cannot do without its normative dimension. It is in the state that fundamental (constitutional) political decisions are made, and democracy is about who makes those decisions. This is the deepest problem of democracies today, and of Latin American democracies in particular, because they project an image of a continent suspended in a state of mediocrity in terms of access to power and in its exercise, due to the dislocation between the legality that prevails and the purposes of a state for which democracies supposedly exist.[14] Hence, evading the democratic or authoritarian character of a state prevents us from clearly seeing the nature of the democratic problem and its practical situation.

Thus, in arguing against the canonical soundness of the distinction between democracy (reduced to the regime) and the state (reduced to the administration) as a general research strategy, there is evidence that democratization as a process involving political actors under the condition of individual and collective citizenship, whether rulers or ruled, is not limited to the regime, but is also projected in the relationship between citizens and government in daily interaction, and impacts the state through the reflexivity of the dynamics of the binomial representatives-represented. Or, in the words of Charles Tilly in summarizing his argument in *Democracy:*

> it took up the impact of three fundamental processes: first, integration of interpersonal trust networks into public politics; second, insulation of public politics from categorical inequality; and third, reduction of autonomous coercive power centers, with the consequences of increasing influence of ordinary people over public politics and *rising control of public politics over state performance.* (Tilly, 2007, p. 188, emphasis added)

Finally, the incorporation of the relationship of representation in the political process has involved the regime, the government, and the state in a long tradition that goes back to the modern classics. It would be unthinkable to understand Montesquieu's distinction between tyranny and democracy without considering the organization of the exercise of power in the state and government, or J.S. Mill's understanding of government separately from "discussion", since, for Mill, "government by discussion" is the distinctive sign of democracy. The intersections between regime, government, and state are essential to understanding democracy in each of them and in their interrelationships. Identifying these interrelations cannot be likened to a "confusion"

---

14 (Valdés-Ugalde and Ansolabehere, 2012; Ansolabehere, et al., 2015 and 2020; Mazzuca and Munck, 2020).

that is attributed to the literature on the quality of democracy when such studies accept this non-minimalist definition of democracy (Mazzuca, 2010).[15]

The reduction of democracy to the exclusive dimension of the political regime makes it impossible to explain its interaction with the government and the state, and to understand the exercise of government power and the functioning of the state in accordance to, or in defiance of, the principles that define it. Democracy or, alternatively, that which is democratic, is a property of all three entities, but this property or set of properties emanates from the citizen agency that derives from sovereignty. Propositional action is the origin of politics, and politics is the space in which actors process the conflicts arising from the search for cooperation through political-ideological projects. In democracy, this action requires two principles: equality and majority (Beetham, 1999, p. 153 and *passim*). The first principle is required because the condition of equality of all members of the *demos* is a requirement for their equal inclusion in public decisions.[16] The second because it is the elementary, but not exclusive, method of collective decision-making. None of these principles is exhausted in the electoral ballots that citizens cast at the ballot box when electing their representatives. Each of them can, in principle, *be present* at all times in all the decisions of the regime, the government, and the state.

1.4 The democratic state as a procedural structure

Anticipating the theoretical foundations of representative democracy that we will unpack in Chapter 3, we propose a way of solving this problem by allowing the democratic features of the regime, on the one hand, and those of the state, on the other, not to be one and the same thing, but to be differentiated conceptually and empirically. Above all, we must recognize that the democratic content of both is procedural and that therein lies their "substantive" essence. Contemporary efforts to reconceptualize representative democracy have made it possible to observe that voting by citizens is one of its fundamental pieces, insofar as it is the way to

---

15 The distinction between regime and state to determine the presence or absence of certain attributes is the result of a methodological decision to examine the problem on the basis of dichotomous variables (yes/no), but this option is not necessarily more fertile than studying the issue on the basis of continuous variables that make it possible to observe the nuances of the quality spectrum.

16 The majority principle is incomprehensible without the principle of equality. The condition of equal rights is the backbone that justifies the fact that the majority can make decisions. Equal voting conditions cannot be violated by a majority that arises through elections (Valdés-Ugalde, 2023).

decide who governs, how and for what purpose; that is, to transform citizens' preferences into political will (government, public policy). The other component that continuously permeates the democratic process is opinion, and this element is a permanent interaction between the spheres of citizenship, regime, government and the state.

If the balance between the democratic principles of majority and equality is maintained, the vote leads to the inclusion of citizens' opinion in government action without violating the political rights of minorities. However, if the same principles prevail between elections, i.e., for the duration of governments, a permanent interaction between representatives and constituents develops. This form of agency is different from voting (Urbinati, 2014, pp. 16–80). The interlocution between citizens and rulers occurs permanently and its characteristics depend on the degree to which the state has built forms and procedures capable of giving them a permanent and continuous place in the formation of public decisions (political will). These forms and procedures are the contemporary form of the "assembly" which, parallel to the legislative assembly -but informally- generates, reproduces, and adjusts citizen opinion vis-à-vis public affairs. Just as voting is the inclusion of opinions expressed as ballots cast, which the state guarantees through clean, fair, and transparent elections, public opinion is a sphere of struggle for the inclusion of societal opinions expressed before constituents' representatives to influence the conduct and policies of the government. The protection of the equality of this right to influence political will with one's own opinion does not currently have institutions equivalent to those that protect the integrity of the vote.

This refers to an exercise of positive freedom (which traditional liberalism distrusts -Berlin 1990), emanating from the rights of expression, press, assembly, and organization, which requires protection from the political community and its authority, the government, which, from the normative point of view, is not subject to regressive negotiation as, for example, legislation on the limits of executive power can be. To guarantee this freedom, it must be removed from the political regime and safeguarded in the sphere of the state; like any provision it may be subject to revision, although the criterion that protects it must be subject to different rules of deliberation, just like the right to equal suffrage. If we reduce democracy to the political regime, then we have no criteria for associating state actions with a democratic will. The *agency* of citizens comes from an *opinion* that is shaped into a *will* for decision-making, except for voting (access), which is realized in the regime -but is regulated in the state's constitution. Within the state, political will is exercised and government decisions are made. The bridge between the two is the representative, and both representatives and citizens shape these decisions during the inter-electoral period. This is the irreducible diarchy of democracy that exists since the unity of opinion and good faith in the monarch was dissolved. To control power is to divide it, to separate the sovereign from the public servant, to elect or remove the latter and to monitor them regularly while they exercise power so that they can fully *represent*. Inclusion in political power is not reduced to participation in the regime, but rather it is being actively present in the enveloping character of representative democracy supervising the driving forces of politics. Hence,

> when opinion is introduced in our understanding of democratic participation, then political representation must attend to the question of the circumstances of opinion formation, an issue that pertains to political justice, or the equal opportunity citizens should have to meaningfully enjoy their political rights (Urbinati, 2014, p. 28).

The guarantee and protection of citizens' right "to form, express, voice, and give their ideas public weight and influence" is a function that begins in the citizenry, continues in the regime, and culminates in the state. The right to equal suffrage has achieved extensive equal protection. However, the same has not been true of the right to equal influence in the formation of political will. In fact, this is frequently violated while the integrity of the vote tends to be more protected. This can even be observed in the processes of autocratization in which, while political and civic rights are suppressed, the vote is maintained as the last bastion of authority validation. Recent examples in Latin America are Venezuela and Nicaragua. Equality of opportunity in the exercise of one's opinion does not have an equivalent of equality to vote; it is a debt to political justice, and the criteria of justice cannot be the same as the criteria of ordinary opinion or judgment (Urbinati, 2014, p. 34).

The interrelationships or affinities between principles and institutions are shown in the tables 1.1. and 1.2. Figures 1.1., 1.2. and 1.3. depict the intersection between citizenship, regime, and state in three types of democracy: developed, underdeveloped, and representative.

1.5 Control of elites and reversal of inequality

Representative democracy has normalized political conflict in all its dimensions and has placed it at the center of the public arena. This is the most important mission: It has to make the construction of social cooperation possible. However, on the other side of the same coin, we find the lack of social cooperation in Latin American societies, which makes it easier to understand how intense and polarizing the distributive conflict is. It is a conflict whose origins lie in the dissatisfaction with the "basic structures" that are the systematic generators of injustice. This dissatisfaction does not stem exclusively from, for example, income inequality, but from perceived inequality in the ability to influence spheres of pub-

Tab. 1.1: State, regime and government in democracy and autocracy.

PRINCIPLES AND INSTITUTIONS	State (constituting community) Includes and excludes actors and practices	Regime (processes-includes/excludes)	Government (produces public goods and services)
Democratic	Makes up and safeguards the "basic structure" of democracy, Equality + Majority.	1. Effective participation	1. Elected officials 2. Free, fair, and frequent elections 3. Freedom of expression
		2. Voting equality 3. Gaining enlightened understanding	4. Alternative sources of information
		4. Exercising final control over the agenda	5. Associational autonomy
		5. Inclusion of adults[1]	6. Inclusive citizenship
Authoritarian	Protects the basic components to arbitrarily exercise state authority.	1. Barriers to participation	Patrimonialism
	Inequality + minority	2. Voting inequality	Arbitrariness
		3. Misinformation and "biased knowledge"	Exclusion
		4. Not having a say regarding the agenda	
		5. Exclusion of adults[17]	

lic decisions. The most transcendent phenomenon of democratic expansion is the increased freedom to expand the modalities of *contention* over the scope and dimensions of political, civil, economic, social, and cultural rights. Political openness, despite inadequacies and differential features of political systems, has meant an expansion of welfare expectations, one of which is the search for the expansion of rights. Whether civil and political, cultural or ethnic, economic or social rights, under democratic conditions the demand for democracy has be-

---

17 Dahl, Robert A. 1998:38. The conditions for democratic rule and government come from the same source.

Tab. 1.2: Principles and institutions in democracies.[18]

PRINCIPLES AND INSTITUTIONS	Equality	Majority
State	STATENESS	*Protects the government to comply with the majority's mandate
	*Contains the fundamental rights and procedures in the Constitution.	*Circumscribes the majority if equality is violated
	*Regulates the regime and the government in accordance with the principle of equality.	*Circumscribes and defines the authority of fundamental political goods
Regime	ACCESS	*Guarantee of results
	*Rule of law[19][1]	*Rule of law
	*Fair elections	*Guarantee of rights
	*Civic and political rights	*Rotation guarantee
	*Alternative information	
Government	EXERCISE	*Makes decisions for the majority
	*Conducts itself in accordance with procedures that recognize and treat the governed equally	*Consultation to understand variations within the majority
		*Accountability

come a demand for equal rights within states that are democratic in their rules
and procedures for access to power, but are less democratic or undemocratic in

---

18 The justification for each of these dimensions of the three institutional levels lies in the definition of sovereignty and its implications. Sovereignty resides in the "people," but the "people" is qualified: it is not the disciplined Hitlerian horde, nor Lenin's proletariat, nor the loyal and obedient people of the populists. Its definition refers to the tension that is permanently present within agency in politics between individual autonomy and the need for collective action. The people comprise free individuals, but they have links among themselves that oblige them to communicate. The search for causal relationships in this problematic is secondary to the fundamental task: the mutual reinforcement between the two aspects of this binary condition of agency that drives it. Representative democracy is the engine that explains the movement of the whole mechanism.
19 ...the rule of the state is to protect the flow of information against concentration of powers and that the liberty of those who are in a condition of passivity, like an audience, is the first good to be protected by right." (Urbinati 2014: 64)

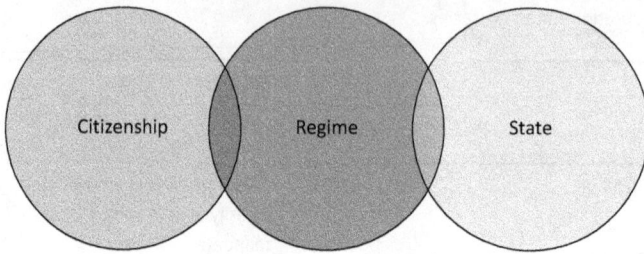

Fig. 1.1: Developed democracies.

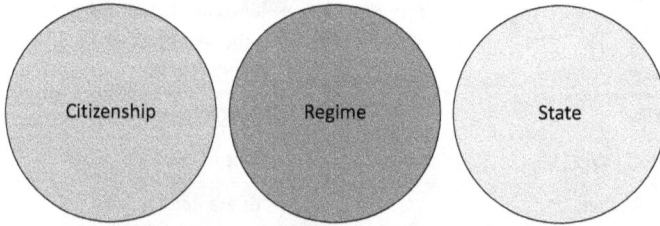

Fig. 1.2: Underdeveloped democracies.

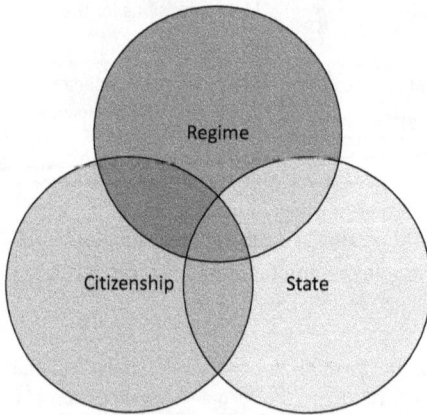

Fig. 1.3: Representative democracies.
NOTE: The intersection of the sets represents different degrees
of fulfillment of representative democracy.

how they exercise it and, consequently, hinder egalitarian change.[20] This trend reflects a challenge to democracy as a political system since it begs the question of whether it can accommodate both the liberal state and the social state at the same time, recalling the warning that "when the liberal state and the democratic state fall, they fall together" (Bobbio, 1992). Except in a few countries, it would stretch the truth to say that democratic development in Latin America has satisfied the criteria of a liberal state. Electoral democracies have been relatively stabilized, but there is a lack of social protection systems and rule of law with the capacity to produce an acceptable political order and the public goods demanded by justice, shortcomings that in turn tend to work against the integrity of electoral democracy.

As seems clear to the average observer, in Latin America there have been two main evolutions in the conformation of democratic political systems. One that remains within the lower limits of the liberal state from the point of view of preserving fundamental freedoms and the balance of powers, and the other one has led to populist formulas in which one or both of these conditions are infringed.[21] The emergence of populism is, at least in part, caused by an inability to establish the social state. From this perspective, a symptom of this evil is the decline in the preference for democracy and the increase in the acceptance of "less" democratic governments that "solve economic problems" (O'Donnell, 2010; see Figs. 1.4 and 1.5).

This trend is linked to another one that is no less worrying: the willingness of some parties and leaders to appeal to the enormous social needs in a quest to establish authoritarian governments that offer "solutions" to the less-favored sectors of society in exchange for support to build monopolies of political power, with the additional support of *de facto* powers -economic, media, military, or religious-, which concentrate and protect the patrimonial practices of power. Relevant citizen groups are dissatisfied with the inadequacy of the political regime to accommodate their demands at the state level, a sphere in which they could be met if the regime were to set it in motion, through the *constitutionalization* of new duties and responsibilities that society and government would be obliged to fulfill and enforce.[22]

Is it possible to get out of the tunnel of precarious democracies with inefficient governments and regressive utopias? The United Nations Development Programme

---

20 Detailed expositions can be found in Valdés-Ugalde and Ansolabehere (2012), Ansolabehere, et al. (2015 and 2020).

21 In the V-Dem 2020 report, only three Latin American countries were in the top 30% of the "liberal democracies" category (Lührmann, 2020, pp. 24–25).

22 Constitutionalization is here understood in the sense of registration of *de jure* inclusion and *de facto* compliance.

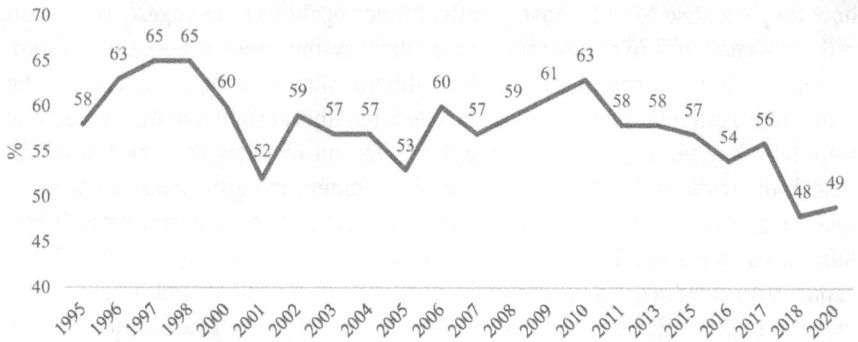

Fig. 1.4: Total Latin America 1995–2020 Which of the following statements do you agree with the most? "Democracy is preferable to any other form of government".
Source: Corporación Latinobarómetro (2020)

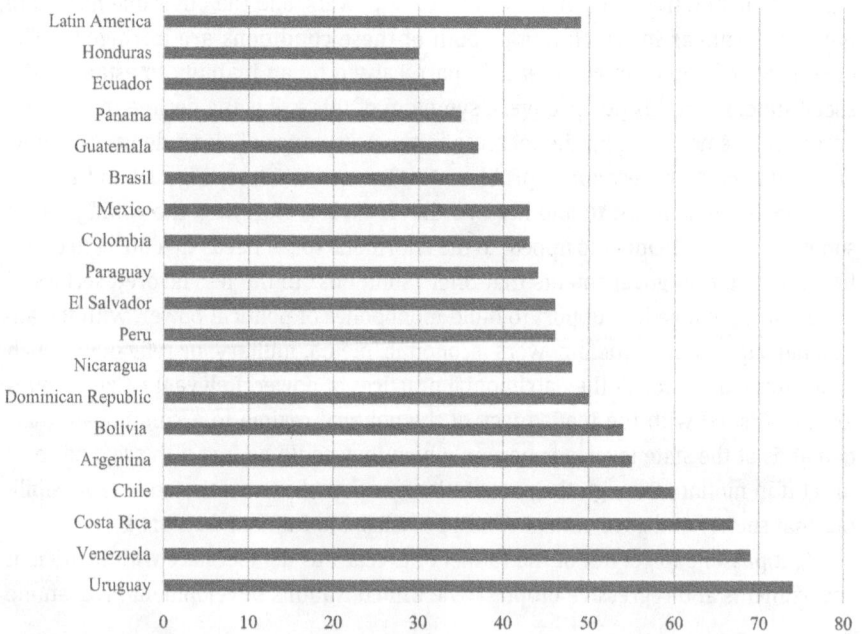

Fig. 1.5: Totals by country 2020 Which of the following statements do you agree with the most? "Democracy is preferable to any other form of government".
Source: Corporación Latinobarómetro (2020)

(UNDP) report on democracy in Latin America (2004)[23] revisited a forgotten topic in Latin American political sociology and put forward a different perspective. The report resorted to T. H. Marshall's famous idea.[24] that democracy is formed at the grassroots by citizens who found in this identity and in its basic tool, suffrage, the vehicle to belong to political society and develop the civil rights "necessary for individual and personal freedom, freedom of speech, thought, and faith, the right to own property, make valid contracts, and the right to justice," as well as social rights, "from the right to basic economic welfare and security to the right to participate fully in social heritage and live the life of a civilized being in accordance with the prevailing standard of society" (PNUD, 2004, p. 33).

The universal extension of citizenship described by Marshall was the result of a complex and conflictive political evolution.[25] This evolution was given a powerful impetus by many of the events that occurred in the nearly 100 years from 1848 to 1945 that saw a racially motivated civil war in the United States, several social revolutions on three continents, countless regional wars, and two world wars that, when concluded, gave rise to the largest massive public investment ever known, the Marshall Plan,[26] which is symbolic of capitalism's distributive turn in the 20th century.[27]

Millions of people lost their lives directly or indirectly as a result of the conflicts that arose in the construction of political democracy and in linking it to the production of forms of collective welfare. One of the keys to understanding the political evolution of the contemporary world is that the liberal state was open to an increasing number of citizens who contributed to its enrichment and received bene-

---

23 This report had a relevant impact due to the change in the approach taken by a group of social scientists led by Guillermo O'Donnell. PNUD, (2004). See also a follow up in PNUD, 2010.

24 Marshall, T. H. "Sociology at the Crossroads. An inaugural lecture delivered on 21st. Feb. 1946 at the London School of Economics and Political Science," London, New York, Longmans, Green, 1947. This conference was later compiled in Marshall (1950).

25 In a different register, Adam Przeworski proposes a precise and detailed explanation of the moments in which the extension of suffrage (one of the rights of citizenship) was a conquest of excluded groups or a concession of the elites (Przeworski, 2009).

26 Between 1948 and 1951 the European reconstruction program implemented by Secretary of State George C. Marshall channeled more than twelve billion dollars of money from the American public to contribute to the reconstruction of democratic Europe. This figure equaled approximately 3.4% of 1951 U.S. GDP and $134 billion at 2022 values.

27 This turn is itself related to the need to demonstrate the ability to generate welfare similar or superior to that of the communist bloc (Judt, 2006, p. 165 *and passim*). From the neoconservative point of view, this path must be abandoned because it leads to "socialism". The Trilateral Commission's report was not deluded in this respect (Crozier, et al. 1975). The development of the social state probably leads to fundamental changes in social cooperation that can peacefully bring about a transformation of capitalism into a different form of productive organization.

fits and entitlements from its institutions. What was initially a system of thought limited to building governments with restricted participation, guaranteeing basic liberties to the small group of people who in the 18th and 19th centuries were citizens, -limited almost completely to minority elites- opened up to egalitarian pressures that gave way to a more complex, less unjust, and more educated society. This was not a fortuitous or marginal evolution, but a development that has ended up proving to be *a royal road*. Without the Marshall Plan, democracy in Europe would not have taken the path we know today. Economic and social stability and the broad horizons open to economic development, although they originated differently, were equally decisive in consolidating democracy. The characteristic development of the advanced economies of the North Atlantic and other countries such as Japan cannot be explained without two institutions of the greatest relevance to egalitarianism: impersonality and free access. These characteristics are indispensable for understanding the link between advanced economic-technical development and modern democracy. The replacement of personal relationships (patrimonialism, serfdom, etc.) by impersonal relationships between individuals and the establishment of rules allowing the free entry and exit of individuals from economic, political, and social "games", i.e., the freedom to decide what kind of ties to adopt, acquired a centrality that made them expand rapidly (North et al., 2009, pp. 148–250).[28]

In contrast, the endemic dislocation of democratic state institutions in Latin America is directly related to the continuing divorce between liberalism, civil rights, and social and human development, leading to great inequality. On the one hand, powerful groups have a hypertrophied dominance of public decisions and policies that reduces state autonomy and the representation of other socially relevant agents in their making. This is due both to the state's institutional (fiscal and legal) weakness and to the presence of public-private coalitions of a mainly rentier sector -and not infrequently kleptocratic- that have traditionally placed themselves above written legal rules and manipulate them in their favor. On the other hand, disadvantaged, endemically marginalized groups see their interests in making public decisions and policies constantly postponed or thoroughly subordinated to the elites. The vicious circle of exclusion and lack of political autonomy is self-reinforcing. Exclusion leads to weakness and a diminished ability to organize and mobilize which, in turn, feeds back into exclusion. In addition, the social segmentation that underpins inequality is also a segmentation of systems of norms and rules of action that establish differential channels of access to vari-

---

28 These two conditions are related to the character of "civilization" referred to in the UNDP Report. Lacking them as a fundamental component, the modern economy and the modern state are not possible or are only partially possible.

ous "goods" for each social group. For this reason, the general rules that are characteristic of legal equality have a low capacity or occupy a secondary place in controlling the patterns and courses of action iterated in political relations. One of these channels is clientelism, which is the common tactic used by dominant groups to come to, and stay in, power.

Under these conditions, neither impersonality nor free access are present in the social conditions that are prerequisites for democracy and advanced economic development. This is one of the main reasons why in most of Latin America, liberalism and democracy do not complement or provide feedback to each other, but rather clash. When distributive conflict appears, the socially dominant groups resort to the most hardened political (or military) options and the socially dominated groups promote the emergence of leaderships and forms of political action which, for the sake of "social democratization", throw liberal "forms" out the window through violence or populism. Distributive conflict becomes endemic without producing a new type of state equilibrium.

The poor fortune of democracy in Latin America is associated with this self-reinforcing divorce between the liberal political state and the civil and social rights of the broadest groups in society. This separation throws even more light on the barriers that the state places on political interaction in the regime. The results of this interaction often have no continuity in the formation of public policies and in the state's constituent mechanisms. As a way out of this contradiction, Latin America has resorted to forms of populism or *Caesarism* which, although they respond to diverse conditions due to the internal structure of each society and its political system, have as a common denominator in the curtailment or suppression of political rights. This is justified in the interest of expanding social rights under the presence of charismatic and authoritarian leaderships which, once deteriorated by the absence of counterweights, tend to fall apart with everything else, as Bobbio points out.

Why have Latin American states been unable to harmonize democratic political systems and modern economic and social development? The answer to this question can have many variants and nuances, but there is a central aspect supported by historical literature and overwhelming empirical evidence. This is the aforementioned ability of the economic and political power elites to maintain, through patrimonial practices, control of the fundamental levers of the political system in order to protect their social, political, and economic privileges. On the other side of the same coin are vast social sectors, especially the working and professional middle classes, who are excluded from access to the means of control of the state government. Regardless of the fact that all citizens have the right to vote, political systems do not have the rules and institutions that would enable them to control the exercise of power and counterbalance extra-state ("*de facto*") powers with the formal regulations of the rule of law and improve citizens' representation in terms of political equality. This gap explains to a large extent the conflict within the sphere of political regimes that deal with it according to rules ("state agreements") that make it difficult or even impossible to transform the spheres of government decision-making and state ability to guarantee the broad protection of rights. The problem lies not only in the instability caused by citizens' rejection of economic inequality, but also in the fact that political equality is denied by elites in the interest of preserving the *status quo*. The feeling that peoples' voices does not count exacerbates other differences and becomes a time bomb that, when it explodes, turns against democratic institutions.

Hence, Latin American political systems, although they regulate access to power through the vote, lack other equally crucial conditions to ensure the quality of democracy in state building. It is at the thresholds between citizenship, regime, and state that the democratization process encounters its greatest obstacles. And this is where representative democracy makes a difference that can be observed in the experiences that have succeeded in consolidating it.

These conditions can be summarized as a lack of political equality of all participants in the "demos" (Dahl, 2006, p. 14; Valdés-Ugalde and Salazar, 2015). Underlying the lack of political equality are the absence of impersonality and free access, which are not institutions rooted in the social relations of Latin American countries. This fact draws attention to the non-existence or insufficiency of existing mechanisms to induce citizen equalization vis-à-vis political power, conditions of equity between society and power and, finally, of *de jure* and *de facto* institutionalization of the expansion of rights achieved through the democratic process.

The explanation of this specific (but not exclusive) problem of the Latin American state has been previously explored (Guerra, 1995; Annino and Guerra, 2003; Coatsworth, 1990). Likewise, recent studies have shed light on the way in which 40 years of more-or-less democratic, more-or-less stable, and more-or-less efficient regimes for conducting economic-political modernization have caused tension in the traditional institutional forms of the Latin American formula (Mazzuca and Munck 2020; Kapiszewski et al., 2021; O'Donnell, 2010). The arguments for this approach are generally the following. The trajectory of state formation in Latin America had a different outcome than in the North Atlantic countries (Coatsworth, 1978, Mazzuca 2020). Both economically and in terms of state capacities, Latin America was reducing the proportions of its economy and its relative importance in the world context between the end of the 18th and 19th centuries. In the 20th century, however, industrial development created a working class that demanded and obtained, at least in the larger countries, a relative incorporation into the political system (Collier and Collier, 1991) that ended around 1980 when ISI (import substitution industrialization) was exhausted. In the third wave of democracy, Latin America experienced a new process of inclusion, as paradoxical as it is illustrative. Paradoxical because, contrary to widespread rhetoric, the inclusion of the popular sectors in economies that had adopted neoliberal policies at the same time as they initiated a new democratic stage in their political systems would be unthinkable, and illustrative because, in spite of this, the combination of the fight against inequality and social policies resulted in a considerable degree of inclusion (see *infra*, Chapter 2). Recent research (Kapiszewski et al., 2021) offers important findings on the post-transition period. The sources of inclusion lie in the persistent struggle against inequality within democratic political systems. Inclusion occurs with advances in "recognition, access, and resources", and the processes that explain such inclusion are characterized as "parchment amendments". Naturally, multiparty conflict leads to actions and reactions for and against inclusion. The sources of resistance to inclusion are concentrated in the conservative forces, i.e., economic elites who question the distribution and the courts' favoritism of the powerful in judicial processes. In some cases, however, the courts have favored broad processes of inclusion.

"Yet paradoxically, opposition to inclusion also creates incentives for some inclusionary governments to weaken the very democratic institutions that enabled their rise in the first place." (Kapiszewski et al., 2021, p. 35) These are the caesaristic forms ("delegative democracies" according to O'Donnell's terminology), that try to cut off the path to inclusion by avoiding the democratization of the state in order to, in the end, replace it with the traditional legitimacy of a charismatic leader. Since democracy admits pluralism, opposition to inclusion takes on various forms; the authors mentioned previously call it "paradoxes" of democracy, although the term is, in my view, inappropriate because it avoids recognizing that the inclusion achieved in democracy can be reversed, unless another type of inclusion occurs: that which interweaves representatives and constituents at the very heart of the *exercise of state power*. The authors of *The Inclusionary Turn* highlight the precise symptom of this more than frequent impossibility: ("While effective state institutions are essential for inclusion, *they only matter to the degree that political actors deploy them for inclusionary ends")* (Kapiszewski et al., 2021, p. 41, emphasis added). The fragmentation of pressure from the popular classes works against inclusion unless a political will for autonomous political organization emerges from them. Thus the differences between Europe and Latin America. Once the unification of territory, population, and legitimate violence was achieved – similarly in both cases – while in Europe local oligarchies that hindered national unification were subdued, with political and military support from popular groups, in Latin America the political elites and other "powers that be" were strengthened and became interwoven. In Europe, the United States, and Canada, the original "European" course of building national unity continued *pari passu* with the establishment of a state with strong military and administrative capabilities. In Latin America a different phenomenon took place. Instead of *state building* there is the consolidation of "patrimonial bastions" with three types of domination: territorial, political party, or power-sharing alliances (Mazzuca, 2021, p. 398, Fig. 11.1). This difference in trajectories means that the process of institutionalization of law and rights is also different. Unlike in Europe where, thanks to the organizational capacity of the popular sectors, it was necessary to negotiate with them the means of waging war and establish permanent distributive concessions (Tilly, 1999), the dynamics that state formation followed in Latin America did not require deep and lasting alliances with the people, but rather among the elites themselves, so as to avert the risks of rebellion of the popular classes (Keane 2009, p. 393 and *passim*). This means that state formation was not followed by modern state building (Mazzuca, 2021), at least in European terms, but rather it produced a different, hybrid state, whose personality has been inscribed in the typology of political systems (Linz and Valenzuela, 1994). It follows that the negotiation between elites and subordinate classes had different effects in Latin America and in Europe. The main difference between the two subcontinents is that while in Europe multiple wars served to unify the elites with the popular classes through the negotiation of rights in exchange for loyalty and military services, in Latin America there was no equivalent bargaining/distribution relationship during the process of state formation, but rather a relationship of unconditional subordination ("dogs that didn't bark" -Fukuyama, 2014, Chapter 7). Consequently, in the former case the state gradually acquired obligations that ultimately shaped citizenship rights and mechanisms for the extension of rights as a legitimate trajectory, while in the latter case this process was delayed until well into the 20th century and has been mired in the endemic conflict at the stage of democratic generalization. The difference in the political balance between society and state was thus very different in the two cases. The first path intertwined political rights and then social rights with the formation of political power, while in the second path the construction of the edifice of power was done with less support from the popular classes, with the consequence of their lesser weight in the formation of political power, that is, the interactions between citizenship, political regime, and state. This problem is discussed in detail in the following chapter.

Chapter 2
The performance of the state. Inequality and exclusion

But, large or small, this state scarcely functions as a propeller of the extension of civil and
cultural rights and, even less so, of social rights
Guillermo O'Donnell

2.1 Approaching the structure of the exercise of power

The institutions created to produce certain desired effects mediate between the democratic nature of the regime and the effects of governance. Their quality depends on the quality of these institutions. Assuming for the sake of the argument that the state is composed of a monopoly of legitimate violence and the bureaucracy, which is partially a consequence of that monopoly, both components can only be explained by the existence of a "political community" (Weber) that makes use of both. Such a community has certain characteristic features that are not limited to the monopoly of violence, and it is logical that the state should be tinged in some way with these features. To paraphrase Montesquieu, such a community may be more or less oligarchic, more or less tyrannical, more or less aristocratic, or more or less democratic. The democratic regime does something right or wrong in order for that political community to produce (or not) the public goods required by society, the citizenry, and its representatives. Hence, a democratic or non-democratic character can be assigned to the state, in addition to other qualities, and "the democratic nature" cannot be reduced exclusively to the regime, which does not mean that we must incur in the tautology of thinking that the distinctive democratic features of the regime and of the state are the same. A non-reductionist reading of the legitimacy of power opens up this perspective and circumvents the technocratic bias that limits the state to its bureaucratic and coercive capacities.

Detailed studies of state performance (Mazzuca and Munck, 2020) (Brinks et al., 2020), (Fukuyama, 2008), (Soifer, 2015) and democracy inclusion (Tilly, 2007), (Pinto and Flisfisch, 2011), (Kapiszewski et al., 2021), and rights (Ansolabehere et al., 2015, 2020) during the "democratic (or transitional) era" agree that there is relevant progress in some areas of state performance and citizen inclusion, although in both cases they are far from reaching the standards established in their constitutions and expressed in the aspirations posed to the regime by a plurality of social groups. Analyzing the World Bank's World Government Indicators, we find states whose underperformance is remarkable. But before studying them, we examine the socio-

https://doi.org/10.1515/9783110773675-003

economic inequality that exists and then discuss a study of these indicators for certain countries we have selected.[29] We will combine them with the V-Dem exclusion index and the degree of fulfillment of a set of rights, in order to associate state performance with the degree of social and political inclusion in public life.

2.1.1 Inequality

According to recent figures (2021) from ECLAC,[30] Latin America and the Caribbean have a population of 665 million people, of which more than half (341 million) live in Brazil and Mexico, where profound social inequality exists. By 2020, in Brazil, the poorest quintile of the population received 3.7% of national income and the top quintile 56.9%. In the same year, in Mexico, the income of the lowest quintile was 5.1% while for the highest quintile it was 51.1% of the total. Nevertheless, between 2006 and 2020, the Gini coefficient for Brazil fell from 0.556 to 0.489 (−0.67) and in Mexico from 0.489 to 0.454 (−0.35).[31] Although inequality has decreased, especially in Brazil, it is clear that profound social inequality persists in Latin America's two most populous countries. The rest of the region is not much different. Available data for 17 countries indicate that in 2020, the highest inequalities were recorded in Guatemala (0.535), Colombia (0.552), and the lowest in Venezuela (0.378).[32] In any event, the outlook is discouraging.

Yet, disconcerting but favorable data for the prospects of democracy are reported by the life satisfaction index.[33] According to this source, among the emerging economies, in Mexico and Brazil the middle and lower strata are most satisfied with their lives. The emergence of middle classes in these countries is one of their most characteristic advances. The case of China has become exemplary, but Latin America and the Caribbean, although in a more modest way, are also posting notable growth. According to the aforementioned report, the subcontinent increased the number of people who have overcome poverty and live with an average income, from 277 million in 1990 to 362 million in 2005, which means that the number of people in this stratum increased by 76%.

---

29 See Methodological Note at the end of this chapter.
30 CEPAL (2022, August 1).
31 World Bank (2022, May 18).
32 Note that these calculations were made with government-issued figures and should be taken with reservations, given the autonomy and suitability of the offices mandated with keeping statistics, particularly in Venezuela during the Chávez and Maduro governments.
33 The Economist (2009, February 14).

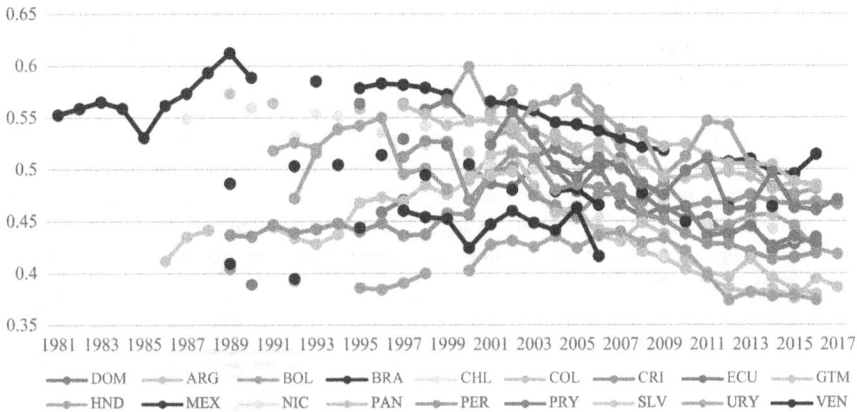

Fig. 2.1: Income inequality in Latin America 1981 to 2017.
Source: Gini Index (CEDLAS, 2018).

According to ECLAC data (CEPAL, 2019), in several Latin American countries, the high-income population more than doubled. In Colombia it grew from 0.6 to 1.5 million and in Argentina from 0.4 to 1.6 million. In Ecuador, for example, from 2001 to 2011 the upper middle class grew from 0.4 to 1.5 million. Between 2001 and 2011, in Brazil the lower classes shrank, increasing the population in the middle, upper middle, and upper classes; the middle class grew from 31 to 54.8 million people. In Mexico, this population increased from 2001 to 2011 by 14 million people; analyzing by income, we observe an increase in the population of the middle, upper middle and upper classes. The middle class increased the most as a whole, growing from

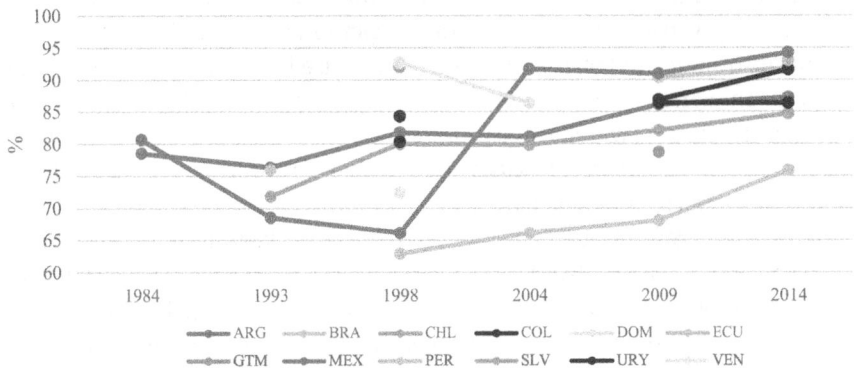

Fig. 2.2: Share of people who say they are happy in Latin America, 1984 to 2014.
Source: World Value Survey (Inglehart et al., 2014)

17.8 to 30.70 million. It is likely that this increase in the middle-income population influences a greater perception of well-being (Fig. 2.2).

ECLAC (Fig. 2.3.) reports that

the share of middle-income strata in the total population of Latin America increased from 26.9% in 2002 to 41.1% in 2017. The population of low-income strata (i.e., the sum of the population in extreme poverty, non-extreme poverty, and low non-poor sectors) decreased from 70.9% to 55.9%. There is also a slight increase in the high-income stratum (people whose per capita income exceeds 10 poverty lines): from 2.2% to 3.0% of the population. (CEPAL, 2019, p. 27)

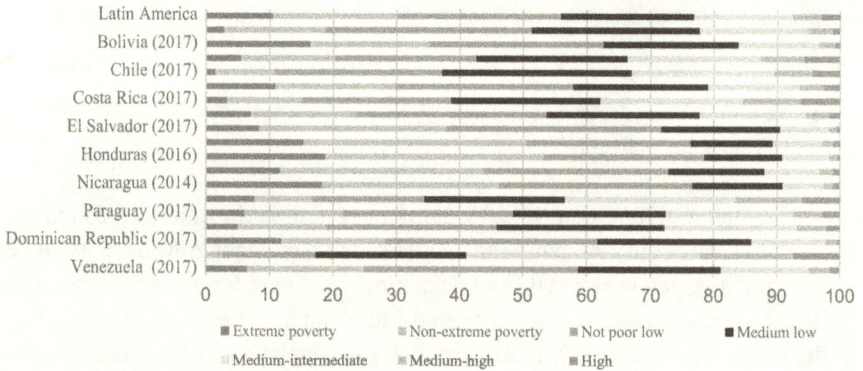

Fig. 2.3: Population by income strata in Latin America.
Source: (CEPAL, 2019, p. 60).

This growth of the middle sectors is partially due to the commodity boom of the first 15 years of the 21st century (2000–2014). Once this growth came to an end, a regression in distribution between strata began to take place. This reveals that income distribution in favor of the more marginalized sectors depends almost exclusively on market behavior. However, during the growth cycle, democratic representation did not favorably impact the structure of income distribution, nor did it improve permanent state capacities for protection and distribution in accordance with recognized rights. As the pace of growth slowed, market distribution was reversed and governments found themselves deprived of the distributive institutions that compensate for this deterioration in advanced democracies. As we shall see below, this evolution brought enormous social pressure on political regimes, which increased conflict and distributive demands on the state, the barriers that oppose them, and shows the poor response they receive from the state.

Figure 2.1. reveals a gradual decrease in inequality in general terms. But if we analyze the Latin American index before and after distribution in comparison with other countries outside the region (Fig. 2.4.),[34] there are countries whose per-capita market income shows a high GINI coefficient, such as Ireland with 0.58, but once the public sector intervenes in the distribution it falls to 0.31; or the Nordic countries whose index after distribution is around 0.25, while before state intervention they have high levels of inequality (Finland 0.50, Denmark 0.44, Norway 0.41). In Belgium, the Gini coefficient would be 0.49 (i.e., almost the same as in Chile, Brazil, or Mexico) before taxes and transfers, but due to a government sector that generates public goods, its coefficient decreases to 0.27. Similarly, Australia reduces its inequality from 0.48 to 0.34, Italy from 0.52 to 0.33, the United States from 0.51 to 0.39, and Japan from 0.49 to 0.33. In contrast, in Latin American countries, the difference before and after is much smaller. For example, the difference before and after public intervention in Chile is 0.50 to 0.47, and in Mexico it is 0.48 to 0.46. The mediocrity of this performance is evident.

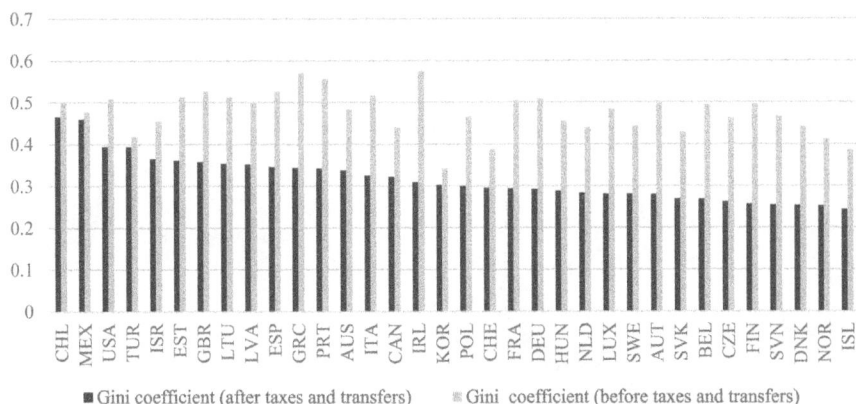

Fig. 2.4: Inequality of incomes before and after redistribution.
Source: OECD (2016). For the years 2012 to 2014 data depend on country availability.

This means that, in general terms, market inequality does not distinguish greatly between more or less "developed" countries, but rather the difference comes from the distribution made through state intervention and this, in turn, is determined by different political histories. The radical difference between countries that reduce inequality through public action and those that do not depends on the levels of tax collection in their economies and the allocation of resources to

---

34 Roser, M. and Ortiz-Ospina, E. (2022, November 23).

public policies that improve citizens' quality of life.[35] A World Bank study (De Ferranti et al., 2003) calculates that between 1990 and 1999, the central governments of Latin America collected 15.15% of GDP from tax contributions, while between 1991 and 2000, developed countries collected 28.7% (Fig. 2.5). Furthermore, the relationship between social spending as a percentage of GDP and the total share of public spending allocated to the social sector places Latin American countries in different positions. In Mexico, total public spending is below 20% of GDP and 9.1% is allocated to social spending, which makes it similar in relative terms to Guatemala and Paraguay. In contrast, Brazil, Argentina, and Uruguay allocate more than 30% of GDP to fiscal spending and channel more than 60% to social spending.

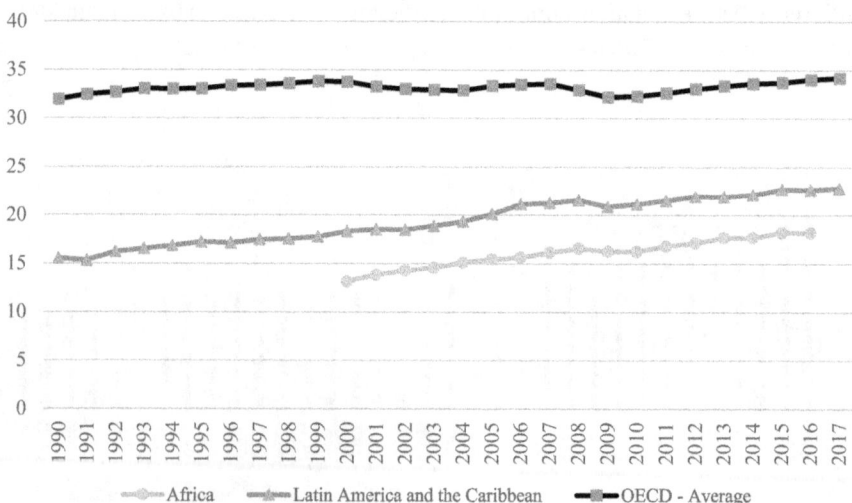

Fig. 2.5: Tax revenue as share of GDP 1990 to 2017.
Source: OECD (2018).

Thus, low tax collection, the scarce amount of resources allocated to social security and social spending, persistent inequality and poor income distribution re-

---

35 One fact not considered here is the different bargaining capacities between workers and employers that create market distribution differentials on their own, prior to state intervention. However, we argue that the degree to which the state intervenes in post-market distribution results precisely from this differential. The more or less asymmetrical, but socially accepted, forms of income bargaining are part of different economic and political cultures (political economies). At the extremes of these cultures are, on the one hand, the countries in which social democracy has had the greatest influence and, on the other, those with a largely oligarchic and patrimonial origin or with strong market fundamentalism.

veal a condition that we would not dare equate with political equality of citizens or, in Dahl's words, "members of the demos," despite the promising data on the growth of the middle stratum.

Latin American states suffer from fundamental flaws that make them weak and conducive to structural entrenchment of special interests. Part of this distributive gap originates in states that lack arrangements for generating social protection and welfare. The absence of progressive income taxation is partially offset by migrants' remittances, a palliative that mitigates distributive pressure (Tab. 2.1.). This brings us to another factor, migration, involving the expulsion of 40.5 million people for economic reasons, or 6% of the population of Latin America and 15% of total world migration (CEPAL, 2019, p. 32).

Tab. 2.1: Poverty with and without migrant remittances.

	Poverty rate of the population			Poverty rate of the population in households receiving remittances		
	Total	No remittances	Difference	Total	No remittances	Difference
Bolivia (Plurinational state of) (2017)	35.1	35.9	0.8	27.3	39.9	12.5
Chile (2017)	10.7	10.8	0.1	15.5	24.8	9.4
Colombia (2017)	29.8	30	0.2	21.1	31.2	10.1
Costa Rica (2017)	15.1	15.2	0.1	8.8	19.6	10.8
Ecuador (2017)	23.6	24.1	0.5	12.7	29.9	17.2
El Salvador (2017)	37.8	39.9	2.1	41.5	54.1	12.6
Guatemala (2014)	50.5	52	1.5	39.5	57.2	17.7
Honduras (2016)	53.1	55.5	2.4	39.5	53.3	13.8
Mexico (2016)	43.7	44.4	0.7	46.2	61.7	15.5
Paraguay (2017)	21.5	22.1	0.6	26.1	33.5	7.4
Peru (2017)	18.9	18.9	0.1	4.1	8.2	4.1
Dominican Republic (2017)	25	27.2	2.2	33.3	60.8	27.6
Uruguay (2017)	2.7	2.7	0.1	3.3	15.7	12.4

Source: (CEPAL, 2019, p.34)

Regarding health spending as a percentage of GDP allocated by Latin American countries, in 2018 the regional average was 7.2%, with the following countries allocating the most: Cuba (11.2%), Argentina (9.6%), and Uruguay (9.2%). The countries that spent the least on health in 2018 were Peru (5.2%), Mexico (5.4%), Guatemala (5.7%). Public spending on education as a percentage of GDP reported by ECLAC.[36] in 2020 shows that of the countries we selected, the ones that invested the least are Venezuela (1.3%), Panama (3.1%), and Paraguay (3.5%), in contrast to the countries with the highest spending on education: Costa Rica (6.8%) and Brazil (6.1%). The OECD.[37] reports that in 2019, the average social spending as a percentage of the GDP of member countries was 20%; France (31%), Finland (29.1%), and Belgium (28.9) have the highest social spending. In comparison, the Latin American members of the OECD spent less than the group average, for example Colombia (13.1%), Costa Rica (12.2%), Chile (11.4%), and Mexico (7.5%). Mexico spent the least of the 37 member countries.

2.1.2 Kratos excludes demos

These peculiarities of inequality and the relative indifference of the state are associated with the non-existence of transversal agreements among political forces regarding the minimum levels of welfare for which the state is responsible, i.e., the range of social welfare that is acceptable, necessary, and desired by society.[38] The non-existence of these agreements is actively or passively accepted by these actors and by civil society. Political forces tend to dispute the constitutional arrangements referring to the rights of the majorities, making them depend on short-term agreements, normally restricted to competition between parties and to the short cycles in which competition takes place by definition: periods of government or even less, drastic changes in the same governmental term. In this dispute there is no previous collective consensus regarding the *de facto status quo*. Despite the existence of constitutions whose values and norms should inform actors' behavior, these do not translate into "elective affinities" of political forces and movements.[39] In what follows we show in detail the evidence supporting this hypothesis based on the World Bank's indicators in the World Governance Index. These indicators are focused on six factors: 1. Rule of Law, 2. Voice and accountability, 3. Political stability, 4 Govern-

---

36 CEPAL (2021).

37 Organisation for Economic Co-operation and Development (OECD, 2022).

38 Welfare interval is the distance between the low- and high-income strata that are tolerable in a society, as well as the standards by which the condition of each is judged. The "tolerability" of the interval can be measured by the level of social instability derived from inequality, as well as by effective pressure (ideological + coercive) on the political regime to address inequality.

39 We use Max Weber's concept (who took it from Goethe) in the sense of empathy between values and beliefs, on the one hand, and social practices on the other. For Weber it was about affinities between religious beliefs and professional ethics (frugality, honesty, etc.). This idea can be applied to economic cultures in the sense indicated in previous notes (27 and 34).

ment effectiveness, 5. Regulatory quality, and 6. Control of corruption.[40] Later we will add the V-Dem indicators that measure exclusion due to different causes.

2.1.3 Rule of law

Most Latin American countries considered herein perform poorly in the enforcement of legal norms. Almost all are below the world average on the rule of law index. This means that there is widespread perception that agents distrust and evade social rules. In particular, they are wary of "contract enforcement, property rights, the police, and the courts, as well as the likelihood of crime and violence".[41] As shown in Fig. 2.6, at the beginning of the period under consideration, four countries (Chile, Costa Rica, Uruguay, and Argentina) were above average in terms of compliance with rules. However, the latter country very soon (1998) dropped out of this group and joined the majority of low performers. Brazil and Panama briefly exceed the average but soon fell below average again. Venezuela had the worst trajectory. Its score dropped from low performance and almost reached a point where the conditions that define the rule of law are nonexistent.

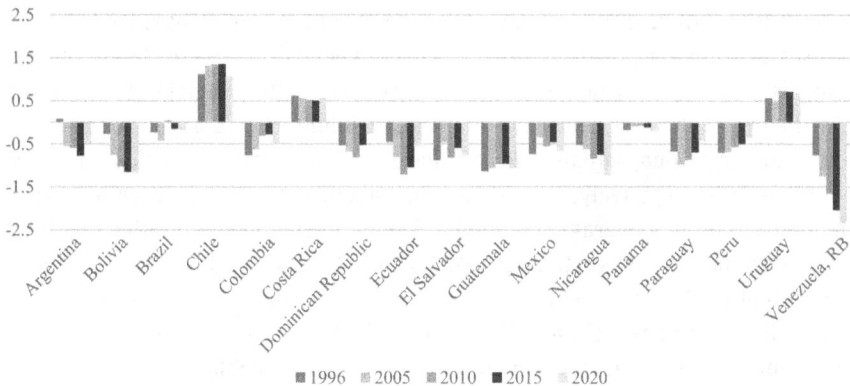

Fig. 2.6: Rule of Law.
Source: Kaufmann et al. (2022).[42]

---

40 (Kaufmann, D., et al., 2022).
41 Rule of law (Kaufmann, D., et al., 2010).
42 Figures 2.6 to 2.11 the composite measures of governance are in units of a standard normal distribution, with **mean zero**, standard deviation of one, and spanning from approximately −2.5 to 2.5, with higher values corresponding to better governance Worldwide Governance Indicators (WGI) (2022, December 23).

In other words, it fell to the level where arbitrariness prevails over what is to be expected in a reliable legal system. Most of the 17 countries considered herein are concentrated around the lower end of the world average. Only four of them (Brazil, Panama, Dominican Republic, and Peru) are above the global average and the vast majority fall below it (10). Thus, most Latin American democracies have rule of law standards below the world average and below average for this group. Chile, Costa Rica, and Uruguay boost the average, while the rest lower it. With the exception of Venezuela, the group remained relatively stable over the 25 years they were measured in this regard.

2.1.4 Voice and accountability

Latin America is above the world average in this indicator, meaning that it has a better relative performance regarding the way in which "a country's citizens are able to participate in selecting their government, and enjoy freedom of expression, freedom of association, and a free media".[43] This definition lends greater weight to "voice" and its effects such as "vertical accountability," i.e., citizens' ability to hold the government accountable, contrasting starkly to the level of corruption (Fig. 2.7.). In 2020, 12 countries ranked above the global average (which is below the sample mean) and only five ranked below it. However, the sample average is on the side of positive performance, with eight countries above it and nine below it. The best performer is Uruguay, followed by Costa Rica and Chile, and then Argentina, Panama, Brazil, Peru, and the Dominican Republic. The others perform negatively, with Mexico just above the world average but below the Latin American average. Venezuela, having started in the positive quadrant in 1995, slipped to the worst score (−1.5), below Nicaragua, Guatemala, and Bolivia. Except for Uruguay, which shows an almost continuous improvement over the period, and Venezuela and Nicaragua, which worsen dramatically, over 25 years our selected countries as a whole tend to remain stable around their original score.

2.1.5 Political stability

Turning now to the political stability indicator, the average of our selected countries is below the world average, which means that the "likelihood of political in-

---

43 Voice and accountability (WGI, 2022, December 23).

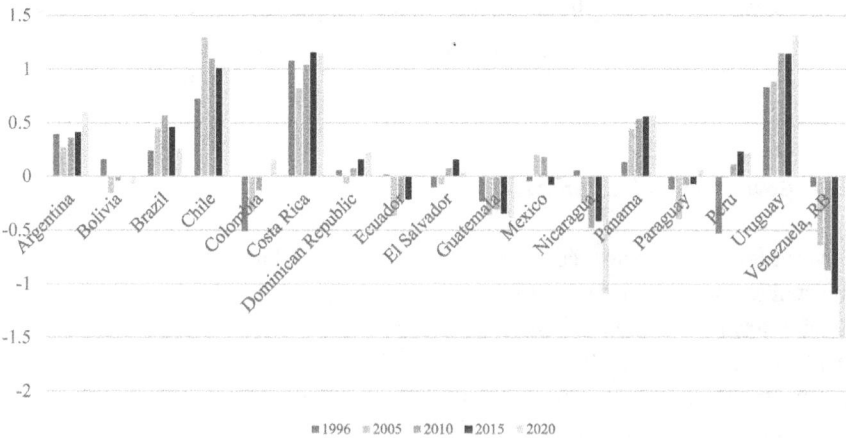

Fig. 2.7: Voice and accountability.
Source: Kaufmann et al. (2022)

stability and/or politically-motivated violence, including terrorism"[44] would be higher (Fig. 2.8.). Only five countries remain above average throughout the period (Uruguay, Costa Rica, Dominican Republic, Chile, and Panama, the latter of which joined this group in the last decade). Chile recorded a continuous drop in this indicator between the beginning of the century and the end of the second decade, before falling to the world average. Argentina, like Mexico, rose and fell around

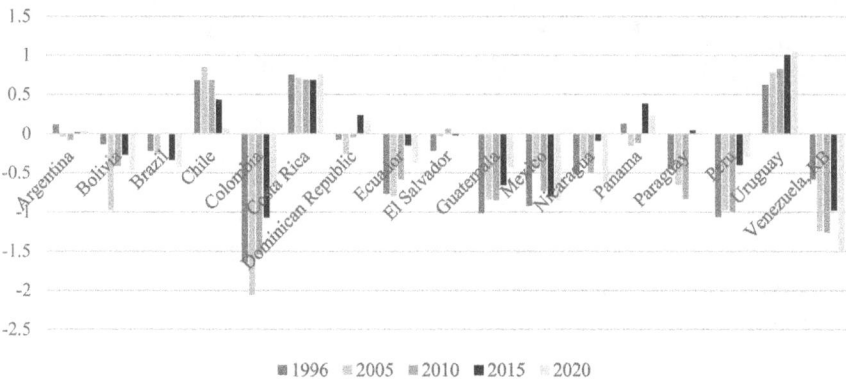

Fig. 2.8: Political Stability and Absence of Violence/Terrorism.
Source: Kaufmann et al. (2022)

---

44 Political stability (WGI, 2022, December 23).

the world average, and Colombia consistently improved its score, crossing Venezuela's line descending in the opposite direction. The majority is grouped below both averages, reflecting a trend towards chronic political instability.

2.1.6 Government effectiveness

Government effectiveness consists of the "quality of public services, the quality of the civil service, the degree of its independence from political pressures, the quality of policy formulation and implementation, as well as the credibility of the government's commitment to such policies."[45] Thus it reflects the quality of public administration and its autonomy, as well as the quality of public policies and the government's commitment to them. It is an approximation to the quality of the government and the public goods it produces. Once more, we find wide dispersion in country performance (Fig. 2.9). Chile, Uruguay, and Costa Rica again are leaders with positive ratings. A second group follows with Panama and Mexico (the latter of which slips towards the Latin American average) and then the rest of the countries bring up the rear with stable negative ratings, except for Paraguay, which shows improvement, and Venezuela, which again places last with low government effectiveness.

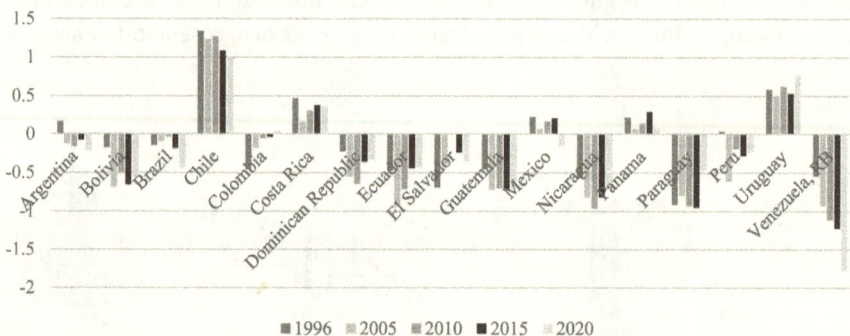

Fig. 2.9: Government Effectiveness.
Source: Kaufmann et al. (2022)

---

45 Government effectiveness (WGI, 2022, December 23).

2.1.7 Regulatory quality

This indicator reveals the "ability of the government to formulate and implement sound policies and regulations that permit and promote private sector development".[46] Chile stands out well above the rest of the countries, followed by Uruguay. Notably, seven more countries (Uruguay and Costa Rica, Peru, Panama, Colombia, Mexico, and El Salvador) post positive performances. This group with positive ratings helps the sample average to almost tie the world average. The rest are located on the negative side: Argentina, Nicaragua, Ecuador, Bolivia, while Venezuela posts the largest drop in score (Fig. 2.10). This result requires special mention. Since this indicator reflects increasing governmental support to the private sector, the greater effort that public policies put into caring for this sector contrasts with the other indicators. The idea of supporting investment and taking care of the "business climate" predominates over any other indicator that reflects the benefit of the public interest, such as political stability, control of corruption, rule of law, or efficiency in providing public services to the population. Certainly these indicators reveal positive state capacity in one aspect (permit and promote the private sector) to the neglect of the other factors discussed here.

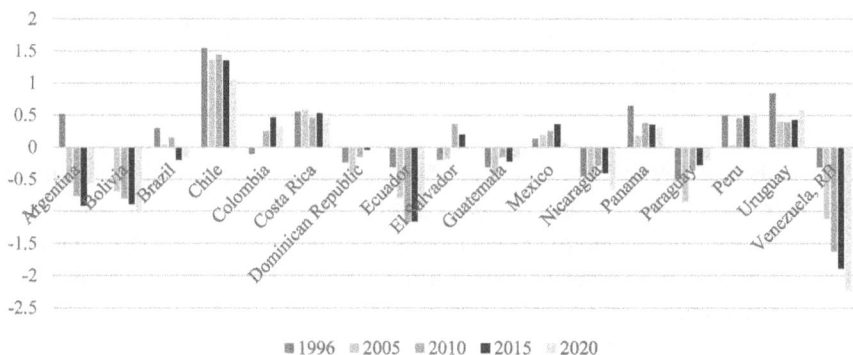

Fig. 2.10: Regulatory Quality.
Source: Kaufmann et al. (2022)

2.1.8 Control of corruption

Control of corruption shows "the extent to which public power is exercised for private gain, including both petty and grand forms of corruption, as well as 'cap-

---

[46] Regulatory quality (WGI, 2022, December 23).

ture' of the state by elites and private interests."[47] It is an indicator that comple-ments how the state's institutional performance rates in most countries. As de-picted in Fig. 2.11, control of corruption is the indicator in which most of the countries obtain the lowest score (–0.25 average), registering at several tenths below the world average. The three countries that continue to stand out with scores above the world average are Uruguay, Chile, and Costa Rica, while Argen-tina and Colombia are found between the two averages. With the exception of these 3 or 5 countries, depending on how they are counted, the remaining 15 or 12 perform negatively.

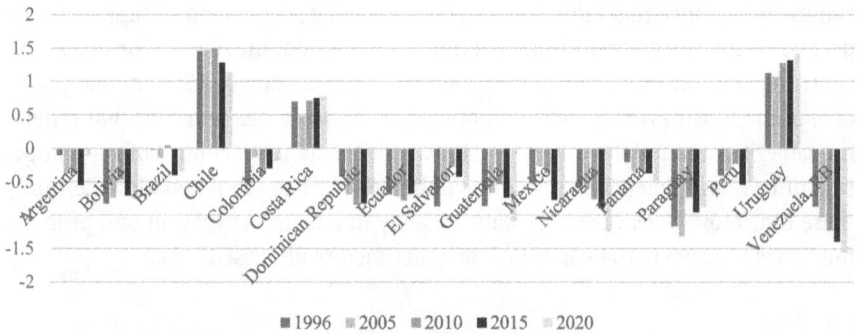

Fig. 2.11: Control of Corruption.
Source: Kaufmann et al. (2022)

These indicators prompt a number of reflections. The first aspect that stands out is the contradiction between the relatively good overall performance in "voice and accountability" and the poor performance in "control of corruption". This contrast is indeed revealing. The former measures the degree to which there are freedoms to elect governments, freedom of expression, association, and the media, and the vertical accountability that citizens exercise over government performance, while the latter refers to the exercise of power over private interests that misappropriate public resources. Greater freedom of choice is real and is explained by the wide-spread presence of electoral systems with legal and legitimate parties. In other words, these countries have a democratic political regime in which it is possible to peacefully resolve conflicts and make decisions through political negotiation. How-ever, there is less state will and means of enforcement to control corruption. The public's perception of widespread corruption corroborates the distance between the exercise of freedoms where they are fastidiously put into practice, which is the

---

47 Control of corruption (WGI, 2022, December 23).

political regime, and the exercise of power in government and its regulation by the state, areas in which the exercise of freedoms should be translated into political will and action. Secondly, a lack of stability, combined with the enjoyment of freedoms without the state being efficient in producing the public goods demanded by society, is also indicative of the obstacles that representative democracy encounters. The higher quality of state regulation, which reflects support for improving conditions for private investment, reveals the privilege that this sector enjoys in public policies, while in the production of other public goods, aimed at favoring public interests over private ones (such as the rule of law and control of corruption), the performance of institutions reveals a lower capacity for action. The data allow us to venture certain valid generalizations. The first and most obvious is that there is no state that offers sufficient guarantees in the face of expectations of actions that promote the collective interest or, in other words, the state is not characterized by solid institutions capable of translating articulated social demands into collective action so as to satisfy the public interest. Second, it follows from the above that state institutions allow a high degree of free-riding or simple arbitrariness on the part of actors who, occupying a favorable position in the economic-social structure, can benefit disproportionately from public resources, whether material, monetary, or exercise of power, thanks to their heightened ability to influence governments. Third, the flip side of poor performance is good performance *localized* in regulatory quality. The positive regulatory quality contrasts with the low level of rule of law, stability, control of corruption, and production of public goods, a situation that is indicative of the degree to which patrimonialism remains the measure of elite's power, i.e., a practice that takes precedence over the public interest. At the same time, this state of affairs demonstrates that there is indeed a capacity for a rational ordering of government action in the public interest when a representative force is present to carry it out. Fourth, we can conjecture that the political party system ill represents the population as a whole and must face invisible, intangible barriers composed of vested, often invisible, interests that political parties dare not touch -and/or participate in- which otherwise would make it possible to translate representative demands into social change. Under these circumstances, citizens naturally tend to become disillusioned with political parties and dissatisfied with governments in general. This leads to a vicious circle that can only be broken by redefining representative democracy as a system authorized to reform the state based on collective interests that are duly expressed, i.e., constitutionally expressed, in the public sphere. The search for political alternatives channeled outside institutions, as seen by uprisings and social turbulence, refer to this condition which, when in crisis, are fertile ground for populism and all manner of radicalisms. We will refer to this problem at greater length later on.

2.1.9 Political exclusion and dissatisfaction with democracy

Let us now turn to the state in terms of its ability to provide essential elements that guarantee an equal and level playing field for people. Exclusion is very acute in Latin America. As seen in Tab. 2.2, V-Dem provides data on exclusion for different groups: socioeconomic, gender, rural-urban, political, and social.[48]

Tab. 2.2: Exclusion, definitions, and scale.

Exclusion by Socio-Economic Group

Access to public services distributed by socio-economic position
Access to state jobs by socio-economic position
Access to state business opportunities by socio-economic position

Exclusion by Gender

Gender equality in respect for civil liberties
Access to public services distributed by gender
Access to state jobs by gender
Access to state business opportunities by gender

Exclusion by Urban-Rural Location

Power distributed by urban-rural location
Urban-rural location equality in respect for civil liberties
Access to public services distributed by urban-rural location
Access to state jobs by urban-rural location
Access to state business opportunities by urban-rural location

Exclusion by Social Group

Access to public services distributed by social group
Access to state jobs by social group
Access to state business opportunities by social group

Note: The scales are Ordinal, converted to interval by the measurement model: 0: Extreme. 75 percent (%) or more of the population lack access; 1: Unequal. 25 percent(%) or more of population lack acces; 2: Somewhat Equal. 10 to 25 percent (%) of the population lack access; 3: Relatively Equal. only 5 to 10 percent (%) of the population lack access; 4: Equal. less than 5 percent (%) of the population lack access.
Source: Coppedge, et al. (2022a, pp. 212–222).

---

48 The content of each variable can be found in Coppedge, et al. (2022a, p. 212) and ss. and the definitions are in Appendix B: Glossary. (Coppedge, et al., 2022a, p. 391).

Latin America is not only the most unequal region in the world, it is also one of the most excluding. One situation goes hand in glove with the other, but there are differences in each country. The differences within the region are also substantial.

Now, by comparing two groups, our sample of selected countries and a set of European countries (Tab. 2.3), the great contrast between the two demonstrates how exclusions exacerbate inequality. In all indicators, a higher score means greater inclusion. In a first aggregate approach[49] spanning 1990–2021 we see that all the European countries are located in the upper part of the scale (relatively equal) while only one of seventeen Latin American countries is located in the same interval (Uruguay). In the same period, of the two countries with the largest populations (Brazil and Mexico), the former is below the lower limit of the highest interval, while Mexico is quite distant with almost half of Brazil's values. These two countries are home to 51 percent of the total Latin American population and their level of exclusion is more severe and greater than any European country considered.

Tab. 2.3: Exclusion averages.

Exclusion averages

1950–1989				1990–2021			
Latin America		**Europe**		**Latin America**		**Europe**	
URY	3.06	SWE	3.87	URY	3.72	SWE	3.95
ARG	2.72	DNK	3.87	CRI	3.48	DNK	3.95
VEN	2.64	NOR	3.78	ARG	3.36	DEU	3.94
CRI	2.62	DEU	3.75	BRA	3.12	NOR	3.9
BRA	1.77	BEL	3.59	CHL	2.92	BEL	3.88
PAN	1.53	FRA	3.41	PAN	2.78	GRC	3.87
CHL	1.43	ITA	3.34	VEN	2.64	CZE	3.85
COL	1.28	POL	2.8	BOL	2.26	ITA	3.83
ECU	1.16	IRL	2.77	ECU	2.13	FRA	3.68
HND	1.11	HUN	2.61	HND	2.12	IRL	3.66
MEX	0.99	GRC	2.5	COL	2.09	POL	3.63
BOL	0.84	ESP	2.26	PER	1.84	ESP	3.6
PER	0.8	PRT	2.25	PRY	1.68	PRT	3.57
PRY	0.63	RUS	2.08	MEX	1.64	BLR	3.54
DOM	0.6	CZE	1.99	GTM	1.39	HUN	3.4
GTM	0.57			NIC	1.37	UKR	3.12

---

49 Sum of each country's scores for the variables in Table 2.

Tab. 2.3 (continued)

Exclusion averages							
1950–1989				**1990–2021**			
Latin America		**Europe**		**Latin America**		**Europe**	
NIC	0.53			DOM	1.31	RUS	2.99
SLV	0.47			SLV	1.25		
Average region	**1.38**	**Average region**	**2.99**	**Average region**	**2.28**	**Average region**	**3.66**

Source: Prepared by the authors with data from V-Dem 12 (Coppedge et al., 2022b).
NOTE Tab. 2.3: The data are country averages for the period indicated, and for all the variables included in V-dem for each of the exclusion groups (Exclusion by Socio-Economic Group, Exclusion by Gender, Exclusion by Urban-Rural Location, Exclusion by Political Group, Exclusion by Social Group). The range is 0 to 4:
0: Extreme. 75 percent (%) or more of the population lacks access.
1: Unequal. 25 percent (%) or more of the population lacks access.
2: Somewhat Equal. 10 to 25 percent (%) of the population lacks access.
3: Relatively Equal. only 5 to 10 percent (%) of the population lacks access.
4: Equal. less than 5 percent (%) of the population lacks access.

When comparing Latin America and Europe from 1950 to 1989,[50] the former's average is 1.38 and 2.9 for the latter. Latin America has a low level of inclusion ("unequal"), while Europe is two steps ahead in the lower zone of "relatively equal". In Latin America, around 25% of the population is excluded from public services and basic freedoms, while Europe has considerably more services and freedoms. The difference between countries in Latin America ranges from 0.53 (Nicaragua) to around 3 (Argentina and Uruguay), and from 1.99 (Czech Republic) to almost 4 (Denmark and Sweden). In terms of population, in Latin America Brazil and Mexico posted the lowest score (1 "unequal") while the countries that account for 60% of the European population were at 3 ("relatively equal").

Aggregating all scores during 1990–2021 gives a better picture (Tab. 2.4). An average of 2.3 for Latin America (one point higher than in the previous stage) and 3.6 for Europe (0.7 higher than in the previous stage). Our selected countries in Latin America post a borderline lower value in the "somewhat equal" rating, while Europe obtains close to the highest possible value (4) on the inclusion scale (0 extreme exclusion and 4 maximum inclusion). If we were to round the result, Latin America would be at 2 ("Somewhat Equal. 10 to 25 percent (%) of the population lacks access

---

50 See Methodological Note at the end of the chapter.

to good-quality, basic public services"), and Europe at 4 ("Equal. Less than 5 percent (%) of the population lacks access to good-quality, basic public services"). The difference between countries in Latin America ranges from 1.25 to 3.7 and in Europe from 2.9 to 3.9. If we take into account countries with more than 60% of the population, the result is practically the same. In Latin America, 60% of the population (Brazil, Mexico and Colombia) experience a degree of inclusion of 2.3 ("somewhat equal"), while in Europe 60% of the population (Russia, Germany, France, Italy, Spain, Poland and Belgium) experience a high degree of inclusion, i.e., 3.6 ("relatively equal").

Tab. 2.4: Degree of inclusion (average and factor).

Degree of inclusion (average and factor)	Latin America		Europe		Spain, Portugal and Greece	
	1950–1989	1990–2021	1950–1989	1990–2021	1950–1989	1990–2021
Socioeconomic	0.9	1.6	1.7	3.3	2.8	3.5
Gender	1.4	2.6	1.8	3.8	2.8	3.8
Urban-rural	1.3	2.1	2.7	3.6	3.1	3.5
Political group	1.4	2.7	1.6	3.9	2.6	3.7
Social group	1.3	2.2	2.3	3.8	3	3.6
General Average	**1.3**	**2.3 (+1)**	**2**	**3.7 (+1.7)**	**2.9**	**3.6 (+0.7)**

Zero = absolute exclusion. Four = ideal inclusion.
Source: V-Dem 12 (Coppedge et al., 2022b).

When analyzing exclusion in its different aspects (socioeconomic, gender, urban-rural, political group and social group), we see that during both periods in Latin America socioeconomic exclusion accounts for the greatest amount of exclusion, having posted the smallest change between periods, moving from extremely unequal to somewhat unequal. Exclusion by political group changed the most, moving from 1.4 (unequal) to 2.7 (somewhat equal). In other words, with the exception of exclusion by socioeconomic group, the other indicators advanced to somewhat equal. As for Europe, in general, exclusion went from somewhat equal (2.9) to relatively equal (3.6); yet when analyzed by aspects, socioeconomic exclusion took a huge leap of almost 100 percent between the first and second periods, and the exclusion by gender and by political group are the ones that decreased the most. Comparing Latin America with Europe, exclusion by political group has the smallest difference, with an average of 1 point between both groups, and the highest average score for Latin America, that is, inclusion by political group is on average the better indicator, although it is still somewhat equal. Despite its progress, on average Latin America has not been able to reach a relatively equal level, while the European countries are relatively equal in all aspects, with gender inclusion having advanced the most.

If we compare the Latin American average with just the three European countries that experienced democratic transitions during the early stage of the third wave of democratization (Spain, Portugal, and Greece), which had the lowest development indexes in Western Europe, the result is that these three countries had greater advances towards inclusion than Latin America. The transitions in these European countries coincided with those in Latin America. Even if we take into account only this trio of less-developed countries in southern Europe that experienced dictatorships before joining the democratic community, the contrast is revealing: they shift from lower levels of exclusion than Europe as a whole to the same level as the average for their region, while more than doubling their levels of inclusion during 1990–2021. This qualitative leap cannot be explained by material improvements alone, but by deliberate action from collective actors and states to produce equality.

In addition to the previous factors of exclusion, we can examine to what extent fundamental rights are respected or violated as another window into the problem of political inequality. Without going into a detailed description, which is unnecessary considering the abundance of reports from intergovernmental organizations (such as the UN), and independent organizations (such as Human Rights Watch), Latin America is plagued with problems. Considering Mexico and Brazil again, the structure of political systems produces outcomes such as a lack of general access to the courts, high levels of violence, and human rights violations by various government agencies against the weakest groups as defined by gender, ethnicity, and region.[51]

In Valdés Ugalde-Ansolabehere (2012), we undertook a detailed classification of 20 Latin American countries.[52] by their levels of protection afforded to a selection of human rights (civil, economic, social, ethnic, and gender). Considering the significant variables of each right listed in the Cingranelli-Richards Human Rights Data Set (CIRI), as well as the form and degree of inclusion of each of these rights in the corresponding constitutions, we found that these countries can be divided between those with high or low effectiveness in the fulfillment of rights and those with a basic or high (inclusive) level of incorporation of these rights in their constitutions, giving rise to result shown on Tab. 2.5:[53]

---

51 Human Rights Watch (2008).
52 Argentina, Bolivia, Brazil, Chile, Colombia, Costa Rica, Cuba, Dominican Republic, Ecuador, El Salvador, Guatemala, Haiti, Honduras, Mexico, Nicaragua, Panama, Paraguay, Peru, Uruguay, and Venezuela.
53 In the same text, the precise measurement of compliance for each group of rights can be obtained separately according to CIRI (Tables 5–9 and Annex 3 in the cited source).

Tab. 2.5: Constitutional protection of human rights (1981–2004).

Characteristics of the constitutional text	Effectiveness of rights	
	Low	**High**
Basic	**Excluding** 1. Chile (gray zone) 2. Honduras (gray zone)	**Sincere** 1. Costa Rica 2. El Salvador (gray zone) 3. Dominican Republic (gray zone)
Inclusive	**Cynical** 1. Bolivia (gray zone) 2. Brazil (gray zone) 3. Colombia 4. Ecuador (gray zone) 5. Guatemala (gray zone) 6. Mexico 7. Peru (gray zone)	**Inclusive** 1. Argentina 2. Nicaragua (gray zone) 3. Panama (gray zone) 4. Uruguay 5. Venezuela (gray zone)

"Gray zone" indicates countries that belong to a particular category but share some characteristics of the other category.
Source: Valdés-Ugalde, Ansolabehere (2012, p. 24).

The differences have a historical explanation. In Chapter 1, we referred briefly to what routes Europe followed in its struggle against inequality[54] and what Latin America's trajectory was. The contemporary differences, supported by our data herein, offer several clues. First, there is a greater presence of the regulatory and welfare state in Europe compared to Latin America. Security systems versus weak safety nets, strong popular and left-wing parties versus relatively weak and disjointed parties, greater social organization versus fragmentation of society and its organizations, and economic and political elites that assume collective rights even though such rights do not respond directly to their particular interests versus economic-political oligarchies that resist or reject reforms that identify the public interest with the general interest insofar as they imply distributive effects that are far removed from their particular interests. The lack in practice of protection and enforcement of the rule of law is a fundamental feature of this problem. In Latin America, constitutional compliance is proverbially deficient. There is a wide gap between the rights established by constitutions and effective compliance, thus cre-

---

[54] Russia does not follow the same pattern as Western Europe. The same can be said of the other countries that belonged to the Soviet bloc. In these countries, the course of the struggle against inequality followed the authoritarian distributive pattern of the communist parties.

ating a constitutional conflict between right holders and governmental authorities (Ansolabehere, Valdés-Ugalde 2012).[55] Democratic inclusion is expected to mean that the arrangements negotiated in a political regime space become fundamental state norms, i.e., become an integral part of the *polity* and that the gap between words and deeds, between promises and the realization of rights becomes smaller or even closes. Gutmann, et al. (2022a) developed a database that depicts the gap between *de jure* and *de facto* constitutional compliance in 168 countries from 1900 to 2020. This effort was aimed at measuring 14 rights summarized in four factors: "[1] property rights and the rule of law, [2] political rights, [3] civil rights, and [4] basic human rights" (Gutmann et al.: 2022a, p. 3).[56] The methodology employed allows researchers to choose an indicator that concentrates the four factors into one ("CC_T"), measuring "the mean value of the non-missing gap" (Gutmann et al., 2022a, p. 12–13).[57]

Examining this database, and similarly to the references to exclusion above, we observe two periods that contrast sharply with each other, both in the case of Latin American and European countries (Fig. 2.12 to 2.15).

The story told by the graphs and the table is eloquent. In the post-war period and up to the dawn of the third wave of democratization, Latin American countries had a large gap in constitutional compliance. Only four countries closed the gap to some degree. The rest were openly non-compliant, with a substantial gap between constitutional promises and effective compliance. In the same period, Eu-

---

55 In this text, we define constitutional conflict as "the growing strategic disposition of political actors with respect to the norms that define the so-called 'constitutional pact'. If we accept that this pact constitutes a stable arrangement under certain conditions, the presence of more or less permanent situations of conflict within it implies a crisis in the stability of the arrangement, defined by the incursion of forces with power to alter the rules and terms of the constitutional pact. When something like this occurs, there is a crisis of equilibrium in which the active forces therein seek conditions and strategies to create a new equilibrium" beyond the established norms. Constitutional compliance in human rights can also be observed in Ansolabehere et al. (2015 and 2020).

56 Although this scale does not measure the totality of the human rights subscribed to by the countries analyzed, the distance between promise and fulfillment can be seen in the texts referred to in the previous footnote.

57 The methodology used for the development of this database is described in the article by Gutmann et al. (2022a, p. 3). The database covers 168 countries from 1900 to 2020. The construction of its indicators "involves matching information on *de jure* constitutional rules from the Comparative Constitutions Project [. . .] to data on these rules' *de facto* implementation according to the Varieties of Democracy project". In the comparison, the authors take into account other measurements and find similarity in the data found, which is equivalent to corroboration of the gap between text and effective enforcement of rights. Our selection of country indicators is taken from this database Comparative Constitutional Compliance (Gutmann et al., 2022b).

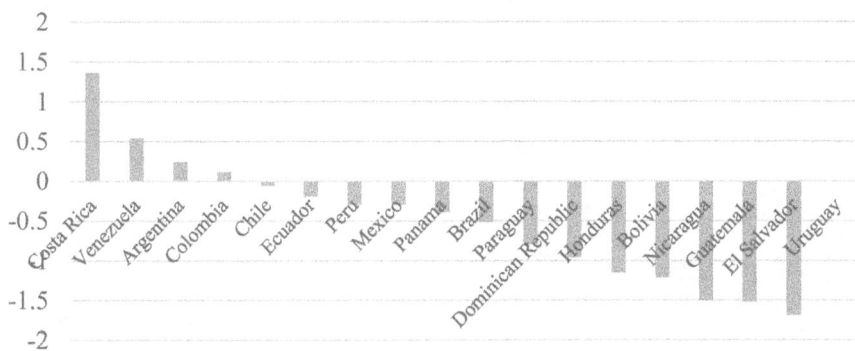

Fig. 2.12: Constitutional compliance indicator, Latin America, 1950–1979.
Source: Gutmann et al. (2022b)

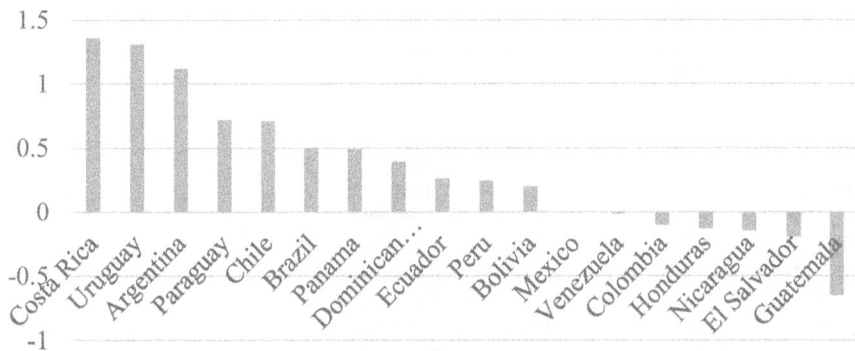

Fig. 2.13: Constitutional compliance indicator, Latin America, 1980–2021.
Source: Gutmann et al. (2022b)

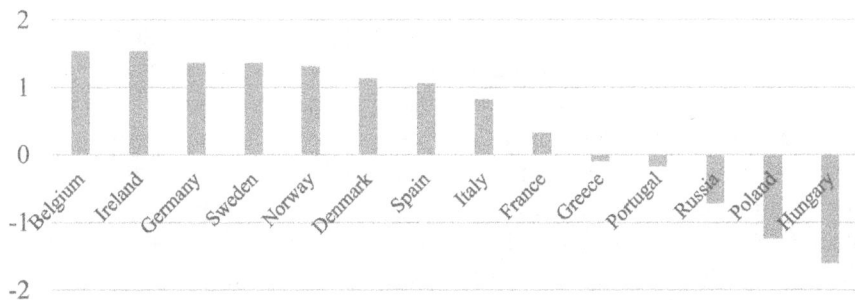

Fig. 2.14: Constitutional compliance indicator, Europe, 1950–1979.
Source: Gutmann et al. (2022b)

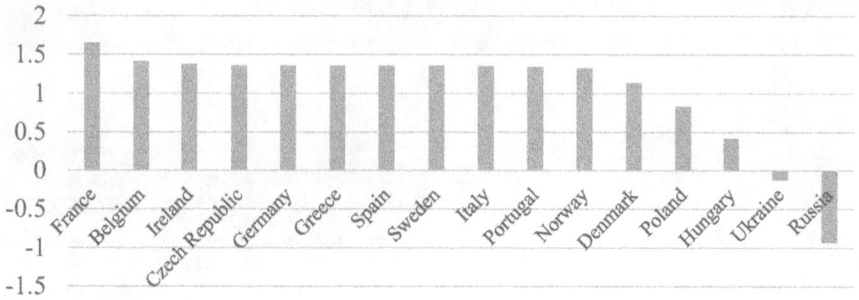

Fig. 2.15: Constitutional compliance indicator, Europe, 1980–2021.
Source: Gutmann et al. (2022b)

Tab. 2.6: *De jure-de facto* constitutional compliance (CC_T) average.
Latin America and Europe.

De jure-de facto constitutional compliance (CC_T) average.		
	Latin America	**Europe**
1950–1979	−0.49	0.47
1980–2021	0.34	1.04

Source: Gutmann et al. (2022b).
Note: We used the database found in the article "The Comparative
Constitutional Compliance Database". Of the indicators, cc_t was
used, which is an indicator generated by the authors from the
averages of the four specific legal areas (the other indicators they
developed are: cc_r, cc_p, cc_c, and cc_b) This aggregate indicator
(as a complete base) has a minimum value of −2.05 and a
maximum of 1.65.

ropean countries displayed an almost symmetrical opposite trend. Beginning in the
1980s, this situation began to shift in Latin America. Everything indicates that constitutions acquire a different meaning than in the previous stage. The countries
that reduced the gap, Colombia and Venezuela, regressed to the negative side, but
notwithstanding these exceptions, the others tended to close the gap, although
some of them did not manage to move from the negative to the positive side of this
story. In Europe, Greece, Portugal, and Spain make a spectacular leap by closing
the gap considerably and the ex-Soviet republics, Russia and Ukraine (which became independent) remain in the non-compliance gap, while the Czech Republic,
Poland, and Hungary post positive values by closing the gap in compliance with the
constitution.

After World War II, Europe began its unification process and gradually included the Mediterranean states that transitioned to democracy and, later, admitted some ex-Soviet states. The trend towards greater constitutional compliance is more pronounced in these countries, both in Western and Eastern Europe. Undoubtedly, the European Union is at the root of this change. However, Spain, Portugal, and Greece all emerged from dictatorships -two of them quite lengthy- to transition to democratic regimes whose endogenous change is explained more by long-term political agreements that led to new constitutions (1975, 1976, and 1978, respectively). The same can be said of the momentum brought by new constitutions in the Czech Republic (1993), Poland (1997), and Hungary (2011). Democracy matters for constitutional compliance, especially when changing from an authoritarian regime to a democratic one, as in the case of these six countries that agreed on new constitutions after submitting the new arrangements to public debate under democratic procedures.

2.2 Weak states, powerful elites, fragile democracies, and precarious citizenship

Studies are beginning to appear in political literature on citizen inclusion or social inclusion -which are not the same thing- during the forty years of Latin American democratization.[58] They all coincide on an empirical confirmation: democracy has favored the inclusion of social conflict in the political regime. Yet, the feedback between citizens and the state through the political regime does not necessarily lead to demands being translated into legal-political arrangements that bring about the provision of rights and public goods necessary to satisfy social demands.

The first "inclusionary wave" in Latin America (Collier and Collier, 1991) had a concentrated effect in the region, both by country and by level, while the second one that takes place during the third wave of democratization, although more fragmented, was also more dispersed. Judging by exclusion indicators, the difference between Argentina (3) on the one hand and Mexico (1) and Brazil (1) on the other is noteworthy (see Tab. 2.3). In all three, workers' organization and bargaining power had a strong impact, but produced very different results for the general population. An explanation for the difference can probably be found in the greater level of equality in Argentina in the 20th century, which contrasts with the extreme in-

---

58 (Pinto and Flisfisch, 2011; Flisfisch et al., 2014; Kapizewski et al., 2021; O'Donnell 2010; Ansolabehere et al. 2015).

equality in Brazil and Mexico, in addition to both of the latter countries having a large rural sector living in precarious conditions.

Democracy has allowed the widening of the spaces for the fight against inequality, although, as shown by Kapiszewski et. al (2021), how wide those spaces become for political inclusion are varied and uneven. The data do not show that average inclusion has improved as might be expected in a *representative* democracy. The variations between countries are very significant, since the tendency towards heterogeneity in the region persists and contrasts with the homogeneity of European countries. History matters and the present cannot be abstracted from it, as studies that offer historical explanations have shown. However, the quality of democracy also matters. Certainly Europe's path, mainly Western Europe's, to political democracy cannot be compared with that of Latin American countries. However, the comparison is valid in order to confirm that in the 40 years that Latin America has had democratic systems, it has not seemed capable of overcoming obstacles that were present in previous periods and that led to dictatorships or authoritarian systems. These features have undoubtedly been attenuated at different times, but currently tensions have surfaced that seem to lead to a conundrum: either more radical changes to reduce inequality emanating from the democratic state or diminish the overflow of political conflict outside its channels with the consequent increase in the probability of failure of democracies and political freedoms.

Despite Latin America's transition to democracy, the elites' politicization has not changed essential aspects of the oligarchic and patrimonial nature of the political society that dominates the state. The exceptions are countries in which governing elites are replaced with people with democratizing ambitions. In Europe this occurred in Spain, Greece, Portugal, Poland, the Czech Republic, and Hungary. In Latin America this happened in Costa Rica, with a democracy that pre-exists the third wave, Uruguay, and, to a lesser extent, Chile. The characteristics of state performance, and, despite the improvement of inclusion indexes on average and by indicator, a pronounced discrepancy between countries continues to exist, as well as in terms of constitutional compliance. The *de jure/de facto* gap in Latin America remains larger than in other regions.

All indications are that the standards required for obedience to authoritarian elites remain very low; the weakness of the citizenry willing to take public action through legal channels and discrepancies between the center and progressive left parties combine with growing tendencies towards autocratization. Elkins (2020) traces the good intentions of the ruling classes through an analysis of the region's constitutions and the changes undertaken in the period of representative democracy. To illustrate this, he highlights the "Bolivarian" inclusion spearheaded by Hugo Chavez and disseminated to Bolivia and Ecuador. But while his analysis recognizes that this type of inclusion is "president's will-dependent," he overlooks the fact that this type of "will" is far removed from the genuine attainment of inclusion that derives from citizen equality vis-à-vis *kratia*. Yet, the fundamental difference between the first and the second "inclusionary turns", as outlined by the authors compiled by Kapiszewski et al. (2021), is that in the latter, for the first time, citizens' political rights are fully recognized, at least formally, allowing them to shape political opinion and make political decisions, central elements of the diarchy of democracy Cfr. Chapter 3. In the same volume, Kenneth M. Roberts brands these elements "pluralization".

> The new inclusion encompassed a plethora of social actors, interests, identities, and organizational forms, as individuals engaged in collective action not only as producers but also as consumers, pensioners, neighborhood residents, women, indigenous peoples, unemployed workers, or simply as rights-bearing citizens. (Roberts, 2021, p. 527).

Improvements in constitutional compliance and state performance (i.e. regulatory quality) support the hypothesis of greater inclusion. Still, a general characteristic is the lack of access.[59] Inclusion in Latin America can be defined as "inclusion without representation" as analyzed by Htun (2016), (cit. by Roberts, 2021, p.533), and this "new inclusion [Roberts concludes] has surely left its mark on the region's policy landscape going forward, but its institutional legacies remain uncertain." (Roberts, 2021, p. 527).

In my opinion, the democratic period of the last 40 years is a stage in which the formation of citizens has reached a new level of development and deployment, albeit with its limits and obvious deficits, which we will see in Chapter 4 when we evaluate them from the point of view of representative democracy. For now, let us limit our assessment to positing that citizens at this stage have had a greater presence in the public space than the more inclusive groups in the previous period had in terms of corporate presence. Following the terminology of Kapiszewski et al. (2021), inclusion in resources and recognition has led to agreement that access is the modality of inclusion that has lagged the most. The dissatisfaction with democracy may well be located there, at the threshold between regime and state in which the combination of forces concentrated in political struggles is not aimed at access to the exercise of state power in the sense of collective benefit. In our reading, the state lags behind in terms of including a new type of forces in the political regime that aspires to representative democracy beyond the electoral process and the traditional workings of politics. Apparently, this situation opens up a quandary in

---

[59] "Recognition, access, and resources" are the three types of inclusion they identify, of which access is significantly the most limited.

which many of the democracies currently find themselves, i.e., between a qualitative democratic leap or an autocratic regression.

As has been widely noted, Latin America's democratic transition went hand in glove with market economic reforms that transformed the institutional landscape which societies faced in their dispute over resource distribution and decision-making. The transition from corporative models to citizen, partisan, and diverse ("fragmentary") forms pulverized and pluralized collective action. These two "episodes of substantial change" (Lührman and Lindberg, 2019) indicate an epochal change in which the old forms of relationship between state and society were substantially modified. From corporative and bloc forms with an elevated social-class content in their interlocution with states whose authoritarian traits prevail over democratic ones, there is a shift to the dispersion of relations that is a characteristic of market societies that downplay or eliminate the previous links and open the way to the third wave of democracy by forming political regimes with a low capacity to achieve political equality beyond universal suffrage, which is a basic challenge for the proper functioning of democracy.

2.3 Methodological note to Chapter 2

In this chapter, we begin our empirical observation using two databases: World Governance Indicators (WGI) and Varieties of Democracy (V-Dem V. 12). The former contains a solid combination and organization of available observations to measure governance performance in the following categories: voice and accountability (VA), political stability and absence of violence/terrorism (PV), government effectiveness (GE), regulatory quality (RQ), rule of law (RL), and control of corruption (CC). Our use of these indicators was based on a broad selection of Latin American countries from North, Central, and South America. Cuba, Haiti, and Honduras were excluded because they are not republican democratic systems or experienced situations that interrupted democratic development, making it difficult to include them in the period we selected to study (1990–2021). However, we include Venezuela, which until 1999 was still one of the most consistent democracies in Latin America, becoming an autocracy during the governments of Chávez and Maduro, a situation that continues to date. Venezuela and Nicaragua are examples of the transition from democracy to closed systems and as a comparative contrast of state performance with the indicators mentioned previously. As depicted in the graphs and tables, the measurement of each category includes the world average, according to the total number of countries included in the WGI sample and the average of our sample of countries.

The V-Dem database was used to observe the levels of exclusion based on the factors and scale shown in Tab. 2.2. Honduras was included in the sample, although it was not taken into account in the previous exercise. The reason is that measuring the exclusion of the population from public services or civil liberties provides a general picture that can be observed independently of the state performance measured in the previous exercise. This section of Chapter 2 ("political exclusion and dissatisfaction with democracy") examines a group of European countries inside and outside the European Union, in order to contrast a region that shows greater progress in inclusion, made up of countries that are both old and new entrants to the realm of democracy.

This arbitrary selection of countries does not produce a significant distortion because it does not exclude a large number of countries or countries with large populations. In Latin America, what justifies the selection of countries is that all are "representative democracies" (only two -Nicaragua and Venezuela- ceased to be so during the period, and Honduras briefly), all have new constitutions or re-implemented constitutions suspended by dictatorships. To a greater or lesser extent, all reformed their constitutions with the aim of improving political representation, social inclusion, greater adherence to the rule of law, increasing control of the president, greater society-media-party relations, greater civic culture, and other improvements. Latin American countries are classified by the origin of their political regimes, i.e., previously democratic; military dictatorships; and old-style civilian authoritarianisms that transition to civilian governments. All have one form or another of "crony capitalism," with the relative exceptions of Uruguay, Costa Rica, and (with reservations) Chile, whose high-income concentration puts it at a disadvantage compared to the first two.

The European countries were chosen at random in an attempt to combine countries of greater and lesser development, old and new democracies, and countries that abandoned the Soviet sphere at the end of the 20th century. They are included here exclusively for comparative and not analytical purposes, which is also true of the comparative approach we carry out in Chapter 4 between the results of the factor analysis of representative democracy for Latin America and the proxy indicators from the same database (V-Dem) for the European countries. As indicated in Chapter 3, the exploratory factor analysis with the principal-component method with varimax rotation was only done on the Latin American countries. For this reason, comparable data are not provided for the European countries we selected. The application of the same factor analysis to the entire V-Dem base is a work in progress. Nevertheless, the results for Latin America are consistent and the comparison, using the same items separately for Europe that were considered in the factor analysis, is illustrative of the differences between the two regions.

The comparison between 1950–1989 and 1980/90–2021 is intended to show the difference in the degree of inclusion by country and region measured in averages over the two periods. The rationale behind this division is that the first, 1950–1989, covers the period between the immediate post-war period and the Cold War until the fall of the Berlin Wall and the beginning of the disintegration of the USSR and the European communist bloc. The second period, 1990–2021, covers the era of unipolarity, greater democratic expansion until the end of the third democratic wave, and the appearance of the first tendencies towards autocratization.

Chapter 3
What is representative democracy and how do we measure it?

> *Political representation is a circular process (susceptible to friction) between state institutions and social practices. As such, representative democracy is neither aristocratic nor a defective substitute for direct democracy, but a way for democracy to constantly recreate itself and improve. Popular sovereignty, understood as an as if regulating principle guiding citizens' political judgment and action, is a central motor for democratizing representation.*
>
> Nadia Urbinati

3.1 Measuring democracy

Few concepts have been discussed and evaluated as much as the concept of democracy. Efforts to measure it have generated an abundant literature and led to important international projects aimed at developing indicators to classify countries according to their level of democracy. This is an ongoing discussion that began more than 30 years ago. The debates have acquired different dynamics and the accumulated knowledge continues to generate important projects aimed at resolving theoretical, methodological, and technical problems that hinder the measurement of this concept.

The great majority of debates about the measurement of democracy have been framed in terms of its conceptualization. There is no single definition of democracy; on the contrary, there are multiple theoretical approaches to address this concept and diverse measurement efforts have been attempted (Dahl, 1971; Przeworski et al. 2000; Sartori, 1987; Schmitter and Karl, 1991; Saward, 1994; Schumpeter, 1992; Vanhanen, 1997; Lindberg et al. 2014; IDEA, 2017; Lührmann et al. 2017; Skaaning et al. 2015; Boix et al. 2013; Bertelsmann Stiftung, 2020). Despite the abundant literature on the topic, consensus still seems distant. Social scientists agree on the need to construct better ways of measuring democracy. The only consensus appears to indicate that the difficulty in measurement lies in its conceptualization and definition. This dilemma is what was called the "defining enigma" (Coppedge et al. 2011) and since it is not possible to arrive at a universally accepted definition of democracy, the debate on measurement will continue to generate discussions.

Note: The literature review and methodological design used in this chapter benefited greatly from the input of Georgina Flores-Ivich. What I argue herein is my sole responsibility.

https://doi.org/10.1515/9783110773675-004

Munck and Verkuilen (2002) identified three challenges in measuring democracy: conceptual, measurement, and aggregation. For Coppedge et al. (2011), in addition to the conceptual difficulty, there are five methodological problems found in the indicators of democracy: their precision, sources and coverage, the coding process, aggregation methods, in addition to validity and reliability. Today we can say that most of the debates addressing the measurement of democracy are grouped into two types: conceptual-methodological or technical. The first is the most problematic, since democracy is an abstract and controversial concept, which by its nature has important problems of conceptualization and measurement that *"will not be definitively resolved"* (Coppedge et al, 2011). I would add, along with Keane (2009), that definitions also change because what they designate can undergo transformation.

Moreover, the debate is complex because it involves both descriptive and normative aspects, i.e., *what* political regimes *are* and *what they should be like* (Coppedge et al. 2011), in addition to the general theoretical dimensions of the content of the concept -what democracy is and what it can be-, as we will see below (next section). Regardless of the discussion on the technical nature of the indices for measuring democracy, i.e., on aspects related to coding, aggregation methods, or the reliability and validity that characterize them, the problems begin (and end) with definitions (Coppedge et al. 2011).

The very nature of democracy is multidimensional and there are multiple competing conceptions and models of democracy (Schmitter and Karl, 1991; Cunningham, 2002; Held, 2006; Møller and Skaaning 2013). From its beginnings and to date, the discussion on measurements of democracy has always had a conceptual dimension in the background. Thus, efforts have ranged from minimalist conceptions (Schumpeter, 1992) to broader conceptions such as that of Robert Dahl (1998), which includes the rights that pertain to and surround the electoral sphere. Today there is an important diversity of perspectives to approach the study of democracy, as well as many definitions of democracy.

In this diversity of perspectives and definitions lies the complexity of its measurement. For this reason, one of the most recurrent criticisms of measurements has been their inability to capture the "full" meaning of democracy (Munck, 2011). Thus, the relevance of including imperfect indicators in measures of democracy rather than overlooking important aspects of its meaning (Bollen, 2001, p. 7283). Moreover, whatever concept of democracy is chosen has direct implications for measurement. Defining democracy institutionally implies difficulties in drawing conclusions about its effectiveness. These difficulties center on the limits of the definition and are visible for any conception of democracy (Knutsen, 2010).

One of the most productive discussions centers on whether democracy should be treated as a discrete or continuous variable. This conceptual distinction has an important methodological and technical implication. The discussion focuses on defining whether democracy is dichotomous, that is, whether it is sufficient to classify countries as democratic and non-democratic or democratic and autocratic, or whether it should be viewed as a continuum with different possibilities and levels along the continuum. This discussion permeated the first indicators of democracy and we note that, to date, there is increasing agreement that it should be seen as a continuum.

Authors such as Huntington (1993), Alvarez et al. (1996), Przeworski et al. (1996, 2000), and Cheibub et al. (2010) saw democracy as a phenomenon of a dichotomous nature (democracy/autocracy). Indeed, in 2000, Adam Przeworski (2000:57) stated that "democracy can be more or less advanced, but it cannot be half-democratic. It is a natural zero point". Likewise, Cheibub et al. (2010) also rejected the idea that there is "something in the middle" between democracies and dictatorships, even though they recognized that there are different types of democracies and dictatorships. Other researchers such as Huntington (1993, p. 11) expressed their opposition to the use of continuums due to the impossibility of weighting and calibrating the indicators.

At the opposite end of this discussion, researchers such as Arat (1991), Bollen (1980), Hadenius (1992), Vanhanen (1990), and others saw democracy as a continuum. Naturally, the argument for defending democracy as a continuum is to avoid information loss (Hadenius and Teorell, 2005; Elkins, 2000). Further, some of the arguments for defending this position are to be found in reality itself: Many countries are close to a cut-off point that is difficult to place in a dichotomous measure (Vanhanen, 1990, p. 13). Collier and Adcock (1999) also defend "degrees" of democracy: "In our view, it is not clear why a regime that has competitive elections for the presidency, turnover in the presidential office, and more than one party, but lacks competitive elections for legislative office, is not at least partially democratic" (Collier and Adcock, 1999, p. 549).

This defense of democracy as a continuum rests on the need for indicators that can capture changes and differences in the quality of democracies, which may be small on paper, but can make relevant differences in people's lives. In addition, there are those who advocate measuring democracy by indices rather than dichotomous measures in order to capture the relationships between various elements that are part of democracy separately, and evaluate the effectiveness of promoting democracy in countries around the world.

In the 1990s, multiple initiatives were developed to measure democracy. Coppedge and Reinicke (1990) constructed a measure based on Dahl's (1971) concept of polyarchy that included five main indicators: freedom of expression, freedom of organization, media pluralism, extension of suffrage, and fair elections. Arat's (1991) measure consisted of four dimensions of popular sovereignty: participation, inclusion, competitiveness, and civil liberties. The indicator constructed by Hadenius (1992) consisted of two dimensions: elections and political freedoms.

Based on these efforts, multiple measurement projects began to be developed with some variations in the concept of origin. Given the proliferation of diverse ways of measuring democracy, several studies showed that the different measures were highly correlated with each other (Arat, 1991; Bollen, 1980; Coppedge and Reinicke, 1990), leading to a conclusion about their validity (Bollen, 1980). The fact that these indicators correlate highly with each other can be interpreted as an indication of consistency, since they measure the same phenomenon. However, Pemstein et al. (2010) found discrepancies in various measures of democracy and their scores for different countries even though the correlations between the measures were quite high.

Table. 3.1 summarizes the most relevant democracy measurement indices. Many of these projects are still in force and others have ceased to be updated. The variety of indicators available today is abundant. Two of the most widely used measures are those of Freedom House and Polity IV. The former was described by Diamond as the "best available empirical indicator of liberal democracy" (1999, p. 12). This measure is based on two components: civil liberties and political rights. The category of civil liberties is composed of freedom of expression and belief, rights of association and organization, rule of law and personal autonomy, and individual rights. In the category of political rights are aspects related to the electoral system, pluralism and participation, and the functioning of government. One of the main advantages of this indicator is the breadth of its databases in terms of geographic and temporal coverage. Data are available from 1982 to 2019. The 2020 edition (with 2019 data) of Freedom in the World covered 195 countries in 15 territories. The index is composed of 10 political rights indicators and 15 civil liberties indicators. Each country is ranked on a scale of 0 to 4 for each of these indicators.

Polity IV is also widely used in scientific work. This database is part of a set of measurement projects carried out by the Center for Systemic Peace. This database operates with a continuum from −10 to +10 in which the level of autocracy, anocracy, or democracy is depicted. The availability of information is quite broad (1800–2018) and covers 167 countries. This continuum is based on 6 indicators comprising regulations and competition in the election of the executive, regulation and competitiveness in participation, decision rules, and openness in electoral processes.

Tab. 3.1: Democracy indexes.

Index	Geographic and temporal coverage	Components	Scale
Freedom House	1973–2022	Civil rights	Scale from 1 to 7 where 1 is indicative of a higher level of freedom.
	195 countries	Political rights	Possible results:
			Free countries
			Partially free countries
			Non-free countries
Democracy Index	2006–2020	Election process	Scale of 0 to 10 points. Higher levels indicate more complete democracies.
(Intelligence Unit, The Economist)	167 countries	Pluralism	Possible results:
		Civil liberties	Countries with a full democracy
		Working government	Countries with an imperfect democracy
		Political participation	Countries with hybrid regimes
		Political culture	Countries with authoritarian regimes

(continued)

Tab. 3.1 (continued)

Index	Geographic and temporal coverage	Components	Scale
Polity Data Series	1800–2018	Regulation of Chief Executive Recruitment	Scale from –10 to +10
	167 countries	-Competitiveness of Executive Recruitment	
		Openness of Executive Recruitment	–10 (hereditary monarchy)
		Executive Constraints (Decision Rules)	+10 (consolidated democracy)
		Regulation of Participation	
		The competitiveness of participation	Autocracies: –10 a –6
			Anocracies: –5 a +5
			Democracies: +6 to +10
Democracy Barometer	1990–2020	The quality of democracy is made up of:	Collection of indicators from various sources, standardized on a scale of 0–100, where 0 represents the worst practices and 100 the best.
	70 countries	Liberty (Individual liberties, rule of law and public sphere)	
		Control (competence, mutual constraints and government capacity)	
		Equality (transparency, participation and representation)	

Index	Coverage	Component	Description
Lexical Index of Electoral Democracy	1800–2020 All countries	Elected Legislature Executive elected Opposition -uffrage for men Suffrage for women Electoral competition	Scores from 0 to 6 composed of a scale of 0 and 1 with 6 binary variables. Higher scores are indicative of a more complete democracy.
Vanhanen Index of Democratization	1810–2000 187 countries	Competition	The competition variable is calculated by subtracting from 100 the percentage of votes won by the party that wins the most votes in parliamentary elections or by the party of the candidate selected in presidential elections.
		Political participation	The political participation variable is calculated as the percentage of the total population that voted in the elections. In the case of indirect elections, only votes cast in the final election are taken into account.
		Democratization	The democratization index is formed by multiplying the values of competence and participation and dividing the result by 100.

(continued)

Tab. 3.1 (continued)

Index	Geographic and temporal coverage	Components	Scale
Democracy-Dictatorship Index (DD)	1946–2008	To classify a democracy:	Binary classification: democracies and dictatorships.
	199 countries	Executive elected by popular election	Democracies: parliamentary, semi-presidential and presidential
		Popularly elected legislature	Dictatorships: monarchy, military, and civilian dictatorship
		More than one political party competing	
		There must be alternation in power under electoral rules identical to those that brought the incumbent to office.	
V DEM Project	1789–2021	Indicators organized into five principles or traditions of democracy:	Ordinal scales.
	177 countries	Electoral	
		Liberal	
		Participatory	
		Deliberative	
		Equal	
The Global State of Democracy	1975–2021	Indicators organized into 5 attributes: Representative Government, Fundamental Rights,	Normalized on a scale of 0 to 1

(International IDEA)	155 countries	Checks on Government, Impartial Administration and Participatory Engagement.	Three forms of aggregation were used: IRT modelling, BFA, and standard mathematical operators.
Regimes of the World	1789–2021	It classifies countries into 4 regimes:	4 classifications.
Lührmann et al. 2017	It is based on the V-dem variables	Closed Autocracies	Closed autocracies:
		Electoral Autocracies	Citizens do not have the right to elect the head of the executive or the legislature through elections.
		Electoral Democracies	Electoral autocracies:
		Liberal democracies	Citizens have the right to elect the head of the executive and the legislature through elections but they lack some freedoms, such as freedom of association, freedom of speech, to make elections free and fair.
			Electoral democracies:
			Citizens have the right to participate in meaningful, fair, and multiparty elections.
			Liberal democracies:
			Citizens have more individual and minority rights, are equal before the law, and the actions of the executive are restricted by the legislature and the courts.

(continued)

Tab. 3.1 (continued)

Index	Geographic and temporal coverage	Components	Scale
Bertelsmann Foundation's Transformation Index (BTI)	2006–2022	There are 18 indicators grouped into 5 criteria:	The criteria have values from 1 to 10.
	137 countries	Stateness	The "Status Index" is the average of the criteria scores.
		Political Participation	They are also used to determine whether a country is classified as an autocracy or a democracy.
		Rule of Law	
		Stability of democratic institutions	
		Political and social integration	

The index developed by the Economist Intelligence Unit (EIU) consists of five dimensions: electoral process and pluralism, civil liberties, government functioning, political participation, and political culture. There are other efforts to measure democracy that consist of dichotomous measurements and seek to classify countries into autocracies and democracies. This is the case of the Democracy-Dictatorship Index, developed by Alvarez, Cheibub, Limongi, and Przeworski (1996), which has been used in a number of scientific articles. In this measurement, countries are classified as democracies if they meet the following criteria: 1) the executive is elected; 2) the legislature is elected; 3) there is more than one political party; 4) there is alternation in power.

In 2011, Coppedge et al. (2011) centered the discussion on the fact that there are different ways of understanding what "government of the people" means. There cannot be a single conception of democracy that incorporates all meanings of democracy. They argued that there are (at least) six main ones with different principles and institutions: electoral, liberal, majoritarian, participatory, deliberative, and egalitarian. Each of these conceptions differs from the other in terms of its principles, core values, and institutions that have greater weight. Therefore, the authors believe each of them should have a different measurement.

While electoral democracy focuses on free and fair elections in multiparty contexts, liberal democracy refers to the decentralization of power, majoritarian democracy means majority rule and vertical accountability, participatory democracy refers to the way in which citizens can participate in politics, deliberative democracy speaks to political decisions as a product of public deliberation and, finally, egalitarian democracy refers to the equal empowerment of citizens.

This is how one of the most recent and complete projects for measuring democracy, *"Varieties of Democracy"* (V-DEM), came about. This project aims to improve the ways in which democracy is measured by considering it a "multidimensional entity". In order to facilitate research that adopts one of these starting points, the project does not comprise a single definition of democracy, but rather it looks at multiple variations of democracy, hence its name. It includes five of the six principles or traditions mentioned above that offer approaches to defining (and measuring) democracy: electoral, liberal, participatory, deliberative, and egalitarian. The database is organized by components based on these traditions that are designed to be conceptually distinct even though they are empirically correlated.

The ways of measuring democracy will continue to develop as its very subject undergoes mutations and offers distinct points of observation. In short, the discussions on the conceptualization and measurement of democracy have certainly not ended; rather that they will be updated to the extent democracy changes, which is a system in constant evolution (Urbinati, 2006, p. 223 ff.). However, it is possible to identify some consensus: First, scholars accept that democracy is a multidimensional concept. This has had a direct impact on constructing indicators, the upshot being that dichotomous measures are used less and less or are reserved solely for certain study purposes. Also, the discussion on the dichotomic or continuous approach to democracy occupies only one place in a broader discussion that encompasses aspects of democracy that are not captured in the continuous-discontinuous polarity. Second, there is a widespread perception that democracy is much better measured by indices than by specific disaggregated indicators. This perception implies that measurements must identify critical thresholds. For this reason, many measurement efforts work with sets of indicators produced either through the aggregation of different indicators developed by international organizations or through surveys of experts. Thinking about multiple conceptions or "varieties" of democracy has also been well received because of the number of factors that can be analyzed.

3.1.1 Measuring representation in democracies

We now refer to the most important studies that have conceptualized and measured political representation. We can observe therein a way to gauge to what extent a political party coincides with the preferences of its voters, a field that has generated a very abundant body of literature. In general terms, these studies refer to the extent to which political parties or rulers and citizens have clear and consistent preferences regarding a set of relevant political dimensions (Achen, 1978; Converse and Pierce, 1986; Dalton, 1985; Iversen, 1994a, 1994b; Powell, 1982, 1989; Przeworski, Stokes and Manin, 1999; Ranney, 1962; Schmitt and Thomassen, 1999, Gerber and Lewis 2004).

In this group of studies, some conceptual variations are important to highlight. For example, Pitkin's (1967) notion refers to the extent to which representatives act in accordance with the public interest, while Achen (1978) and Gerber (2004) see representation as a normative property of the relationship between legislators' opinions and those of their constituencies. This type of operationalization of representation requires data from elites and voters and poses important challenges, such as the ability to distinguish representation on various policy issues, since the electorate is unlikely to express consistent views across diverse policy spectrums.

In a classic study, Dalton (1985) used survey data from parallel surveys of voters and party elites in Europe to analyze how representatives performed. Dalton showed that in matters of the economy and security policy, there is a close correspondence between the two views, but not on foreign policy. Furthermore, Dalton concluded, the clarity of party positions, articulated by a centralized party structure, strongly influences the efficiency of the outreach process.

Along the same lines, Luna and Zechmeister (2005) combined data from surveys of elites and the public to create indicators of representation in nine Latin American countries and quantify the extent to which political parties represent voters' political preferences in those countries. These authors found that party system institutionalization and socioeconomic development are positively related to representation and that left-wing parties contribute to the representative structures of political systems. Notably, their findings also provide evidence that perceptions of fraud in an electoral system are correlated at a fairly high level with representation. This points to the idea that citizens' perceptions of a system are consistent with its reality.

Achen (1978) uses three measures of representativeness that attempt to reflect the liberal democratic concepts of citizen equality, neutrality towards alternatives and popular sovereignty. He uses indicators of proximity, i.e., the ideological distance between representatives and voters; responsiveness and centrism, which is the difference between the proximity of the representative and the variance of opinion in the electoral district. Page and Shapiro (1983) analyze public opinion data on policies in the United States over a period of more than 40 years to analyze the responsiveness of government policies to citizens' preferences. To do so, they document the relationship between changes in preferences and changes in U.S. policy to assess whether public policy moves in the same direction as opinion.

Bartels (1991) also carried out work along the same lines, analyzing the votes of representatives in a series of hearings on the defense budget and their relationship with voters' opinions on defense spending during the 1980 election campaign. This study follows the same line as previous studies: To estimate representatives' stances on a public policy issue, it measured the relationship between representatives' characteristics and those of their districts, as well as their individual voting behavior. These data were compared with voters' opinions gathered by a national public opinion measurement project.

Other authors have used the concept of dynamic representation, which refers to situations in which there is a change in public opinion and public policy responds accordingly. Stimson, MacKuen, and Erikson (1995) indicate that there are two mechanisms through which this type of representation occurs: (1) elections change the political composition of government, which is then reflected in new policy, and (2) policymakers calculate the future implications (mainly electoral) of current public opinions and act accordingly (rational anticipation).

This entire line of work uses various measures of public opinion contained in opinion barometers or policy mood measurement projects, such as the Domestic Policy Mood (Stimson, 1991). Annual congressional performance indicators or surveys designed to measure elite responses to public policy issues are generally used to measure elite behavior or opinion. Other research projects, such as that of Ansolabehere, Snyder, and Stewart (2001), have relied on their own databases containing information on the policy positions of congressional candidates, as well as surveys designed specifically to measure candidates' positions on public policy issues.

Another way of approaching the measurement of representation consists of coding legal instruments. For example, Lax and Phillips (2009) studied the effects of public opinion on the adoption of specific gay-rights policies. For this purpose, different laws against discrimination and on same-sex civil unions, among others, were codified and a positioning index was constructed. The results indicated a high degree of response, controlling for interest group pressure and voter ideology.

Some approaches, such as that of Bafumi and Herron (2010) measure representation in terms of ideal points. An ideal point is the position of a person or institution on a scale that spans from liberalism to conservatism. To do so, the votes cast by congresses and presidential positions were measured. An online survey, conducted by the Cooperative Congressional Election Study, focused on representation and electoral competition and was used to measure voters' ideal points. The study asked people to vote for or against a proposition as if they were members of the Senate or House of Representatives.

This body of work seems to model a single type of relationship, leaving aside other types of links established between representatives and their constituents. Mansbridge (2003) questions the types of linear and unidirectional relationships that do not meet the traditional criteria of democratic accountability and proposes including new types in the study such as "anticipatory representation" (representatives act according to what, according to their prediction, voters will approve in the next election), "gyroscopic representation" (representatives act according to their own principles, common sense, and interests), "surrogate representation" (occurs when legislators represent constituents outside their own electoral district).

Gilens and Page's (2014) main interest is with actors who have the power to influence public policies. These can be very diverse actors: citizens, economic elites, various organized and mass interest groups. This study used an original dataset that measured over 1500 public policy issues and concluded that citizens and mass interest groups have little influence, while organizations representing commercial interests have substantive impacts on U.S. government policy. These results support theories of economic elite dominance and biased pluralism.

In all previous studies, representation is analyzed based on the relationship between a legislator's behavior and the interests of the electorate. This measurement option had a fundamental interest in territorial distribution. Sartori (1999) and Urbinati and Warren (2008) have problematized this way of looking at representation. Among their concerns are population growth, subject overload, and the existence of extraterritorial issues. Urbinati and Warren (2008) argue that representation is more than a division of labor between political elites and citizens, and we should see it as an intrinsic and dynamic part of the elements that make democracy possible.

Recent discussions have endeavored to distinguish measurements focused on territorially-based electoral representation from new, more complex forms of representation that have focused on a set of elements such as institutional design, citizen-power linkages, legitimacy, justice, political judgment, and participation. Existing theoretical and empirical evidence suggests a series of political, social, and economic factors that are associated with levels of representation. According to Luna and Zechmeister (2005), these factors are the level of institutionalization, policy change, the personalism of the electoral system, the strength of left-wing parties, the presence of horizontal links, perceptions of electoral fraud, levels of economic and social development, and economic change. For Urbinati and Warren (2008), electoral representation is shaped by constitutional design, the design of the electoral system, political parties, representatives' ethical obligations, and citizens' deliberation and judgment.

All of the above has led to a discussion of representation in democracies, its implications, challenges, and what difficulties exist in its measurement. Modern democracy consists of a very complex sum of institutions involving multiple channels of representation. Thus, it is important to add the dimension of institutional designs to the measurement of representation and analyze whether political institutions articulate patterns of inclusion (Tilly 2007). Naturally, these elements add complexity to the measurement and represent a challenge in quantitative terms. Therefore, this book seeks to help address such challenges.

3.2 What is representative democracy today?

In our view, of the ways in which democracy is conceptualized, the one that best responds to the characteristics and needs of democratic systems in today's world is representative democracy. Representative democracy is usually considered insufficient, and is identified with obsolete forms of institutional organization that are judged, sometimes with good reason, as unproductive or inefficient. Thus, REPRESENTATIVE DEMOCRACY is underestimated or set aside as a relic of the past. Although this unproductiveness may originate in institutions that have ceased to serve their purpose, it does not stop there.

Conversely, it can be argued that these and other institutions are the result of earlier evolutionary processes. As such, it is possible that, as they age, they may become obstacles to new democratic demands. This was the case with electoral legislation that limited the right to vote to just a sector of the adult population. Electoral legislation, and indeed constitutions, eventually accepted the right of all adults to vote, whether rich or poor, male or female, young or old. For a long time, parliaments were largely made up of men belonging to dominant ethnic, religious, or regional groups. However, demands for gender parity, ethnic, and religious inclusion, among others, have led to a diversified parliamentary composition that is more representative of national populations and better represents them. Recently, legislatures have also opened up to representation of diasporas and other "postnational" minorities. These examples show that the old institutions can adapt to the new realities that democracy must incorporate: new demands and requirements, changes in the composition of political actors, diversification of political preferences and mentalities, etc. In opposition to academic currents that consider representative democracy to be exhausted and have shifted their focus to other varieties, such as direct or participatory democracy, we share the hypothesis that the demands for representation expressed against the grain of existing institutional structures are challenges that representative democracy can deal with, forcing us to rethink the institutions in which, as a product of past collective decisions, it has materialized up to the present (Urbinati 2006, Alonso et al., 2011).

Since it began and expanded as a form of organizing political power two centuries ago, representative democracy has modified its forms of institutional organization. The way in which institutions adjust the relationship between political power and society has changed substantially. However, it has since been driven by two main engines: a) incorporation of new groups into political rights (extension of suffrage, of the rights of association and participation in public office, gender and ethnic parity, etc.) and, consequently, the uptake of issues that these citizens promote in the legislative and government agenda, and b) the transformation of the relationship between these citizens and their elected representatives through the continuous interaction between the two. Thus, representative democracy is not tied to a single predefined institutional structure, but has taken on different guises at different times. Historical evidence supports this position and from it new theories and innovations have been produced to further its development (Manin, 1997; Dunn, 2019; Drake, 2009).

Latin America's recent political development has been characterized by an expansion of democratic regimes that regulate access to power and a resistance, active or passive, by governmental and state structures to respond in accordance with this expansion. In a region where, as we saw in Chapter 1, there has been a historic relationship of constant subordination and non-negotiation of access to power between the elites and the majorities, during the stage of democratic expansion it was to be expected that growing political freedoms would lead to open confrontation centered on income and power distribution. Among the hypotheses circulating at the beginning of the transitions (O'Donnell, Schmitter, and Whitehead 1986), some speculated about the future such changeovers would have. These authors chose the metaphor of a multi-layered or overlapping chess game in which a large number of players would be involved in myriad moves with uncertain outcomes. Almost 40 years later, we can see some results of this complex game called representative democracy. Let us first dwell on the definition of this concept.

3.2.1 Democratic theory of representative democracy

If we judge representative democracy from the perspectives of its conservative traditions of thought, mostly rooted in the 19th century, we can appreciate the changes it has undergone up until today: universal suffrage, pluralism and party diversity, civil liberties, multiple individual and collective autonomies, and a dynamic of exchange between rulers and ruled that has no previous parallel. If, on the other hand, we judge it with a negative lens, the great problems that currently arouse malaise and anger manifest themselves: disaffection and distrust of institutions, reprehension of politicians and parties, demoralization of the citizenry, media stridency, anti-system protests, and the emergence of all manner of impostors on the political scene. We could erroneously conclude that the era of representative democracy has come to an end. Further, the responses offered in the face of widespread dissatisfactions, once they have seduced a majority, have led to real vortexes of destruction. The evidence of these shifts has led many to call for "direct" forms of democracy, *replacing* representative forms. Removing political professionals, limiting their power, forcing them to answer to their base through plebiscitary forms have been and continue to be sometimes commendable efforts, sometimes deplorable. Incorporating variations on direct democracy is not a substitute for representative institutions. In fact, in all systems in which innovations have been introduced, such as the assembly, the popular initiative of law, referendums and plebiscites, the recall, etc.,[60] they coexist and stimulate representation. So far, representative democracy has incorporated additional mechanisms, in some cases successfully, and are maintained as institutions in which the public interest and

---

[60] These practices have been grouped into several categories: direct democracy, deliberative democracy, and participatory democracy (Altmann, 2010; Welp, 2022).

citizen control thereof prevail. In other cases, for example in populist experiences, they have fallen prey to manipulation by those in power.

The theory of representative democracy has the greatest capacity to balance the virtues and defects of what are generically called "parliamentary democracies". Theoretical debate on representative democracy has developed significantly based on the academic and public attention that the worldwide expansion of this form of government has attracted. Theories of representation have come under close scrutiny to demonstrate that in many contemporary trends, citizen participation in multiple manifestations, the tumultuous proliferation of specialized or lay public opinion in all media and its spread in the digital universe, the discrediting of traditional modes of political representation, the crises of democracies, and the return of autocracies are all phenomena that have forced a rethinking of the relationship between democracy and representation, and the very idea of "representative democracy."

The dichotomy between the two terms was born with "census suffrage", which reserved the right to vote to the owners of considerable wealth and restricted political representation to certain issues that were not reserved for the crown. In other words, representative democracy began in the modern era with the monarchy's recognition of the right of the nobility, the wealthy, or the enlightened classes to vote to elect rulers, but limiting the issues on which their opinion was taken into account for decisions. Thus, the further development of democracy is inextricably linked to the idea of citizenship and its extension to new groups previously excluded, to the incorporation of matters on which citizens can make decisions; in other words, the transfer of sovereignty from the various elites to the people, establishing a germinal tendency to subsume the elites to the sovereignty of the people as a whole, under the principle of one individual, one vote. This was a first stage of equality of all citizens before the ballot box that, in the end, seeks to extend itself to new territories of the public sphere. Democratic representation neither begins nor ends with elections. It requires elections as a precondition of existence; the electoral decision authorizes certain individuals to legislate and make government decisions for a period after which they must alternate through new elections. The tradition of the moderns claimed that, once elected, representatives had autonomy with respect to the electors and acted according to their judgment and reason in matters they had to resolve. Representation was a total surrender of sovereignty. In this view, there was no need and even less an obligation to maintain a relationship, whether sporadic or constant, with constituents. However, this definition was always surpassed by a "surplus of politics", which is behind its constant evolution (Urbinati, 2006, p. 223 and passim).

The history of the extension of suffrage is to a large extent the history of political movements that strived to be included in the public agenda and of the commitments made to recognize the access of previously excluded groups therein (Tilly, 1999, p. 81; Przeworski, 2009). This increase in the number of people entitled to vote gradually changed the meaning of representation. From a representation restricted to the interests and preferences of the elites (bourgeoisie and aristocracy), there was a multiplication of groups of individuals endowed with the power to send their representatives to government bodies, especially to parliament. Men of legal age and later women were enfranchised; in quite a few locales ethnic or national minorities also became empowered. The increase in the voting population exposed democracy to the natural political turbulence caused by the raising of demands and expectations of non-elite sectors to the traditional spaces of representation. In addition, we should highlight that the extension of suffrage was significantly correlated to the drop in inequality between social classes (Marshall, 1950).

The prevalence of democratic systems cannot be understood without the relationship between representatives and constituents, or without the effects produced by the dynamics between the two groups. Moreover, the stability of democracy depends on the degree to which constituents are satisfied with their representative institutions. It is normally assumed that, *caeteris paribus*, the more satisfied constituents are with their representatives, the lower the probability that the former will question the legitimacy of the political-representation cycle (elections-government-elections) and want to move away from democratic systems.

As the diversity of the population with citizenship rights expands, constituencies increase in number and their preferences become more varied and divergent. Thus, they obtain satisfaction with their representatives if preferences can be articulated and processed into legislation and state action. By its nature, representation is present in the feedback continuum of politics (reflexivity) where the circulation of preferences and opinions takes place. This circulation tends to increase during the runup to elections and remains active in public opinion afterwards, although it tends to diminish between elections. Elections are thus high points when the electorate's decisions can change regarding who is fit to hold office. Following elections, the government undertakes its duties, which in turn constitutes a continuous source of interaction through political opinion and action. Now, the question is no longer *who* the elected official represents, but about *how* those elected to office represent their constituents.

In the conservative tradition of representation, being elected to office authorizes representatives to conduct themselves independently with respect to the constituency. This is because, upon being elected, they become general representatives and not only of the particular interests of their electors, although they emerged from therein, since they inevitably enter into interaction with other interests, motivations, and preferences that are at play in politics. Thus, elections produce governments that are responsible and limited (by the constitution), but not necessarily representative, paradoxically demonstrated by the permanent deficit of representation with respect to evolving constituent demands. To develop a "democratic theory of representative democracy" (Urbinati, 2006, p. 224) requires, then, an interruption in this rigid tradition and the uptake of citizens' permanent interaction between representatives and their constituents as drivers of democratic expansion. Without ignoring the importance of the electoral process, by reexamining the representative cycle, we can observe shortcomings in the representative-constituents relationship and, at the same time, draw attention to the possible innovations that could strengthen it institutionally.

After the third wave of democracy (1972–2016), there have been political regressions that, should they become an ongoing trend, will signal a shift towards autocracy: "the third wave of autocracy" or "illiberal democracy" as they are known (Sigmann and Lindberg 2015; Zakaria, 1997). In many countries satisfaction with democracy has declined. This is due to citizens' perceptions that political elites, the governments they head, and the institutions in which they serve, despite arising from legitimate constitutional decisions and periodic and fair elections, are insufficient, unproductive, inefficient, corrupt, and favor elite interests, while relegating other social groups. The participation of many countries in this third democratic wave has been followed by a stage that was first thought of as "consolidation of democracy", but which in reality has led to what today we perceive as a pendulum swing between oligarchic, or populist, deformation of democracy (Urbinati, 2014). Both options place us at the gates of autocratization.

In the former option, political representation is captured by elites that isolate the state from the majority of citizens. Private and public powers appropriate the institutions and isolate them from opinion, in an effort to prevent public voices from influencing decisions; they create barriers in the political regime to avert the waves of social demands from being included in the state. By so proceeding, the principle of equality is compromised, which, while respected in the voting process, is shipwrecked on the shores of representative "infidelity," giving rise to dissatisfaction that grows as long as this *oligarchization* is not counteracted. If this deformation is not corrected, the electorate usually favors alternatives promoted by providential leaders who appeal to the people for support in order to replace elite "capture" with an authentic popular representation that drifts again towards the hijacking of power by leaders and the elite around them, turning the people into an "audience" (Urbinati, 2019a). The populist drift is a "mono-archic emendation of democracy" (Urbinati, 2014, p. 153), a transmutation of the majority into a leadership that "*embodies*" it, that polarizes (people/non-people) and reduces its followers to the category of spectators, i.e., an "audience". Here again, the principle of political equality is compromised by ignoring any voice that dissents with the leader who controls the will, regardless of whether it is the people's will that he/she claims to represent or that of the political opposition. Typically, when representatives come to power, their appropriation of the government is reflected in an exclusive monopoly of power, which leads to the development of a state which is no longer based on representing general opinion but rather represents the will of the group that controls access to the state. Moving from one extreme to the other, this pendulum tends to lead to political decomposition and instability in which democracy is challenged as a viable and ideal form of government. These crises leave deep scars on political development and place democracies on the brink of autocracy.

The relationship between democracy and representation is at the heart of this problem. When the former moves away from the latter, it loses plasticity and becomes petrified as it transfers sovereignty to the group or the leader, who exercise power and "representation" as they see fit. And when representation moves away from democracy, it moves away from citizens' sovereignty, making decisions behind their backs or avoiding decisions that respond to the demands and problems of their sovereign. To overcome this dynamic, parallel or alternative forms of democracy have been proposed. Deliberative, participatory, direct, egalitarian, and liberal democracy are the best defined, each of which, or in combination, has an extensive literature (Coppedge, 2011; Coppedge et al. 2020). We posit the hypothesis that representative democracy encompasses responses to the problems that each of these forms seeks to address and integrates them into a single conceptual unit.

> Representative democracy is the antithesis of both delegated democracy and en masse types of representative populistic or plebiscitary democracy that identify the people with the person of the leader. In both cases the citizenry is conceived as an atomistic gathering with no intermediary political associations and ideological narratives. (Urbinati, 2006, p. 227).

The judgment of the citizenry and the plurality of its political will are continuous flows. Elections are a "snapshot" of voters' judgments, a moment when such judgments turn into a will to vote, but which are not fully expressed at the ballot box. Elections are correlated with polls: We can get an idea of the sample population's opinions at the moment surveys are taken, but they cannot predict how those opinions will shift in the future. The weight and effects of elections continue during the period in which elected officials are in office. The widespread practice of undertaking opinion polls or voting intention surveys proves that citizens' opinions are constant and variable, and also demonstrates the need to understand shifting opinion over time, although this "consultation" is rarely formally institutionalized in political systems.[61]

---

[61] Although forms of direct decision-making have begun to proliferate in matters occasionally submitted to a vote.

In the conservative conception of representation, the electoral photograph of people's opinions was frozen until new elections were held (Von Beyme, 2011, p. 51). The authorization to make legislative decisions was guaranteed, as if the makeup of parliament in accordance to voters' preferences on election day remained the same throughout elected officials' terms of office. Ratification or rejection during the statutory term of office, such as the "vote of confidence or no confidence," or impeachment allowed people to change their minds at any point during representatives' terms within the same government, thus modifying policies or terminating a government and calling for new elections. However, despite the fact that representation includes the right of citizens to change their minds according to prevailing circumstances, this ability does not always receive the right response at the right time. This is because, unless they have mechanisms and devices for transformation, centuries-old inherited institutions are unable to respond with plasticity to these changes in needs, circumstances, and preferences. If representative democracy contains an electoral moment and a continuum throughout a governmental administration, it is evident that the institutions that guarantee and protect the former are greater in number and stronger than those dedicated to the latter.

The change in democratic demands inevitably makes it necessary to recognize and put into use innumerable new practices and spaces wherever representation is needed. In addition to demands that have been articulated, there are others that are growing daily, such as the presence of large migratory contingents or transnational/multinational populations; there are problems of a magnitude impossible to encompass and manage within the limits of the national state, such as climate change, human rights, migrations, or the regulation of transnational companies. To this list we add the tensions surrounding calls to intervene in decisions made by international bodies in which participation is limited to member states, especially when the connection between these bodies and citizens' interests are weak. Then there is the expansion of civil society organizations and movements that operate as government monitors or that continually propose public policies and legislation in different local or international matters, without their place in decision-making being specified in democratically derived tenets (Alonso et al., 2011, pp. 1–22; Valdés-Ugalde, 2023 Ch. 4).

To accept these influences and translate them into positive institutions, democracy must open its doors to "permanent representation." This capacity is lacking in "delegative" democracy (O'Donnell, 1994) and populism (Urbinati, 2019b), because they restrict democracy to fractional and exclusionary representations that contradict the principle of citizen equality in collective affairs. In addition to the political causes that are at their origin, these two tendencies also stem from the material difficulties to institutionalize permanent representation, a "realistic

utopia" (Rawls) that would require the conjunction of technical-political commu-
nications methods, which has been achieved only in special moments. The dynamics of the demands can only be institutionally integrated into the continuous
and open flow of representative democracy. It is true that the cases in which it is
best realized are still few and far between, so that, to a large extent, this remains
a project whose viability depends on its grounding in the political culture and in
ideological projects competing for power. Hence, subjecting actually existing democracies to the rigorous scrutiny of the basic conditions of representative democracy can give a better idea of the pending tasks of contemporary regimes and
of the principles whose institutionalization should be sought in order to integrate
the political imagination of those "outboard" engines that are the citizen and
their supportive movements.

This dichotomy has been examined as a "democratic diarchy" (Urbinati 2014:
16–80), i.e., the natural separation between citizen *judgment*, that appears as *opinion*, and the *will* of the sovereign, that is manifested through forms and mechanisms of interposition. In the Athenian *ecclesia* (or *ekklesia*), democracy was at the
shortest distance between the two. In the *assembly,* judgment and will could meet
more easily, or rather, the distance between the two was less perceptible, since decisionmakers were subject to the close and direct scrutiny of the same people who
participated in public deliberations. In complex societies, this proximity breaks
down and opens up a problem insufficiently addressed by democratic theory.
When citizens vote, they simultaneously "express their opinion" and grant governmental institutions and the state the authorization to carry out their will through
acts of government. But when they act politically beyond election day, they also
express their opinion. This second opinion, that of citizens as political actors, has
been insufficiently addressed by political institutions. If democracy is essentially
defined by the procedures that protect citizens' freedoms (Urbinati, 2014, p. 21 and
passim), to express their opinions, whatever they may be, and ensure that they
count on equal terms with all others in order to be transformed into their will
through decisions, then the "moment" in which citizens act politically needs to be
incorporated by political institutions. This "moment" is, in reality, an uninterrupted
continuum of acts that make up the public sphere.

Contemporary democracies have in "public opinion" a non-binding pressure
"compass" for political representatives, while in the vote, on the contrary, they
have a binding rule. Sovereign will is strongly concentrated in the vote, while public opinion formation is at the mercy of the powers that be, especially in the institutional structure of the mass media and the "social networks". The imbalance is
evident, which is why it is easier for political parties and rulers to detach themselves from opinion with relative ease. In societies where public opinion is very
robust due to the existence of "high intensity" citizenry, the impact of "opinion" on

"will" is greater, but in weak societies (with "low intensity citizenry") opinion is fickle and its impact on will is more tenuous. This condition provides representatives with an alibi in order to manipulate the electorate through clientelism and cheap propaganda and put themselves out of reach of their constituencies. The difference between the two extremes lies in the greater or lesser capacity to punish the disengagement of the rulers vis-à-vis the opinion of the sovereigns.

3.2.2 Factors of representative democracy: A proposal

V-Dem does not provide an index of representative democracy. Instead, it aims to provide high quality data for the research of those who adopt approaches based on the criteria formed through analyses of electoral democracy, liberal democracy, egalitarian democracy, participatory democracy, and deliberative democracy. Hence its "high level democracy indices" are divided on the basis of this classification. All of them have elements for observing the "character" of representative democracy, but they require a different organization to make a "high level" index of representative democracy. Thus, to observe and evaluate the quality of representation, we must translate the meaning of these dimensions of representative democracy into observables that allow us to identify its behavioral dynamics in concrete political systems. To flesh out this structure, we selected indicators from this database, which, in our opinion, is the most complete to date. This is what the proposal consists of.

We have identified four factors that need to be taken into account to measure the quality of democratic representation beyond the electoral moment. We have also observed them as data that denote minimum conditions that are maintained over time between elections: 1) citizen equality when participating in public decisions, 2) conditions for deliberation, 3) accountability, and 4) political party-ideological maturity. Each of these factors is a proxy for the "environment" of relations between representatives and constituents during that continuum called government. These are minimal conditions because they do not signify the most possibly developed expression of the *kratia* configuration that represents the *demos* in its maximum possibilities of virtuous self-government, i.e., close to the prescriptions of normative theory, but because they indicate the presence or non-presence of the minimal conditions that must be met for its initiation.

3.2.2.1 Equal freedom for public participation

Citizens' political equality is the basis of their independence in the exercise of their sovereignty. This equality of individuals and groups is premised on the absence of obstacles, based on social origin and economic status, to participating in public affairs. Differentials in the capacity for voice and influence in politics, whether during elections -when they are minimized- or in the inter-electoral continuum -when inequalities are normalized- depend on factors that condition the strength of the link between representatives and constituents. In representative democracy, equality simultaneously includes citizens' equity in voting (*isonomia*) and in expressing their voice (*isēgoría*) (Urbinati, 2006, pp. 40–46).

Legal equality is the minimum starting point, but its meaning in representative democracy involves the capacity or freedom to carry out one's own purposes in the public sphere that are not dependent on the dictates of others: neither a predetermined objective in the legal system, nor an order from the ruler. Freedom to express citizens' own judgment against power in order to limit it, or channel it in a different direction. Therefore, legal equality is only the beginning of freedom of public intervention, since this requires favorable conditions and absence of obstacles.

3.2.2.2 Deliberation

Citizens judge public affairs continuously, playing an essential role in bonding with their representatives. Every judgment calls for impartiality. However, this is not and cannot be the same when judges issue sentences, when citizens judge matters based on their interests, or when parliamentarians legislate. From judge to citizen, from a member of parliament to a party candidate, they all exercise public judgment. Throughout its workings, democracy demands impartiality and objectivity, insofar as public life seeks justice above particular biases in favor of, or against, particular groups. However, citizen judgment is an essential component in forming public reason, the most elaborate degree of opinion that has undergone a collective process of deliberation.

The capacity for citizen deliberation develops in close relation to the rights of freedom to express and know judgments that are manifested in ideas, beliefs, and ways of thinking that originate with the individual and the social need to communicate about common issues, which includes communication about the condition of each individual. The control of power and the intervention of individuals in that control is developed through deliberation. The exercise of these rights requires sufficient information about the social environment and, therefore, from varied and alternative sources. It also requires that the practice of rights faces as few obstacles as possible regarding resources, education, time, dialogue, and as much receptivity as possible in the public and social institutional environment created to channel the voice and conversation arising from the exercise of these rights. It also needs institutions to protect and guarantee this exercise, as well as for civil society advocacy.

3.2.2.3 Accountability

Accountability is an essential factor of democratic representation. Thus, representatives are required to report their decisions to competent bodies and directly to the public. The better the accountability, the more information will be available for citizens to judge how representatives are carrying out their duties. The power to call representatives to account between elections depends on the institutional network that compels representatives to account for their performance where required. The link between these requirements and the flow of information to the sovereign completes the information circuit necessary for forming an opinion. Therefore, the relevant requirements are: level of transparency and effectiveness of laws, control of the legislature and other competent bodies over the executive branch, and submission to the judiciary branch.

3.2.2.4 Political party-ideological maturity

The presence of solid ideological currents, political parties and organizations with clear and consistent platforms of thought and programs are key for achieving quality democratic representation. At the same time, quality is associated with the degree of linkage established between ideological and political party alternatives and social groups. The currents and organizations and their degree of linkage with society with the aim of influencing public decisions are the materialization in collective action of a sizable part of the "surplus of politics" that drives the evolution of representation (Urbinati, 2006, p. 223). According to the conceptual structure of representative democracy, these elements are indicative of whether citizens are exposed to a competitive environment in which the exchange of ideas and public debate nourish the capacity of citizens and representatives to visualize horizons of political development. The stronger these actors are, the more possibilities for exchange there are, and the robustness of the state also benefits. The existence of multiparty competition, of political parties with a national presence, grassroots support and outreach, as well as the type of link they maintain with citizens are the elements that allow us to gauge the maturity of this engine of representation of future visions that are being included into the collective agenda.

3.2.3 Analysis technique

The objective of this analysis is to empirically test a proposed structure of representative democracy. For this purpose, V-DEM data from 1990 to 2021 and from 15 Latin American countries were used. Electoral and closed autocracies were not included in the analysis, nor were the Caribbean countries, except for the Dominican

Republic.[62] Initially, we selected a set of items that correspond to the structure of representative democracy that we are examining, based on existing theory.

An exploratory factor analysis was performed using the principal components method with varimax rotation. This technique is useful when gauging from a set of items the underlying structure of that set. The basic assumption of factor analysis is that for a collection of observed variables, there is a set of underlying variables (called factors) that can explain the interrelationships between these variables. In this sense, the technique is used when we wish to locate the components that are part of concepts that, by their nature, are multidimensional. The technique was estimated by excluding items with a factorial weight of less than .40. In this way, the initially proposed indicators were tested and those that did not have the ideal factor load were eliminated.

3.2.3.1 Indicator selection

A measurement of representation that aims at a broader vision of its quality should have, at least, the following dimensions: equal conditions for participation, deliberation, accountability, and political party-ideological maturity. From the set of V-DEM indicators, 23 items were selected as proxies to measure each of these dimensions (see Tab. 3.2).

This proposed form of organization, based on the concept of representative democracy, takes into account indicators of the egalitarian and deliberative components, as well as the indexes of freedom of expression, civil society participation, the rule of law, and the institutionalization of the parties that appear in the V-DEM database. In each of these groups, there are key indicators for measuring representative democracy.

The first component indicates the equality of conditions for participation insofar as it includes protection, access, and distribution of rights for different social groups. For this component, six indicators were chosen from the protection, access, and distribution dimension (see Tab. 3.2). These six indicators represent a sufficiently objective table regarding the degree to which a population is more or less equal in protection, access, and distribution of rights that are considered essential for citizens to publicly have their voice heard. Civil liberties, access to political power, and guaranteed access to education and health indicate to what degree societal equity or inequity exists in terms of the interplay (of greater or lesser quality) between citizens and representatives from the perspective of conditions needed to "initiate" people's social lives.

To incorporate the second component (deliberation), a group of indicators from three indexes was used: freedom of expression and alternative sources of

---

62 Cuba is not included because it is a closed autocracy. The first year of this analysis (1980), Nicaragua and Venezuela were electoral democracies but over time they shifted to electoral autocracies. Therefore, they are excluded from this selection.

information, the deliberative component, and civil society participation. As depicted in table 3.3, these indicators measure the freedom of discussion of different actors, the media's gamut of informative and critical perspectives, as well as the degree of influence of civil society.

Regarding accountability, note that insofar as we are trying to measure the quality of representation between electoral periods, i.e., during governmental exercises, we assume that vertical accountability (elections) is given in the set of countries analyzed.[63] Therefore, we used indicators that measure the existence of transparent laws with predictable application, the executive's respect for the constitution, as well as judicial and legislative constraints. Note also that the most important dimension of accountability in representative democracy is diagonal accountability, that is, the media and civil society's control of the government. These indicators are already included in the other dimensions, insofar as it is a cross-cutting dimension. Finally, the dimension of political party-ideological maturity involves four indicators that account for party organization, platforms, and the quality of the links established with the citizenry.

Tab. 3.2: Selection of items.

Dimension	Items	VDEM component
Equal status for participation	Social class equality in terms of civil liberties	Egalitarian component index
		Equal protection index
	Social group equality in terms of civil liberties	Egalitarian component Index
		Equal protection index
	Power distributed by socioeconomic position	Egalitarian component Index
		Equal access index
	Power distributed by social group	Egalitarian component Index
		Equal access index
	Educational equality	Egalitarian component Index
		Equal distribution of resources
	Health equality	Egalitarian component Index
		Equal distribution of resources

---

63 In any case, we include separately in Chapter 4 the behavior of the electoral component in the countries studied.

Tab. 3.2 (continued)

Dimension	Items	VDEM component
Deliberation	Print/broadcast media perspectives	Freedom of expression and alternative sources of information index
	Freedom of discussion for men	Freedom of expression and alternative sources of information index
	Freedom of discussion for women	Freedom of Expression and alternative sources of information index
	Freedom of academic and cultural expression	Freedom of expression and alternative sources of information index
	Critical print/broadcast media	Freedom of expression and alternative sources of information index
	Engaged society	Deliberative Component Index
	Reasoned justification	Deliberative Component Index
	CSO consultation	Civil Society Participation Index
	CSO entry and exit	Core Civil Society Index
Accountability	Transparent laws with predictable enforcement	Rule of Law Index
	Executive respects constitution	Judicial constraints on the executive index (v2x_jucon)
	Legislature investigates in practice	Legislative constraints on the executive index (v2xlg_legcon)
	Compliance with judiciary	Judicial constraints on the executive index (v2x_jucon)
Party and organizational (ideological) maturity	Party organizations	Party Institutionalization Index
	Distinct party platforms	Party Institutionalization Index
	Party branches	Party Institutionalization Index
	Party linkages	Party Institutionalization Index

Source: Prepared by author based on V-dem codebook 12. (Coppedge et al., 2022a and 2022b).

3.2.3.2 Results

The application of the technique allows us to account for four factors characteristic of representative democracy that have an eigenvalue greater than 1 (Tab. 3.3). Together, these items explain 74 percent of the variance. The results allow us to verify the presence of a structure typical of representative democracy that includes egalitarian, deliberative, accountability, and political-party elements. The structure derived from this analysis suggests a first factor in which most of the items of the egalitarian component are clustered, which implies equality of conditions for participation. In this sense, equality by class and social group, as well as educational and health equality, are the items that are part of this first component. This component also includes the item that tells us how independent public deliberations are in incorporating this element in the degree of societal involvement. This item had been considered one of the deliberation components; however, the factor analysis indicates that it also has weight, and to a greater degree, in the egalitarian component, so it was reassigned therein.

The second factor makes up the deliberation items. This component includes the items of freedom of discussion of all citizens without distinction, of gender, and of cultural and academic expression that make it possible for citizens to enjoy an environment free of obstacles to deliberate and justify their positions. The element of "reasoned justification" is excluded because, although it refers to the degree to which elites explain the reasons that justify their decisions, the sense in which we consider deliberation is therefore relative to society as a whole and not only to decisionmakers in government and other informal spheres of political power.

The third factor refers to accountability. Here there are five items that transcend the traditional view of accountability, including critical media and civil society. This is in line with the diagonal-accountability dimension of representative democracy. This component also includes items that refer to the legislative branch in its investigative function of the executive branch in terms of its respect for the constitution, and of the judiciary for the compliance of government to its provisions.

The last component contains items related to party maturity. This component groups together items that measure the number of parties with permanent organizations in a country, the presence of local party branches and the types of links -clientelist or not- that they build with the citizenry.

This structure is consistent with the theoretically stated dimensions and confirms that representative democracy, in addition to an electoral component, must also consider egalitarian, deliberative, and accountability elements based on formal institutions and public opinion, and the factors of organization and maturity of political parties.

Tab. 3.3: Results of the exploratory factor analysis.

Variable	Factor 1	Factor 2	Factor 3	Factor 4
	Egalitarian	Deliberative	Accountability	Party maturity
Social class equality with respect to civil liberties	0.7546			
Social group equality with respect to civil liberties	0.7742			
Educational equality	0.8968			
Health equality	0.83			
Engaged society	0.6205			
Freedom of discussion for men		0.8704		
Freedom of discussion for women		0.8243		
Freedom of academic and cultural expression		0.6278		
Critical print/broadcast media			0.7606	
Civil society organisation entry and exit			0.5918	
Executive respects constitution			0.4724	
Legislature investigates in practice			0.7533	
Compliance with judiciary			0.63	
Party organisations				0.8812
Party links				0.7834
Party branches				0.7805

Source: prepared by author based on V-dem codebook 12. (Coppedge et al., 2022a and 2022b).

3.3 Final consideration on the method

This analysis is focused on measuring a conceptualization of representative democracy. As we saw above, the classical empirical literature on the measurement of democracy fails to fully operationalize the concept of representation or to capture the broader sense of what representative democracy implies in a new perspective, which includes "judgment-opinion" on the one hand, and "will" on the other (Urbinati). These previous studies generally use indicators to measure the size of districts, the presence of institutionalized parties, and the correspondence between public and representative preferences. Although these variables are important for political representation, by limiting representation to an aspect of territorial, institutional, or declared coincidences, much of its substantive meaning is lost, which should be approached from other conditions that are better captured by equality, deliberation, accountability, and ideological and party maturity as the main dynamics in the formation of public reason.

This chapter is part of the discussion on the measurement of this type of democracy by proposing original scales constructed on the basis of the V-DEM project, which was created to offer better ways of observation, given the weakness of the classic indicators and the need to have measurements of its "varieties". It is thus possible to conceive of representative democracy as a "variety" in the same sense as egalitarian, deliberative, or participatory democracy: all of them with a common electoral component that registers the fulfillment of civil and political rights, but expanding it in order to capture more highly evolved features in actual democracies. By no means is this an attempt to perform an analysis as thorough and methodologically sophisticated as the one V-Dem has carried out by conceptualizing and describing the five varieties defined by its team (liberal, electoral, deliberative, egalitarian, and participatory) (Lührman et al., 2017). This approximation is barely tentative and it attempts to capture dimensions that are otherwise distributed in the V-Dem classification, in order to advance toward a reconceptualization of representative democracy. This concept is empirically tested in the analysis. The results obtained in the statistical analysis allow us to conclude that it is indeed possible to bring together the four factors that make up representative democracy corresponding to the conceptual dimensions described above: the egalitarian factor, the deliberative factor, the accountability factor, and the political party-ideological maturity factor. These four components are independent of each other, but together they capture the maximum variation of representation in democracies.

Our results confirm that the four theoretical dimensions are consistent for measuring representative democracy and have a structure that is empirically sustained. We need, however, to clear up some additional points. The strongest component that explains the structure of representative democracy is the equality condition for participation, which includes the egalitarian and power-sharing elements necessary for representation. The equal status of all members of the *demos* is the starting point of representation. The historical development of representative democracy is inexplicable without the extension of rights that have become universal and comprise both equality of voting and equality of communication. As we have seen, both factors, by extending them to ever increasing sectors of the citizenry, have helped reduce inequality in other dimensions: socioeconomic, gender, ethnic, etc. The core of this effect lies in placing these inequalities at the center of public space and political activity in order to combat them. The resulting factor is composed of the five items with the highest factorial weight.

Deliberation is one of the engines that sets in motion the reasons, judgments, and opinions that are socialized, disseminated, and acquire structure, publicity, and relevance in the public sphere. Hence the importance of this indicator as part of the dimensions of public reason. From the environment closest to the individual, to the wider extension of community and society, meanings are formed and circulate through all available systems of communication. Deliberation is, therefore, a central piece of public reason understood as a process in continuous transformation and, as we can see, the deliberation and accountability indicators cut across the dimensions of public reason, judgment, and opinion, because they best allow us to empirically identify their meaning. In our initial proposal, this component included a broad group of items on deliberation, but also criticism of the media and the freedom of entry and exit of civil society organizations. The component that arose from the factor analysis only includes the items referring to freedoms related to cultural discussion and expression. The items related to media criticism and opportunities for entry and exit of civil society organizations were grouped under the accountability factor.

This result allows us to discuss the notion of accountability in representative democracy, which is different from the traditional one. Vertical accountability is the decisive form of accountability insofar as elections and their consequences are key for citizens to express their judgment on candidates and parties and on the performance of governments in changing electoral preferences. In turn, freedoms of expression and association allow citizen opinions and deliberation on public administration to be reflected in political trends that tip the balance of policies and decisions in a certain direction. Certainly, horizontal accountability, which is essential for maintaining checks and balances of power and good government performance, with its various components (executive respect for the constitution and checks and balances of the legislative and judicial branches), is part of the inter-electoral extension of citizen opinion. However, it is mainly an interplay of instituted power authorities, so that vertical accountability is the closest and strongest indicator that can be obtained of the judgment and opinion that nourish deliberation in the formation of citizen will.

According to our findings, the resulting accountability factor in this structure includes the traditional elements that were proposed at the beginning, i.e., transparent laws with predictable enforcement mechanisms, respect for the constitution by the executive, investigative powers of the legislature, and government compliance with the decisions of the judiciary; the analysis also made it possible to include in this factor what level of media criticism exists, as well as civil organization input and output. This indicates that the dimension of accountability in this type of democracy should include elements for measuring the diagonal accountability that the media and civil society exercise.

The factor of political party-ideological maturity is made up of the items that indicate the number of parties with a permanent organization, their local roots and links with affiliated persons. This is a core indicator of the capacity of citizens and representatives to convert social preferences, values, and desires into legislative and public policy decisions regarding the management of public affairs. Political parties are the borderline that divides opinion from decision; they are a defining part of the will to make projects and aspirations a reality and transform them into government. In this sense, ideological and party maturity is an indicator of the degree, form, and clarity in which the representation of society is translated into political patterns that shape the action of the state, i.e., its capacity to imprint the "surplus of politics" in the fundamental agreements of the state. For this reason, the items that most clearly capture this maturity are those that refer to the link between parties and society (organization, local support, and links with affiliates), while platforms and programs, although they reflect the proposals that guide action, are not necessarily indicative of the interrelationship with citizens.

This shows that, in addition to party organization per se, it is important to measure its scope in terms of territorial and ideological linkage. This is consistent with classic studies of representation. The items of the party component have factor weights greater than .70, thus indicating a strong correlation among themselves, but they explain a smaller percentage of the total variance of the construct than the other components. This means that the party dimension in representative democracy is important but not the only one.

Finally, our analysis indicates that the most important dimension in this type of democracy is equality, since this component explains the greatest percentage of the variance. These results have empirical support in the analysis technique we used and therefore we conclude that they have important implications for a broader understanding of the concept of representative democracy. Let us now turn to the results of the factor analysis when applying the values assigned in each item to countries we are interested in exploring.

Chapter 4
The facets of representative democracy in Latin America

The portrait of representative democracy in Latin America has yet to receive its finishing touches. It will have to be a composite sketch, comprised of many story fragments, told here and there, country by country, one phenomenon and problem at a time. These facets and the history of their development are scattered in hundreds of studies undertaken on constitutions, political processes, executive, legislative, and judicial powers, elections, media, citizenship, and social movements. As far as I have been able to research, there is no comprehensive account of their character nor, consequently, of the problems that progressive forces must face to cross the Rubicon and conquer the "popular, democratic and representative republic", as our 19th-century constitutions aspired and which the Bolivarian reforms (unsuccessfully) tried to leave behind (Gargarella, 2013, p. 196 and *passim*). These attempts are reminders of the imperative need for the return of representative democracy informed by an updated conception for the 21st century.

The quality of representation varies in an analogous manner to the quality of state performance. Without losing a proper perspective in comparisons between governance (Chapter 2) and our factor analysis measurements, Latin America demonstrates that its democratic quality, measured in terms of the relationship between citizen opinion and the political will of those in power, has abysmal gaps. Although there are relevant differences between countries and some of them post favorable scores, the distance between the best- and worst-rated countries is huge. So are the fluctuations over time. In the group of countries we selected, the temporal fluctuations in each indicator vary considerably. We now look at them in detail.

4.1 Democratic diarchy 1. Electoral representation

Voting and elections are a way of controlling governmental power given that at election time rulers are subjected to the will of the citizens. Once the government is formed, parliamentary representation and the judiciary play a role of constitutional control on behalf of the citizenry. Further, citizens remain active through opinion, organization, and participation in common and public affairs. Thus, elections are part of the political decisions made by the citizenry, but they are also an outflow of opinion into political decision-making exercised by individuals who

https://doi.org/10.1515/9783110773675-005

vote. Of all human rights that are in the core of civic-political rights, this one is the best distributed right. In our analysis from the previous chapter, in order to emphasize the items closest to representation in the inter-electoral period, we considered only Latin American countries that are minimally defined as "electoral democracies" in the V-Dem index. We deliberately excluded countries that became electoral autocracies or closed autocracies such as Nicaragua, Venezuela, and Cuba because they lack even the electoral minimum of democratic representation. This is why, although they may have positive ratings in areas such as social participation and other considerations, they cannot be included as representative democracies. This implies considering the electoral factor separately, so we will look discretely at this phase of political representation and its quality.

The V-Dem electoral democracy index contains the elements that help us understand the outcome of the electoral system of the countries considered herein.[64] Next to the scores obtained in this index, we can place the values obtained by our factor analysis of the quality of representation. In the following data, we identify the outcome scale of the countries in question.[65] We can clearly identify three groups with distinct outcome scores: high, medium, and low. Five countries are in the first category (0.8 to 0.9): Costa Rica, Uruguay, Chile, Brazil, and Argentina. Next, Panama, Bolivia, Ecuador, Peru, Mexico, and Colombia posted ratings between 0.6 and 0.79. In third place, Dominican Republic, Paraguay, El Salvador, and Guatemala have scores below 0.6.

As shown in Fig. 4.1, from 1990 to 2021, the entire group averages between 0.5 and 0.9. In other words, they post scores above at least half of the values in the set of indicators summarized in the index. This is explained by the priority that democratization places on the presence of reliable electoral systems and the rights of citizens to freely elect rulers. However, in addition to the average score, the variations of this outcome over time should be noted. The most stable countries are the first three in the first group. The other two, Argentina and Brazil, begin the 1990s at the same level, but dropped to the second group during significant periods, especially Brazil, which dropped from 0.8 in 2016 to 0.7 in 2017, reaching 0.66 in 2021, and Argentina, which remained most of the period in the first group, moved to the second in 2006. El Salvador, Dominican Republic, and Guatemala, which were always in the

---

64 "The index is formed by taking the average of, on the one hand, the weighted average of the indices measuring freedom of association thick (v2x_frassoc_thick), clean elections (v2xel_frefair), freedom of expression (v2x_freexp_altinf), elected officials (v2x_elecoff), and suffrage (v2x_suffr)". V-Dem Codebook V. 12 (Coppedge et al., 2022a, p. 43. The question answered by the index is: To what extent is the ideal of electoral democracy in its fullest sense achieved?

65 The scale ranges from 0 to 1, where 0 is the absence of electoral democracy and 1 would meet all the necessary requirements to qualify as such.

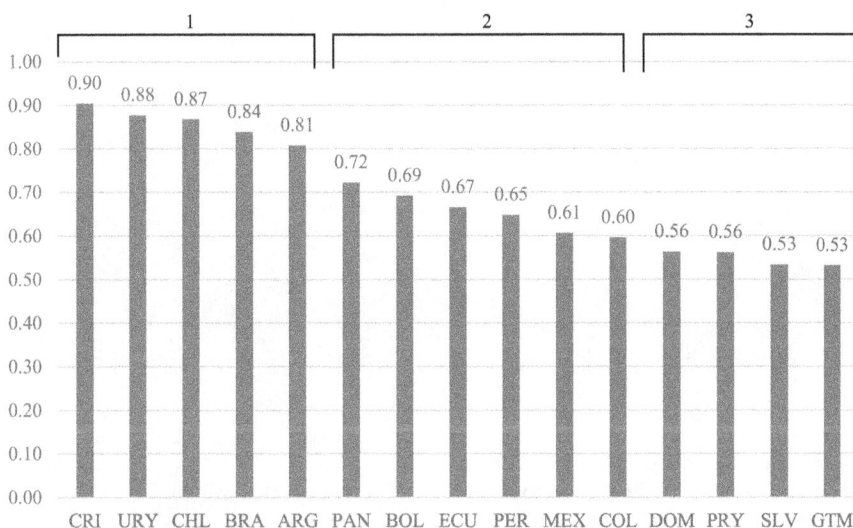

Fig. 4.1: Electoral Democracy Index in Latin America 1990–2021.
Source: Average for each country from 1990 to 2021. The overall average is 0.69. Prepared by the author with data from the V-Dem electoral index (Coppedge et al., 2022b).

third group -reaching the second group for a few years- with their lowest scores in the 1990s. El Salvador reached its highest score (0.69) in 2017, and from there it started to decline; this is one of the countries with the highest variance. Peru rose in the index starting in 2001, and Bolivia, whose values ranged from 0.3 to 0.7, averaged 0.69. The countries whose values changed the most during this period are Peru, El Salvador, Bolivia, and Panama. The main difference between countries is the presence or absence of interference by political power in the control of the electoral system, either through restrictions to the autonomy of the electoral authority or by coercing voters through threats or clientelism. Nevertheless, this group of countries is coherently situated, following the trend of Latin America as a whole, which rose notably between 1980 and 2021, as depicted in the comparative graph with Europe (Fig. 4.2).

If we now look separately at some crucial variables linked to a good outcome of an electoral system, the details are more revealing of some pre-democratic traits that persist in most countries (Fig. 4.3). "Election vote buying" is one of the major vices that crop up during elections. Of all the indicators of the V-Dem electoral index, this is among those with the lowest (worst) average (1.9/4). It exists in practically all countries. Only in Uruguay is there no evidence of vote buying. The other countries practice it to a greater or lesser extent. In Brazil and Mexico, which have the largest populations, there are "non-systematic but rather common

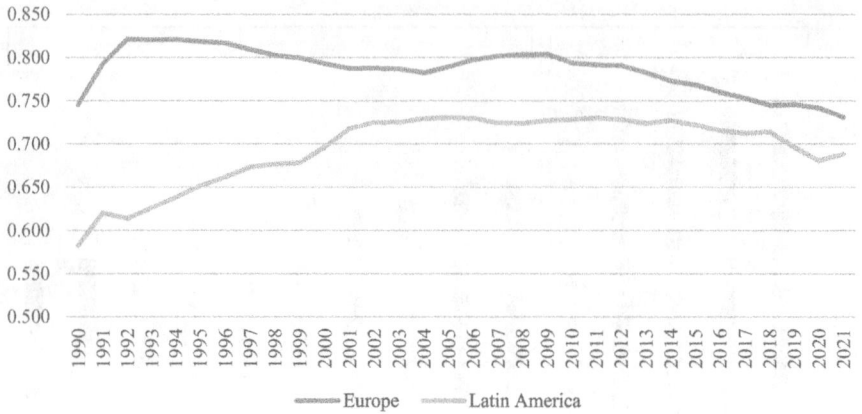

Fig. 4.2: Electoral Democracy Index 1990–2021.
Prepared by the author with data from V-Dem version 12 (Coppedge et al., 2022b).
(Averages per year for the previously selected countries).

vote-buying efforts, even if only in some parts of the country or by one or a few
parties" (Coppedge et al., 2022a). Also notable is the still weak autonomy of the
electoral authority vis-à-vis the government. This institution is autonomous "almost all the time" (average 2.9/4), but nine of the 15 countries in our sample fall
below this borderline score and are located between "somewhat" and "ambiguous". Only Costa Rica and Uruguay have electoral institutions of unquestionable
autonomy.

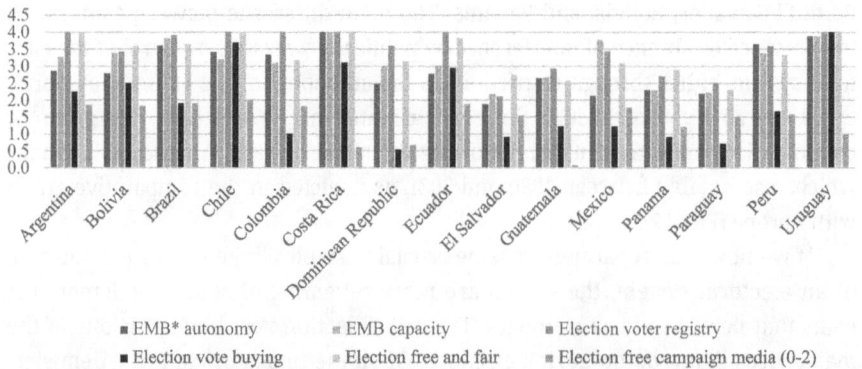

Fig. 4.3: Election Qualities Variables 1980–2021.
Source: Prepared by author based on V-dem codebook 12. (Coppedge et al., 2022a and 2022b).
*Election Management Body

The short period of stability of electoral institutions makes us cautious about their sustainability in most of the region. Most countries have sudden decreases or increases in their ratings over thirty years. However, one thing is clear: the implementation of electoral democracy, although incipient, has engraved in voters' minds that the alternation of parties in power is possible and that political pluralism can be guaranteed. Yet, it is seriously weakened when the results of government action are highly unsatisfactory, as we show with Latinobarómetro data (Chapter 1, Figs. 1.4 and 1.5). Authoritarian urges, aimed at weakening electoral institutions, are also beginning to appear, for example, in Venezuela and Nicaragua, as well as in Brazil and Mexico.

If elections matter, it is because they are an elemental expression of popular sovereignty, i.e., the basic level at which all citizens are equal when casting their ballots. The quality of elections impacts the quality of elected representatives and is, above all, an indicator of the power of citizens to hold them accountable. Ongoing submissiveness through vote buying or intimidation and laying siege to the autonomy of electoral authorities are reminiscent of political backwardness. When the electoral democracy index is low, so is elite sensitivity to public opinion because ignoring it often does not seem to pose a risk. The "harassment of journalists" only decreased by one point (out of 4) between 1980 and 2021, which places the region between a state of generalized harassment and harassment that occurs when journalists "offend powerful actors" (Coppedge et al., 2022a, p.204). When these factors converge, instability and protest ensue and retrospective voting, that is, future electoral punishment for present performance becomes the tool voters use to establish a new governmental direction. However, we can assume with reasonable certainty that not infrequently the electorate sees in the retrospective vote a weak and insufficient tool for exercising its right to change rulers.

In spite of all the shortcomings, we see from the above graph that Latin America as a whole made a very significant leap starting in the 1980s. This change coincided with the initial stage of the third wave of democracy. The gap with Europe closed by almost three points, remaining on a parallel course with a difference of approximately one point, before beginning a decline towards political regression in 2012, ending the last decade slightly distancing itself from Europe -which, at the same time, experienced a slight decline. The question today is whether this decline will trend towards the neutralization of electoral democracy.

4.2 Democratic diarchy 2. Equality, deliberation, accountability, and political parties

In addition to the dimension of voting, the continuous or permanent interaction between society and political power is manifested in the other elements that comprise representative democracy. In the previous chapter, we proposed several factors to approximate a measurement of representative democracy regarding the second pillar of democratic diarchy (judgment-opinion and will). Let us see how they appear in reality.[66]

4.2.1 Equality

Our egalitarian index is composed of five items (Tab. 3.3) measured from 1990 to 2021. By merging these items, we obtain an indicator of minimum equality that reveals the conditions in which most people exercise the basic political freedoms of democracy. Together they give us a picture of whether a country meets the *minimum conditions of equality for the participation* of all members of the demos. In particular, the egalitarian factor reflects the protection that the state provides to individuals and groups for the exercise of these freedoms and abilities by providing the population with the "primary goods" that make up part of the basic basket of equality for the exercise of civil liberties. Once again we have a profoundly uneven picture of the conditions under which citizens can exercise their freedom to influence political decisions on an equal footing. If we consider that just the high values of the index (0.75 to 1.0) (Tab. 4.1) meet the minimum conditions of equality in this factor -and conceding too much- only Costa Rica and Uruguay can be considered representative democracies. A second group (from 0.5 to 0.74) includes Argentina, Panama, Chile, Bolivia, Brazil, and Ecuador. There is insufficient equality in these countries despite the fact that there have been considerable improvements in recent times, demonstrated by the fact that in some countries the distance between minimum and maximum values is significant for each year in the period. For example, in Brazil it is 0.28 points, in Bolivia 0.23, and in Ecuador 0.33, which indicates that the egalitarian improvement is recent and probably oscillates to a high degree. This group is followed by the countries that scored between 0.25 and 0.49, that is, in third place on the scale (Colombia, Dominican Republic, Peru, Mexico, El Salva-

---

66 The four indexes have a scale of 0 to 1; however, each index is composed of different variables that the factor analysis indicated were relevant. The egalitarian index is composed of five variables, the deliberative index of three, the accountability index of five, and the parties index of three.

dor, and Guatemala), with Colombia, Peru and El Salvador showing the greatest fluctuation, which again indicates that their levels of equality are very fragile, with a high possibility of regression in inequality. Finally, Paraguay is barely in the lowest range with an average of 0.23 and an fluctuation interval of 0.04 and 0.14.

If just the first group qualified under equal conditions to exercise minimum-quality democratic representation, the countries between the second and fourth groups would be excluded from practicing democratic representation. Only the first two countries meet the essential requirements needed for citizens to have an opportunity to participate equally in political decisions. From the middle of the scale downwards, and despite oscillations in each country -especially towards a worsening situation-, egalitarian conditions decline significantly, reaching trivial levels of representative democracy. The seven countries in the bottom two groups of the scale have conditions that border on denial of citizenship. In other words, in these countries the state does not protect the basic rights of equality for participation, and society is insufficiently involved to defend these rights. The overall average is eloquent: 0.52 points.

Tab. 4.1: Equality Index.

Equality Index

Average during 1990–2021

Country	Average
Costa Rica	0.89
Uruguay	0.83
Argentina	0.73
Panama	0.71
Chile	0.65
Bolivia	0.56
Brasil	0.55
Ecuador	0.53
Colombia	0.44
Dominican Republic	0.4
Peru	0.38
Mexico	0.34
El Salvador	0.34
Guatemala	0.27
Paraguay	0.23
Average	**0.52**

Source: Prepared by the author with data from V-dem version 12 (Coppedge et al., 2022b).

4.2.2 Deliberation

To analyze the basic conditions for collective deliberation, this factor assesses freedom of discussion for men and women as well academic freedom. These three items measure the degree to which people can exercise political discussion and what respect exists for a country's academic and cultural expression. Together, they reveal whether the essential conditions for public deliberation on political issues in private and public are met. The scale here is from 0 to 1; three variables are considered herein (see Tab. 4.3). The distribution of values across countries is, again, extremely varied. However, it is not as extreme as the low-level egalitarian condition. Costa Rica tops the list with the highest average during 1990–2021 with a value of 1; most of the other countries are located in the highest quartile, i.e., with scores equal to or greater than 0.75 on average. El Salvador has the greatest score fluctuation, ranging from 0.08 to 0.9, and Peru, which ranges from 0.4 to 1. Colombia and Guatemala posted the lowest average scores. The group average is high compared to the previous index: 0.87. The freedoms to engage in deliberative relationships rate highly. The countries obtained the highest positive scores in this factor.

Tab. 4.2: Deliberative Index.

Deliberative Index

Average during 1990–2021

Country	Average
Costa Rica	1
Uruguay	0.99
Argentina	0.99
Panama	0.98
Chile	0.97
Brasil	0.95
Ecuador	0.92
Dominican Republic	0.86
Bolivia	0.85
Mexico	0.83
Paraguay	0.82
El Salvador	0.82
Peru	0.82
Colombia	0.7
Guatemala	0.6
Average	**0.87**

Source: Prepared by the author with data from V-dem version 12 (Coppedge et al., 2022b).

4.2.3 Accountability

The accountability factor includes items that assess the critical role of the print and electronic media, the government's submission to, or independence from, civil society organizations, the executive branch's respect for the constitution, the legislative branch's investigative power, and whether the decisions of the judiciary are respected. The scale is also 0 to 1, and is divided into five variables (Tab. 4.3). Again, this factor was drawn up based on the minimum conditions necessary for representatives' accountability to constituents. Once again, there is a large variation between the best and worst scores. Uruguay, Costa Rica, Chile, and Brazil score between 0.75 and 1. The rest of the countries (11), the majority, score between 0.5 and 0.74. Peru has the greatest variation between values with a difference between minimum and maximum values of 0.55 and an average of 0.64. The overall average is once again very low at 0.67.

Tab. 4.3: Accountability Index.

Accountability Index	
Average during 1990–2021	
Country	**Average**
Uruguay	0.88
Costa Rica	0.85
Chile	0.85
Brasil	0.77
Argentina	0.74
Colombia	0.69
Panama	0.64
Peru	0.64
Guatemala	0.6
Paraguay	0.59
El Salvador	0.58
Mexico	0.58
Ecuador	0.55
Bolivia	0.54
Dominican Republic	0.52
Average	**0.67**

Source: Prepared by the author with data from
V-dem version 12 (Coppedge et al., 2022b).

4.2.4 Party maturity

The minimum amount of party maturity required for representative democracy is determined by factoring three variables: the permanent presence of national party organizations, their outreach through local branches, and the way they relate to the electorate (Tab. 3.3). On the scale of 0 to 1, a higher value indicates that there are well-established national and regional parties in the country and that their relationship with the electorate is more pragmatic as it moves away from clientelism. Dividing the scale into quarters, only Chile obtains a score of 1, while Uruguay, Mexico, El Salvador, and Brazil are also located in the first group (0.75–1) with robust party structures. Argentina, Costa Rica, Bolivia, Dominican Republic, Paraguay, Panama, and Guatemala are in the second quarter (0.5 to 0.74). The others have scores below the middle of the scale in the third group (0.25 to 0.49). A low score indicates precarious party systems in terms of their coverage, with a limited presence among their constituents that hinders their ability to channel popular demands and conflicts of interest to the political regime,

Tab. 4.4: Party index.

Party Index	
Average during 1990–2021	
Country	**Average**
Chile	1
Uruguay	0.9
Mexico	0.8
El Salvador	0.79
Brasil	0.77
Argentina	0.71
Costa Rica	0.68
Bolivia	0.61
Dominican Republic	0.58
Paraguay	0.58
Panama	0.56
Guatemala	0.53
Colombia	0.47
Ecuador	0.41
Peru	0.39
Average	**0.65**

Source: Prepared by the author with data from V-dem version 12. (Coppedge et al., 2022b).

which would contribute to a better quality of governance. The average for all countries tallied here is 0.65.

4.3 The fusion of factors: A poorly representative democracy

The best scores reveal what we might call the least worst democracies in the region. However, when the countries are analyzed as a whole, the result is an average of 0.66 (Tab. 4.5). Latin America excels in the deliberative factor with a score of 0.87. This result for this indicator is outstanding in comparison with the other four, which is both good and bad news. The good news is that there are sufficient margins of freedom to express opinions on political issues, while academic and cultural freedom has advanced considerably. This indicates that governments are more respectful of these freedoms than of social rights (Ansolabehere et al., 2015 and 2020) such as education or health, and that society has low levels of engagement. The freedoms that guarantee voice to the people were won and entrenched. The bad news is that, despite this, the voice of the public does not have enough impact to make political power accountable to society, or for political parties to have a sufficiently competitive level, or to be sufficiently grounded in their constituencies to force accountability. Thus, the regional average for the accountability factor is 0.67. The people's voice is more tolerated than listened to; society has this weapon at its disposal more than in the past, but the weapon is dented from so much pounding on a "rock" of unaccountability and so its bearers tend to lose patience.

The greatest deficit in the region is that of political equality with 0.52. According to the most advanced political theory, this is the most important component for the existence of a representative democracy. This factor plays a role in the weight that citizens can bring to bear -due to conditions of inequality- in public affairs and to participate in political discussion. A combination of a lack of equality, an enhanced capacity to deliberate in an environment with low accountability, weak parties unable to force the government to do its job well, and a mediocre electoral apparatus gives rise to a facet of democracy that contains few ingredients of a representative "bundle."

A brief comparison with Europe shows how far Latin American democracy must still advance, if it does not breakdown first. Although a factor analysis was not undertaken for Europe, if we examine the selected items separately, we observe an abysmal difference, despite the fact that in the European group we take into account countries with very low scores and distant from the average (like Latin America), such as Belarus, Russia, and Ukraine, i.e., three countries in which democracy has had the greatest instability following the fall of the Soviet bloc.[67] In terms of equality, observing the averages, Europe surpasses Latin America with 0.87, that is, 0.3 points more; in deliberation the European countries post 0.95 with a difference of 0.07 with respect to Latin America; in accountability 0.73, with a difference of 0.06; and in political parties 0.88, i.e., a difference of 0.23 points. Taking the overall average, Europe outperforms Latin America by 0.18 index points. Although both regions are similar in terms of deliberation and accountability, they differ strongly in terms of equality and party maturity, which makes an important difference in democratic representativeness.

Tab. 4.5: Comparative averages.

Comparative averages		
Factor	Latin America	Europe
Equality	0.52	0.87
Deliberative	0.87	0.95
Accountability	0.67	0.73
Parties	0.65	0.88
Total	**0.66**	**0.84**

Source: Prepared by the author with data from V-dem version 12 (Coppedge et al., 2022b).

One dimension of the problem remains to be analyzed: Which countries have a high, medium, or low performance in all factors, and which appear at different levels of the scale or in those with the greatest deficiencies? Only two countries, Argentina and Uruguay, have scores at the highest level on the scale of the four factors. Two others, Chile and Costa Rica, have high grades in three factors but fail in one. Chile registered a low score in the egalitarian index (medium level) and Costa Rica in party maturity (medium level). The former has the most notable failure in educational and health equality which are the two basic goods the population has the least access to. The latter fails in the homogeneous presence of its political parties throughout its territory, which means that they are concentrated in the capital. With the exception of Guatemala, Peru, Bolivia, Dominican Republic, and Paraguay that posted the lowest scores, the remaining countries post mid-level or mediocre scores, sometimes scoring high in some variables, but low in others.

---

67 Not so the Czech Republic, which stands out for its high standards.

4.4 Present and absent variables

Pseudo-representation and inequality. The countries with the best performance have less inequality (Costa Rica and Uruguay), with the stipulations noted in Chapter 2. The greater degree of equality in the enjoyment of freedoms and basic services, as well as the involvement of society in public affairs, makes the relationship between representatives and constituencies closer and more continuous. In contrast, the reverse situation significantly deteriorates the quality of representation. With few exceptions, almost all countries enjoy reasonable civil liberties, but not freedoms involving social and economic components, particularly education and health, which are items included in the egalitarian factor. In both of these areas, most of the group performs very poorly. Only three countries (Costa Rica, Uruguay, and Argentina) have an above-average educational and health equality. In the rest, the scores drop alarmingly until they reach the lower end of the scale, i.e., Guatemala, Mexico, Peru, El Salvador, and Paraguay. The latter country is the worst in the education variable, scoring zero, extremely unequal for "75% of citizens' ability to exercise their political rights as adult citizens is undermined".[68] Engaged society is another item in the egalitarian factor, where these same five countries again have very low levels of organized social participation in public affairs. The absence of adequate health and education for the majority of the population overwhelmingly hampers people from becoming involved in everyday affairs. The coexistence of freedoms -which occur to a greater degree than the enjoyment of access to services and goods fundamental to the quality of political life- is a mixture that inevitably leads to instability, conflict not channeled organically by the political regime, and democratic deterioration. Since the egalitarian factor is the most important in this factorial analysis, the alarm signal could not be more worrisome; also unsettling is that, with the passage of time and should the same conditions persist, conflicts and deterioration will only worsen. Thus, despite the improvement in the Gini index (Fig. 2.1), such uneven conditions for public action do not forebode well for inclusion, unless political pressure is increased to bring it about.

Pseudo-representation and Accountability. The five items included in the accountability factor are unevenly balanced. The critical action of the media and the freedom with which civil society organizations act with respect to the government

---

[68] According to the definition of the variable, only four countries reach the "somewhat equal" category, while the remaining 11 definitely fall into the unequal category, meaning that "at least 25 percent of citizens' ability to exercise their political rights as adult citizens is undermined" (Coppedge et al, 2022a, 209).

reveal acceptable levels for creating an environment in which public opinion and the citizenry can demand action. In contrast, the executive tends to have little respect for the constitution, compliance with the judiciary[69] tends to be "about half the time," and the degree to which the legislature investigates is the lowest of all ("as likely as not"). Press and media are more critical than passive, social organizations act freely, but state agencies that should demand accountability and/or be accountable behave far below what is to be expected in a representative democracy. Guatemala, El Salvador, Bolivia, Mexico, and the Dominican Republic, in that order, have legislatures that are the least likely to conduct investigations should the executive incur in "unconstitutional, illegal, or unethical activity". In Guatemala, Paraguay, and the Dominican Republic the executive respects the constitution the least, and Bolivia, Peru, and Ecuador have governments that show the least respect for "important decisions by other courts with which it disagrees".

Pseudo-representation and political parties. Party maturity is low. All parties in Chile, and almost all in Uruguay and Mexico, have a permanent organization. At the other extreme, in Peru, Colombia, Guatemala, Bolivia, and Ecuador, half or less of the political parties fulfill this condition. They also have weak links with the population. Their territorial presence is uneven and even scarce in a large number of countries, and the type of relationship they establish with society is predominantly clientelistic. Overall, in the region the existence of political parties is real, but their representation relations with society are weak because they lack a greater homogeneous presence among the population and due to their patrimonial relations with society; clientelism often points to a greater frequency of normally precarious exchanges of political loyalties in exchange for goods.

Pseudo-representation and deliberation. The deliberation component plays an essential role in the quality of political representation. As previously discussed in Chapter 2, the citizenry makes extensive use of their "voice" to express their opinions and complain to their rulers. The three variables that we included in the factor to make it consistent due to their specific weight (freedom of discussion for men, for women, and academic freedom) are also very heterogeneously distributed. While in Brazil, women's freedom of discussion in the private and public spheres is almost equal to men's, in Mexico, there is a very notable disparity that places women at a disadvantage. Considering that in both countries women account for more than half of the population, the difference is relevant. Colombia and Guatemala also disfavor women in this regard, in addition to the fact that

---

69 This indicator is different from "compliance with high courts". However, the latter is only slightly higher than the one indicated above.

both countries have a very limited degree of "freedom of discussion" for both sexes, as well as in academic and cultural realms. In addition, voice and existing freedoms are not necessarily associated with their influence in decision making. In addition, one of the factors included in the "deliberation component" as presented by V-Dem, i.e., the "range of consultation," is quite low for the entire continent; only Brazil posted above average scores between 2005 and 2015, only to then see them fall sharply. Something similar occurred to a lesser degree in Mexico: The range of consultation increased between 2000 and 2017 and then plummeted after 2017. Naturally, this indicator is a proxy that does not cover what is key to the meaning of deliberation, i.e., the inclusion of citizens' opinions in government decisions and in drafting public policies or making fundamental state decisions ("judgment and will").

A synthesis of findings so far reveals high prevailing inequality in the region, very deficient presence of political parties (because of their predominantly clientelistic links and low presence among the population), very poor vertical, horizontal, and diagonal accountability, and an extremely scarce "range of consultation" between representatives and constituencies. These results paint a desolate political reality that is hardly suitable for democracy to flourish. Unlike the transitional moments that demonstrated a capacity to emerge from authoritarianism and sparked the enthusiasm of progressive actors (omitting the authoritarian radicals at both ends of the political spectrum), this democratic interlude has revealed social, political, and state incapacity to produce a sufficient pace of democratic development that would provide a long-term platform. Unless democratic efforts succeed in changing the configuration of the political community, i.e., the state, and consequently the distribution of societal responsibilities and obligations in general and its political and economic elites in particular, the fate of most Latin American democracies will be uncertain and checkered at best.

As we shall see in the following chapters, the comparison between Latin America and Europe reveals differences not only in degree but also in their nature. While Latin America has not succeeded in reconciling rights and power in its constitutional order, Europe has succeeded to a greater extent and most of its countries have turned that page of political history -except for Russia, Belarus, and Ukraine.[70] The difference originates, first, in history. The defining historical point has been the degree to which majority groups have been able to negotiate wealth and power distribution on more egalitarian terms with economic and political elites (Tilly, 1992 and 1998; Przeworski, 2009; Mazzuca, 2021). In addition,

---

[70] Besides the invasion agains Ukraine, the major conflict facing European countries today in terms of rights is post-national and is centered on the global diaspora of migrant populations.

we should recognize the important role played by Europe's post-nationalization, mainly the foundation of the European Union and other similar institutions, which have contributed to improving democratic standards in the most backward countries, notably Spain's evolution since the Moncloa Pacts. By contrast, in Latin America the equalization that began at the electoral level has not yet permanently extended to other spheres of public life. It is seemingly caught halfway between achieving collective freedom for access to power but not the freedom to control power when it is exercised by governments.

Chapter 5
It's the state, stupid. Institutional obstacles to representative democracy.
The rules of the game

The sense of futility that disadvantaged citizens may have of democratic institutions should be interpreted not as a denunciation of the latter's deficit or inability to amend themselves but as a recognition that in order to be preserved their conditions require being persistently monitored and reasserted, because social inequality does translate into unequal political power.
Nadia Urbinati

The elements provided in the previous chapters demonstrate that Latin American representative democracies suffer from feeble links between representatives and constituents in both "moments" of the diarchy of democracy: the moment of opinion and the moment of will. Thus, there is a "surplus of politics" that gets "stuck" in the political regime when, so to speak, it hits a barricade that the state erects in opposition, showcases that protect, like museum pieces, the structures of vertical and despotic exercise of power.

What are these obstacles that the "surplus of politics" produced by representative democracy must navigate in order to impact the state and make it more inclusive and democratic? A reasonable answer to this question cannot exclusively account for the impediments so that the state can be technically useful to all of society. Rather, it must account for what detains the processes, so that state decisions arise from the will that develops from the complex process of establishing collective judgment. The components of the democratic diarchy discussed in the previous chapter are the containers, the molds, which we can see as half full or half empty, and which point to achievements and shortcomings, advances and setbacks that are the result of political processes within the regime.

The interest in understanding the factors that contribute to consolidating or eroding newly inaugurated democracies is a constant concern of political-science scholars who study the third wave of democratization. Specifically, scholars have studied Southern Europe, Central Europe, the former communist Soviet republics, and Latin America in order to understand these factors and processes. After our journey up to this point, we ought to review some of the ideas in play to understand the half-century of transitions to democracy and the problems of consolidation, durability, and regression. Juan Linz and Alfred Stepan (1996, pp. 151–234) noted three decades ago the constrained character of the transitions in the Americas' Southern Cone. In comparison to what happened in southern Europe, the

https://doi.org/10.1515/9783110773675-006

four Latin American countries Linz and Stepan studied at the time.[71] lacked the functional equivalents that Portugal, Spain, and Greece had back then: market relations and military alliances with democratic countries. On the contrary, they carried heavy economic constraints derived from dictatorships, or presidential systems that hindered the transition to more effective parliamentary models. The Southern Cone countries navigated in an environment of pluralism and with constitutions written or reformed under restrictions imposed by de facto powers or traditions of the past.

As more countries adopted democracy and this form of government reached almost the entire continent (and the Caribbean, with the exception of Cuba and Haiti), several of these features were accentuated or mitigated. Regarding trade, the plethora of interregional or global treaties and agreements increased interaction between countries within and outside the region. Currently, Latin America is connected by multiple trade treaties and most of its countries are signatories of the Inter-American Democratic Charter, as well as other human rights treaties and conventions.[72] Nonetheless, trends away from representative democracy remain an ongoing inertia. The driving forces behind these tendencies continue to be socioeconomic inequality (plus ethnic and racial inequalities), and the providential and patrimonial tradition of power. In terms of political rationale, the main tension derives from the repeat of the separation between democratic regimes capable of processing conflict and low statehood in the institutionalization of lasting responses to the underlying problems of inequality and exclusion.

5.1 The global context

Today, as Latin American democracies transition through the third wave, a growing trend is to question whether democracy is the preferred form of government. After a long period in which democracy was "the only game in town", a number of ideological currents have appeared that compete with democracy. The two main sources are orthodox nationalism and personalist populism. In Latin America, in addition, there is left-wing radicalism, akin to the Castro and Guevarist tradition, which often converges with the nationalist and populist traditions (Mainwaring and Pérez-Liñán, 2013). Chávez, Correa, Ortega, Morales, and López Obrador represent this trend. In turn, the extreme right has also adopted populist forms as an

---

71 Argentina, Brazil, Chile and Uruguay.
72 ALBA (Bolivarian Alliance of the Peoples of America), promoted by Venezuela and Cuba, was formed in 2004 to promote a different form of integration based on Hugo Chávez's idea of 21st Century Socialism. To date, ALBA is defunct.

extreme response to changes produced by leftist governments or movements. The most recent examples are Jair Bolsonaro in Brazil and Nayib Bukele in El Salvador.

This challenge appears in the longest-lived democracies, but is more pronounced in new democracies. There is a growing preference among citizens for governments that offer to "resolve" problems in exchange for ceding political freedoms. However, from the extreme right and sometimes from the extreme left, this preference is encouraged and intensely propagated by autocracies. The Chinese Communist Party propagates its authoritarian system as a functioning people's democracy; the Russian oligarchy has built an apparatus of legitimization of authoritarianism based on orthodox nationalism and the "threat" of the West. Both nations seek a bi-polar world in which they can compete for global hegemony. They promote their ideas with remarkable effects among people who miss the past and believe that the Soviet Union is alive and well in today's Russia, just as there are admirers of the "political capitalism" (Milanovic, 2019, Ch. 3) prevailing in China.[73] In Latin America, we should factor in Cuba and the failed "socialism of the 21st century" promoted by Hugo Chavez. These antipodes encourage the populist and authoritarian impulses that are emerging in various parts of the world, especially those most exposed to globalization without having the necessary adaptations in place. They seek to revive nationalisms and autocratic forms which, according to their believers, will produce "better results" and certainty. Populisms based on these beliefs have mainly developed in Venezuela, Ecuador, Brazil, Mexico, and El Salvador. In certain countries, leaders who follow these ideas have seized power; in others they have built powerful movements and achieved a continuous presence in political systems.

We know that in the long term, democracies began under the influence of the French and American revolutions and were reactivated after the second post-war period. In the short term, democracies began exponential growth with the "third wave" (1974–) and at the end of the Soviet Union and the Warsaw Pact (1991). As depicted in Figures 5.1, 5.2, 5.3 and 5.4, around 2003 in Latin America, electoral democracies reach their highest peak and begin to decline, while electoral autocracies grow slightly and liberal democracies to a lesser extent. Closed autocracies have grown as a result of the decline of electoral democracies.

---

[73] In one sense they are right. Putin and his followers in the United Russia Party vindicate the totalitarianism that began during Czarist rule and continued by Lenin and Stalin, albeit with the doctrine of Russian nationalism instead of Marxist-Leninism. For its part, the Chinese Communist Party offers a "model" of private economy for technological growth with an absolute monopoly of political power.

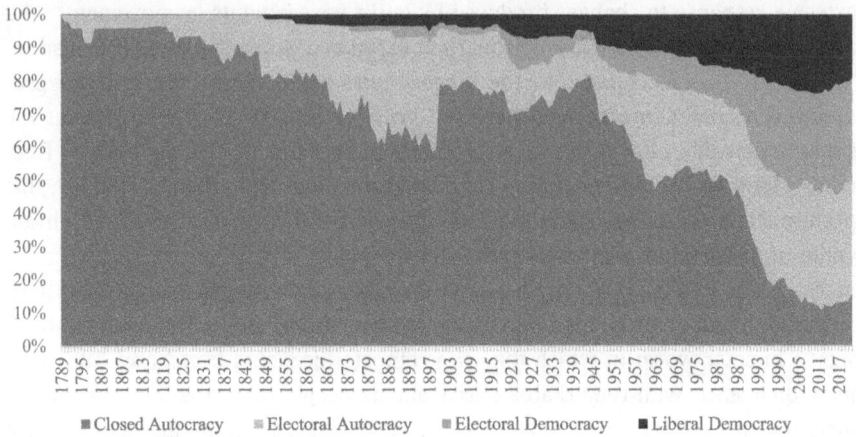

Fig. 5.1: Share of democracies and autocracies. Long Run.
Source: Prepared by the author with data from OWID and Herre (2023).

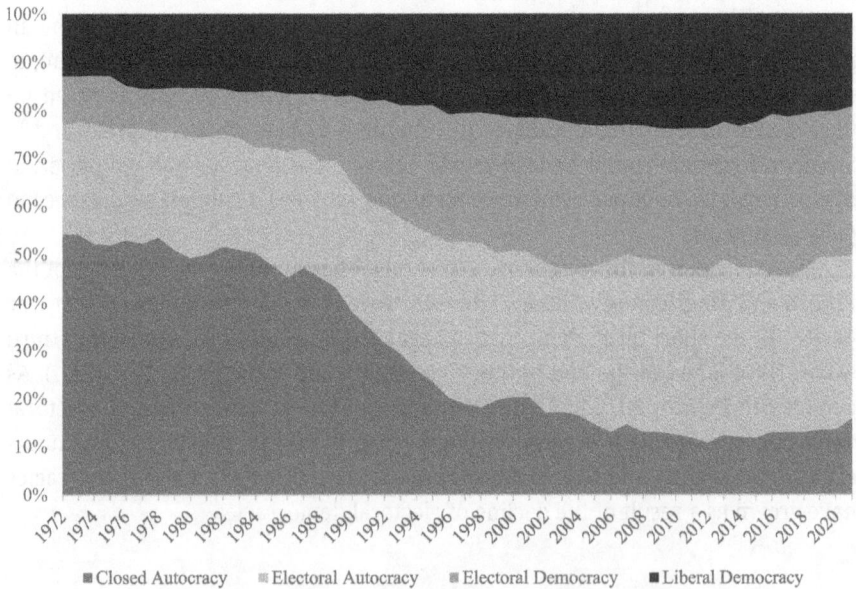

Fig. 5.2: Share of democracies and autocracies since the Third Wave.
Source: Prepared by the author with data from OWID and Herre (2023).

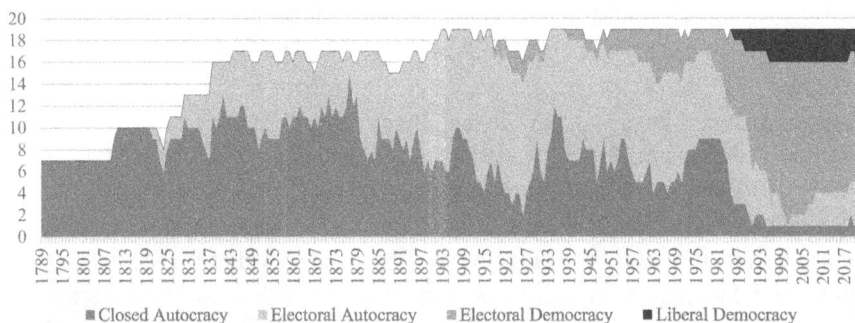

Fig. 5.3: Regime type in Latin America. Long run. 1789–2020.
Source: Prepared by the author with data from OWID and Herre (2023).

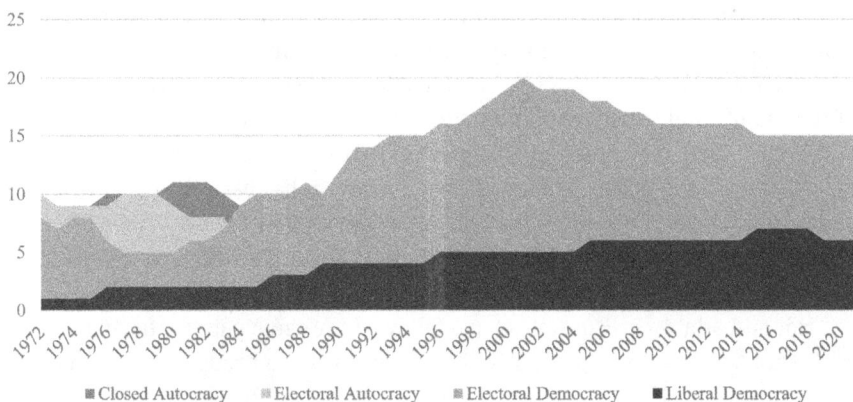

Fig. 5.4: Regime type in the Americas and Latin America. Short term. 1972–2021.
Source: Prepared by the author with data from OWID and Herre (2023).

5.2 Farewell to guns, welcome to politics?

Reversing von Clausewitz's thesis, we can ask ourselves whether politics can be favored as a means to avoid war. The construction of modern democracies is inexplicable without a struggle -peaceful or violent- against inequality. It is no coincidence that all democracies are founded, first and foremost, on enshrining in the constitution the principle of universal equality and the rights that derive from it. Without the principle of equality, the majority principle is not democratic, and when it is separated from the former, authoritarian will and justification of dictatorship begin. From the onset of the Declaration of the Rights of Man and of the Citizen

(1789), to its current transformation into the Universal Declaration of Human Rights (1948), equality has been the fundamental principle of the global community.[74] The tradition of historical sociology, from Barrington Moore to Charles Tilly, explains how, in Europe's journey from the late Middle Ages, war played a fundamental role in the development of distribution and in building the institutions of the modern world. Latin American historiography describes the origin and trajectories of inequality in terms of the absence of mechanisms and moments of negotiation by which wealth and power were distributed. Hence the enduring or repetitive oligarchic, caudillo-style, and populist traditions that originate in societies marked by class and racial inequality, which perdures thanks to the fact that the region's elites have had little need to negotiate with the popular classes. This is also true in most countries, with the notable exceptions of the countries that score highest on the indicators discussed in the previous chapters. In the Americas, with the probable exception of Canada, inclusion has been uncommon and different. Its origin can be more easily traced to the (weak) organization and (erratic) politics that the popular classes have deployed to advance their interests and negotiate an egalitarian sense of community and society with the ruling classes. We could say, following Tönnies and Weber, that the community (*Gemeinschaft*) has been the refuge of equals, united by class and group, while society (*Gesellschaft*) has been the realm of group and class unequals. This difference and the distances they establish have been enshrined in the state, just as in the case of Europe both difference and distances became smaller and shorter, respectively.

Not all Latin American states have followed the same pattern. In some cases, civil wars have led to leaps in this difference that have brought the community closer to society. This occurred following the Mexican Revolution and the civil war in Costa Rica. Some political movements have ended in military dictatorships, for example in Chile, Argentina, and Uruguay. In Central America, war has also

---

74 Here nuance is important. Curiously, the French Assembly wrote the first article as follows: "Men are born and remain free and equal in rights. *Social distinctions can only be based on common utility*", while the 1948 UN Assembly transformed it as follows: "All human beings are born free and equal in dignity and rights and, endowed as they are with reason and conscience, *they should behave fraternally towards one another*" (emphasis added). The difference is historically and semantically relevant. The French Assembly set out to regulate private utility with public utility, while the United Nations Assembly establishes it as a duty. The former is compulsory, while the latter is optional and left to the voluntary fulfillment of the duty. For some, the French declaration, inspired by Rousseau, gives rise to state arbitrariness. The Reign of Terror was based on the declaration and taken as an authorization of class annihilation and was thus handed down to the Marxism of our days. The second is optional and explicitly abandons the obligatory character of solidarity, appealing (ingenuously?) to the imaginary magnanimity of humanity. The ghost of both "constitutions" still haunts the world today.

played a similar role, as have guerrilla wars in different parts of the continent. Political violence and contestation have led to the advancement of social and economic rights in national contexts (Fig. 5.5). Without violence and protest, it is difficult to explain how democracy came to Latin America. Thus, political space opened up, political violence diminished, but the situation began to revert in time with the onset of symptoms of democratic decline.

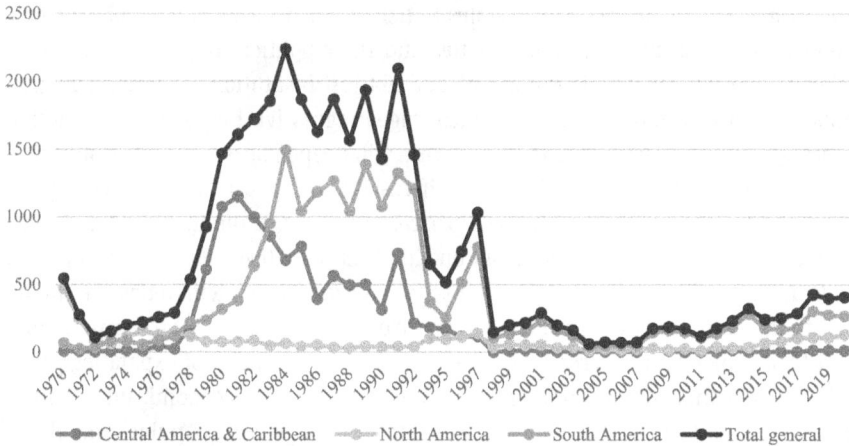

Fig. 5.5: Political violence, number of terrorist attacks.
Source: Prepared by the author with data from START (2022).

In our period of study herein, which roughly covers the last forty years, the extension of neoliberal policies at the global level, notwithstanding their origins in the governments of Ronald Reagan and Margaret Thatcher, coincided with the shift to democracy of Latin American states. The Washington Consensus was the economic policy recipe book for underdeveloped economies and was widely applied in Latin America. The paradox is eloquent: While neoliberalism, or rather market fundamentalism, became dominant in the economies of core states and international financial organizations as a response to the crisis of governance (Crozier et al. 1975), democracy in Latin America became the predominant political form due to the unsustainability of dictatorships and the social unrest produced by the crises of the preceding economic policies. Neoliberalism was born to reform the core economies and overcome the effects in those countries of the "spillover" of democratization into economic distribution exceeding the limits of political structures, which led to a severe fiscal crisis. In Latin America, on the other hand, it was maintained when the democratic form appeared.

The improvement in social inclusion that was encouraged by social policies has not had the same effect at the level of politics. As we have already seen, "access" is the least of the spheres of inclusion compared to the distribution of resources and forms of recognition (according to the classification of Kapiszewski et al. 2021). The political regime and civil society have been the spheres in which political conflict and negotiation have been most apparent. The third sphere, the state, has been the main parapet where the borderline issues of those conflicts are outlined. Latin American democracies lack states to help "crown" or complete political, economic, and social renewal that societies and their political regimes have undertaken through conflict. This is a moral, and not just institutional, shortcoming that puts democratization in crisis and encourages regressive forces to set in motion processes of de-democratization.[75] This crisis will deepen or endure if the obstacles, faced from within by democratic agents themselves or opposed from outside by authoritarian actors, are not addressed programmatically. If the impetus for democracy has come from below and from outside (Axtman 2004: 269 and *passim*), that is, from social discontent and change in the international system, today we should add to this impulse efforts from above and from within. We ought to keep in mind that Latin America democratization is taking place in a context of expanding political processes that go beyond the nation state, and that both economic and political paths respond to these movements: exogenous, endogenous, popular, and elitist. What, then, have been the institutional obstacles that oppose or prevent political representation from achieving the state's democratic transformation? Can democratic politics replace war (a decisive element in other regions of the world to reduce inequality), to produce the distributive changes in political and economic power that this transformation requires?

5.3 The institutions of state decisions

While the nation-states that emerged in the postwar period were predominantly driven by a political economy that heightened their internal domination, the globalization that exploded in the 1980s forced them to internationalize. They were required to develop international linkages while weakening their domestic ones. This was partly because of a requirement of the prevailing economic policy (the "withdrawal" of the state) and partly a consequence of pre-existing weaknesses, the most

---

75 This moral deficiency is a characteristic of both civil society and political elites and is a subject that requires separate examination when it comes to studying the quality of citizenship, which for now is not our objective.

important of which was rentier and crony capitalism. Note that this internationalization was both a phenomenon caused by changes in preferences manifested in political will, i.e. by "neoliberalism", but also responded to a change in the relative prices of the factors of production (capital, labor, and land). Both led to a change in the global economic, social, and political regime that had its intellectual leaders in neoliberal ideologs and "post-national" elites. This strategic command has been undermined in part by political dissent in the main economic powerhouses and in part by economic dissatisfaction in industrially backward countries. In both cases this has led to the emergence of right and left-wing populism and has revived the attraction of old and new left-wing currents. The big question raised by this crisis is whether the Washington Consensus (1989) can be replaced by a new type of agreement or whether, in line with the pattern of behavior followed in the 20th century, this new agreement would be reached as a result of a catastrophic conflict of such magnitude that all parties would be forced to come to an understanding. Such a conflict is potentially looming following the Russian invasion of Ukraine and in the escalating economic war between the United States and China. The resolution of these conflicts will define much of the response.

The very process of economic internationalization and political democratization gave rise to the nemeses of market fundamentalism: nationalism and autocracy. Both have been able to take advantage of the flaws and inadequacies of these processes, not to counteract them, but to eradicate them. The forces of untethered markets led to the growth of exports, creating productive chains whose tasks were assigned to different nations. In Latin America, multiple trade agreements (Looney 2018, Matoo et. al. 2020) drove the export-oriented economic transformation. Yet, trade and geopolitical conflicts have encouraged a return to economic regionalism that is shifting the structure of trade toward regional locations and blocs. At the same time, "accidental" nationalisms have been triggered, such as Brexit,[76] or intentional nationalisms such as Trump's in the United States, which sought to distance its economy from China. Given the prevailing conditions, it would not be impossible to witness a "Mexit" in North America. Other nationalist reactions have appeared and are reshaping the global economic and geopolitical map. Although the scientific and technical bases of globalization and, to a large extent, the social bases will continue to advance, there is a political retreat into national spaces that encourages authoritarian strategies to be pitted against the democratic structures built over the last 40 years. If, as we noted in the two preceding chapters, exclusion and the low quality of representation have been partly the result of the "neoliberal

---

76 The strategic miscalculation of David Cameron's government led to the triumph of the "exit" and the separation of the United Kingdom from the European Union. In that sense it was "accidental".

model", it would be a mistake to attribute both problems solely to that model. In fact, these are very old blemishes that date back to the birth of patrimonialism, classism, and oligarchic and populist tendencies that permeate everyday culture and are recycled in each successive adopted "model" of political economy. Moreover, "neoliberalism" has brought growth, distribution, and modernization that have entailed varieties of inclusion, just as what happened with the import substitution "model" (ISI). This has also been discussed in previous chapters.

Today's conundrum can be summed up in the question of whether a new consensus is possible for a political economy that will make it possible to respond to social discontent through representative democracy, or whether a return to authoritarianism, populist or oligarchic, is inevitable and long-lasting. It is striking how few political proposals there are, other than the extremes. The answer to the question is to be found by examining the central aspects of economic decision-making.

5.3.1 Imaginary economies for real societies

Representative democracy cannot be compatible with a situation in which the state is forced to accept an interpretation of reality isolated from the influence of politics (Habermas, 1999, pp. 120–128). The adoption of systems of thought as state policies has an authoritarian component by which the direction of the state's economic action is delegated to an economic elite with indifference to its consequences for the common interest. It is a mistake to confuse a political party or program elected by a majority to form a government with the granting of a prerogative to that party to impose a single direction on government policies. The grafting on of forms of direct democracy such as popular consultation, referendum, or recall to representative democracy is only the seedling of a tree that will grow towards greater inclusion in public decision-making. However, these forms are often used by non-democratic political forces.

The literature on the systemic segregation that mainstream economic policy causes in sectors of the population that are not important to its priorities is so abundant that it would be pointless to review it here. Privatization of public enterprises and the production of public goods, liberalization of financial markets, and *trickle-down* economics were part of the triangle that framed neoliberalism in Latin America (Stiglitz, 2018). Although the original Washington Consensus documents included fiscal reforms, this component was quickly forgotten. What matters for our purposes is to acknowledge that the way neoliberal economic policies were imposed was an obstacle for representative democracy. More than an economic doctrine, neoliberalism gave rise to market fundamentalism as the dominant ideology among economic and ruling elites. "Fiscal austerity, privatization, and market liberalization were the three pillars of the Washington Consensus throughout the 1980s and 1990s" (Stiglitz, 2018, pp. 149–182). As Stiglitz and others have observed, while markets have appeared in all known civilizations (North and Thomas, 1973, North, 1982), their institutional structuring is much more important than the elementary factors that synchronous economic theories isolate (demand, supply, information, and competition). Institutions are embedded in the specific histories of economic cultures, and thus do not emerge *deus ex machinae* through the dictates of policies such as deregulation, privatization or financial liberalization, or their opposites such as intervention, nationalization, or regulation. On the contrary, market fundamentalism ignored the accumulated knowledge of the societies in which it was imposed as an ideology. Moreover, it deliberately ignored its own knowledge about the history of the societies where capitalism successfully emerged. This deliberate ignorance led to partial successes and failures and to resounding debacles. Two specific elements that have been essential in building modern economies were overlooked in the economic policies implemented in Latin America: the rule of law and economic ethics. We have already observed (Chapter 2, Fig. 2.6) that rule of law standards in Latin America are low, although by contrast regulatory quality (Chapter 2, Fig. 2.10) is significantly higher. We note that this difference lies in the deliberate effort to improve the latter and neglect the former. This difference in political will in the state's legal and administrative reforms coincides with the priorities set by the international organizations that dominated economic cooperation to overcome the economic crises of the 1980s. However, this "overcoming" clashes with the social perception of economic performance and equality before the law, as shown in the Figs 5.6 and 5.7.:

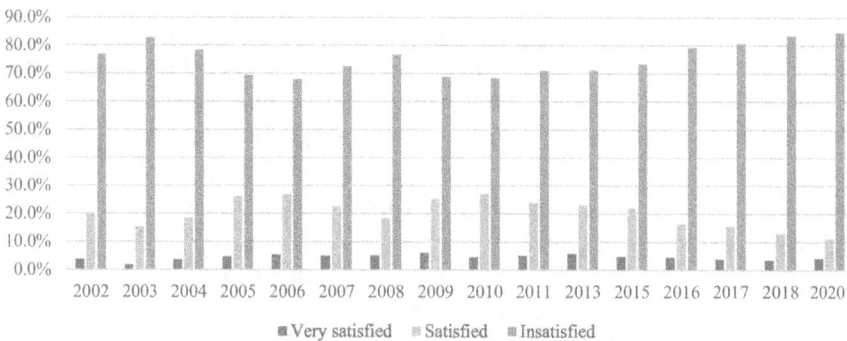

Fig. 5.6: Satisfaction with the performance of the economy in selected countries in Latin America. Source: Prepared by the author with data from Corporación Latinobarómetro (2020).

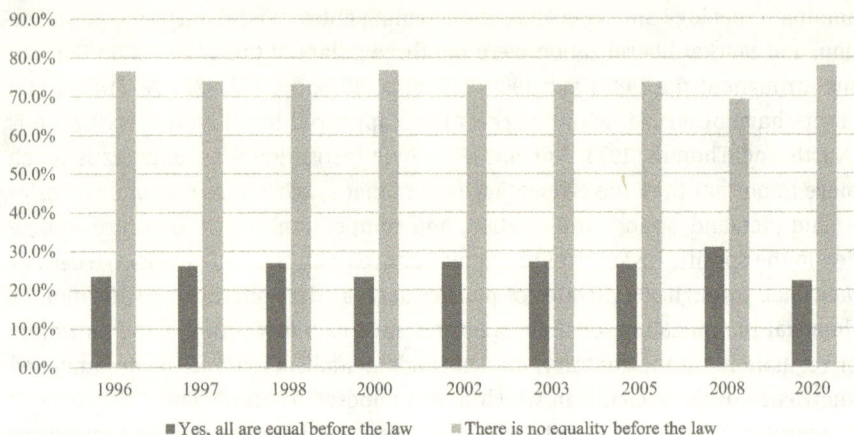

Fig. 5.7: Equality before the law or not in Latin America.
Source: Prepared by the author with data from Corporación Latinobarómetro (2020).
In this question, how the answers are recorded changes: From 1996 to 2000 the question was: "The Political Constitution stipulates that all (NATIONALITY) are equal before the law. Do you think that all (NATIONALITY) are equal before the law or that there is no equality before the law in (COUNTRY)?" "(1) Yes, all are equal before the law, (2) There is no equality before the law." However, starting in 2002 it reads as follows: "Would you say that the (NATIONALITY) . . .: Are equal before the law?". The response options were: a lot, somewhat, a little, and not at all. In order to be able to compare results, "a lot" and "quite a lot" were added with "yes there is" and "little" and "none" with "there is not".

Political representation, understood as the sum of electoral decisions and the continuous interaction between elected authorities and citizens through public opinion and other means of exchange (open parliament, citizen consultations, etc.), has few institutional guarantees beyond individual actors, the media (including social networks), political parties, and social mobilization. In this interaction, encouraging the dissemination of specialized knowledge in order to expose it to public opinion would be useful, thus strengthening its quality in order to improve how it is manifested as an intention of will. There can be no paradigmatic fictions embedded in democracy without the influence of knowledge of economic reality and the implications of public policy alternatives. The potential for public discussion of these alternatives is wasted because it is marginalized or hijacked by specialized economic agencies.

Referencing market fundamentalism, Karl Polanyi noted the "utopia of the self-regulating market" and, beyond his expectations on the welfare state, that utopia was revived when significant failures appeared in the core countries, with repercussions in its imitators in the peripheral countries (and in the communist economies). Market self-regulation is solely ideological and its power lies in the illusion of "a world without politics" (Block and Somers, 2014, p. 219). Polanyi's prophecy about the failure of that utopia did not come true, although the reasons that grounded his critique of market fundamentalism hold true today: society, the type of social relations, culture and history, concrete customs and practices cannot be precluded by the conceptual frameworks that guide state or economic action. Hence, as we previously pointed out, the democratic governance of society is incompatible with a predominant scientific-technical or ideological vision that excludes substantive public discussion and political negotiation.[77]

If the apparent or latent social judgment regarding economic dissatisfaction or inequality before the law had had representative impacts on the state, responses to correct these deviations would have been faster with changes in the government or its policies. However, there are clearly insufficient institutional channels for state action to respond to general opinion in the form of public decision. Instead we have *de facto* powers that promise imaginary societies. Political elites distanced themselves from their role in political representation and left collective decision-making in the hands of experts, instead of promoting dissemination and discussion of the proposals and possibilities put forward by specialized knowledge, as was their duty.

5.3.2 Electoral solipsism

In Latin America, there are so many frequent and varied reforms of the electoral systems that they reflect a permanent and generalized nonconformity with how political parties are setup and how elections are run. This dissention arises mainly from political elites due to changes in voters' preferences. The elites mobilize to change the rules when voters shift preferences in presidential elections. "The change in vote share across political parties from one election to the next at the presidential level may explain the likelihood of electoral reform on any aspect in a country at any given time" (Friedenberg and Gilas, 2022, p. 27). Although electoral reforms have improved some aspects of citizens' interests, such as the expansion of their political rights, the main motive for most reforms has to do with the elites' interest in obtaining more power over their competitors. Securing the presidency is often the most important motive for this jockeying for votes. In countries where reelection is allowed, this is clear. Bolivia is the most illustrative

---

77 This does not mean that a specific economic course should not be pursued, but rather that it cannot be pursued in isolation from the common interest, with which it will be confronted sooner or later.

example, where a grotesque episode played out involving Evo Morales' claim that to stand for reelection in 2019 was "his human right", followed by the alleged coup d'état that led to his downfall.

On more than a few occasions, reforms are attempted or carried out within the term of office of the elected authorities in order to increase their advantage to stay in power. This occurred in Bolivia recently and is being attempted in Mexico, reflecting the ruling parties' clear intention of benefitting themselves, which hardly advances the democratization of the system and even tends to weaken it (Saavedra, 2022, pp. 36–55; Salmorán, 2022, p. 120). Similarly, the constant reforms and attempts to subject the adversary to increasingly extreme conditions of control -that in the end turn against the promoters of the reforms- lead to the "hyper-judicialization of electoral processes" (Marván, 2022, p. 88). This self-serving tendency in electoral reforms weakens the party system and the effectiveness of the legislative branch (Gilas, 2022, pp. 150, 174). Overall, the dynamics of the reforms reflect a tendency to favor party and ruling elites rather than to settle "debts of representation to important parts of their citizenry" (Freidenberg and Gilas, 2022, p. 508), that elites and parties that have benefited from democratization owe to the societies they govern.

The history of the Latin America's transition began with a great social momentum that demanded political openness in dictatorial or authoritarian regimes. The demand focused on equal access to public office through competition between political parties and fair elections. The push for good representation coincides with the need by previously excluded political groups for access to power. Once a step in this direction was taken, these groups, relatively independent of their ideological positions, occupied state structures and offices where power was exercised prior to the establishment of democracy. The three exceptions that stand out in almost all aspects, including this one, are Costa Rica and Uruguay that have a long-standing democratic tradition, or Chile, which had a similar tradition -although it inherited a constitution with stipulations included by the Pinochet dictatorship to preserve guarantees and privileges-, and did not lose a tradition of unyielding observance of the law. In contrast, there are nations with a long authoritarian tradition. In most cases, the new or renovated democratic parties are in government but continue practices of no accountability and weak or nonexistent controls of the civil service, with plentiful opportunities for corruption and ample margins for arbitrary practices by the hierarchies of authority.

The instability of electoral rules poses an obstacle to implementing reforms required by the state in order to serve the public interest. Permanent electoral disagreement is a symptom of a lack of arrangements among political forces regarding minimum norms that should define the general interest: the protection of rights and the production of public goods. This vicious circle can only be broken by including the object of politics in fundamental state agreements.

5.3.3 Presidentialism

Although there is no academic agreement on the superiority or inferiority of presidential systems over parliamentary ones (Sartori, 1994; Cheibub and Limongi, 2002; Colomer and Negretto, 2005; Negretto, 2018), evidence shows that the presidential form has been an obstacle to the social control of power and democratic representation. Early on, Juan Linz captured the essence of the problem, characterizing it as a constitutional conflict between opposing principles, operating against each other. On the one hand, the presidential system seeks "to create a stable, powerful executive endowed with popular legitimacy," while it "introduces many mechanisms that limit that power which might turn out to be arbitrary" such as non-reelection or limited reelection, external comptrollers, etc. (Linz, 1985, p. 5).[78] The good-natured -and patriarchal- idea of an executive that is at once a "representative of the nation," who overcomes the divisions and factionalisms that occur in society and in parliamentary representation, runs up against the need to overcome this factionalism by suppressing political differences, eschewing interaction with legislators and parties different from his/her own, and tending to impose coherence on the government by protecting it from interference from dissidents. Unlike the parliamentary system, in the presidential system changes in public opinion are hardly reflected in government policies, since these are designed, in the best of cases, to fulfill goals within the term of a fixed and inflexible government period.

The social and ideological diversity of societies with presidential regimes is unsurprisingly difficult to make compatible with such a form. Despite little or no experience in developing parliamentary systems in Latin America, the chronic instability under presidential systems and the relatively greater stability of some countries is explained by the fact that in the latter (Uruguay, Chile, and Costa Rica) coalitions have played a decisive role in electoral competition and government formation.[79] However, when entering periods of great polarization due to

---

78 Linz undertook this analysis several times. The most extensive version was published in Linz and Valenzuela (1994, pp. 3–87).

79 Linz (1985, pp. 6–7) notes that the emergence from military dictatorships in several countries was achieved thanks to the concurrence of forces that differed from each other but coincided in the need for democratic systems. Since 1990, Chile has been exemplary in this regard, although it has been losing its initial plasticity.

social and ideological reasons, the president's temptation to separate his/her legitimacy from that of the rest of the political system increases, unlike in parliamentary systems where the opposite is more viable, i.e., the majority party may need to make arrangements with other parties to form a government, which implies mutual concessions and compromises that give policies wider margins to be embodied in robust state agreements. For this reason, the gap in constitutional fulfillment of rights tends to close in parliamentary systems, while in presidential systems it is more difficult to narrow the gap.

In discussing the advantages and disadvantages of both systems, Giovanni Sartori (1994) argued in favor of both, as long as the conditions exist for them to "work", that is, to govern with stability. Yet, when Linz first articulated his argument, he pointed out the obstacle that presidentialism in Latin America represented for incorporating political plurality, facilitating government stability, and assuring the flexibility to adapt policies to changes in preferences. In contrast, parliamentary systems can modify policies or change governments when they fail and need to revise commitments, which in a presidential period is difficult to correct without triggering political crises. Recent research indicates that Latin America has been moving towards reviewing presidential systems that in some cases tend to attenuate the executive's authority and in others to strengthen it (Negretto, 2018, pp. 144–148). In any case, countries with parliamentary systems tend to maintain their democratic character,[80] while those described as presidential are more prone to forgo the parameters of their system and shift towards electoral or closed autocracies, such as Venezuela and Nicaragua. Reforms towards hybrid models that can balance and make the relationship between the executive and the other two branches of government more flexible are more compatible with plurality. This option seems to be gaining acceptance (Negretto, 2018).

However, as shown in Figs. 5.8 and 5.9, the executive branch's respect for decisions rendered by the judicial branch peaked in the first five years of the century, and then slowly declined and fell further in the last two years (2020 and 2022). A similar behavior exists in terms of the legislature's oversight of the executive. In comparison, both Europe as a whole and the European Union in particular, with parliamentary or semi-parliamentary systems, show higher standards of adherence to the balance of powers.

The ability of presidential systems to favor special interests in public policy and select the party and ideological affinities of legislative representation makes

---

80 In an extreme case, such as Peru, the parliamentarization of the presidential system has led to chronic instability of the government as seen by the resignation or dismissal of six presidents in less than a decade.

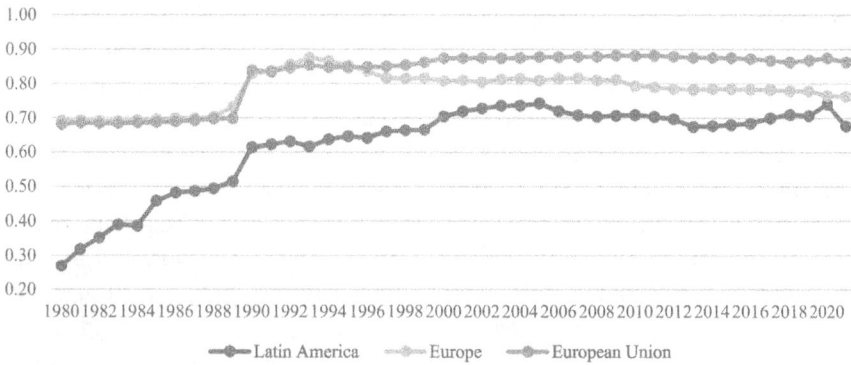

Fig. 5.8: Legislative constraints on The Executive Index.

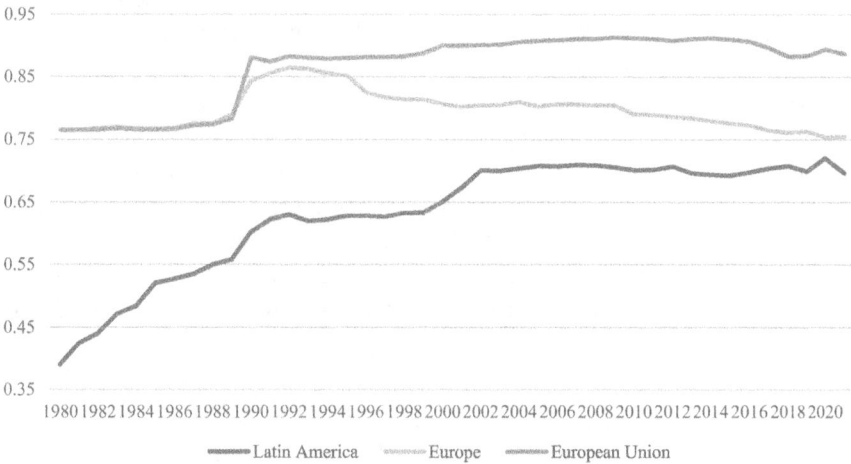

Fig. 5.9: Judicial constraints on The Executive Index.
Prepared by the author with data from V-dem 12 (Coppedge et al., 2022b).
For these two graphs, the averages of the countries selected from Latin America were obtained:
From **Latin America**: Argentina, Bolivia, Brazil, Chile, Colombia, Costa Rica, Dominican Republic, Ecuador, El Salvador, Guatemala, Mexico, Panama, Paraguay, Peru, Uruguay; and from **Europe**: Belarus, Belgium, Czech Republic, Denmark, France, Germany, Greece, Hungary, Ireland, Italy, Norway, Poland, Portugal, Russia, Spain, Sweden, Ukraine.

it more likely that demands for changes in rights will stall or follow a longer path than in parliamentary and mixed systems. Josep Colomer suggested that the social utility of an institution tends to be higher "when the winner includes the preference of the median voter" (Colomer, 2001, p. 227). He also revealed that the most successful democracies (measured in terms of their durability) have adopted par-

liamentary systems with proportional representation, precisely because that regime is more inclined to placing the median voter's interest at the center of governance. As other research has shown (Friedenberg and Gilas, 2022), recurring
electoral reforms in Latin America are a vicious circle largely because presidential systems tend to produce more losers than winners. Thus, the presidential system, and presidentialism to an even greater extent, tend to be an obstacle to the
balance of power that hinders the advancement of most citizens' interests. Recent
analyses of Bolivarian constitutionalism (in Venezuela, Ecuador, and Bolivia)
have pointed to a supposed radical turn towards inclusion through their new constitutions, due to the fact that they combine the incorporation of more rights and
social options for democratic incidence (greater sovereignty) given the political
will of the leaders of these political projects. This "inclusion" depends on two factors: the inscription in the supreme norms of more and new rights and the will of
the president, i.e. the leader of the corresponding Bolivarian revolution (Hugo
Chavez, Nicolas Maduro, Rafael Correa, or Evo Morales) to enforce the rights. The
problem lies, as Elkins had to recognize, in the presence of "two seemingly contradictory elements of Bolivarianism: increasing popular sovereignty and increasing
executive power." (Elkins, 2021, pp. 461–490). The Venezuelan experience disproves
this argument and shows an authoritarian drift that has led to a closed autocracy
in which popular sovereignty has been replaced by a permanent state of exception
(a "sovereignty" a la Carl Schmitt). In Ecuador, we have shown that institutionalizing rights is far from realizing those rights due to the preponderance of the presi-
dentialist variable in the state agreement and the "routinization of charisma"

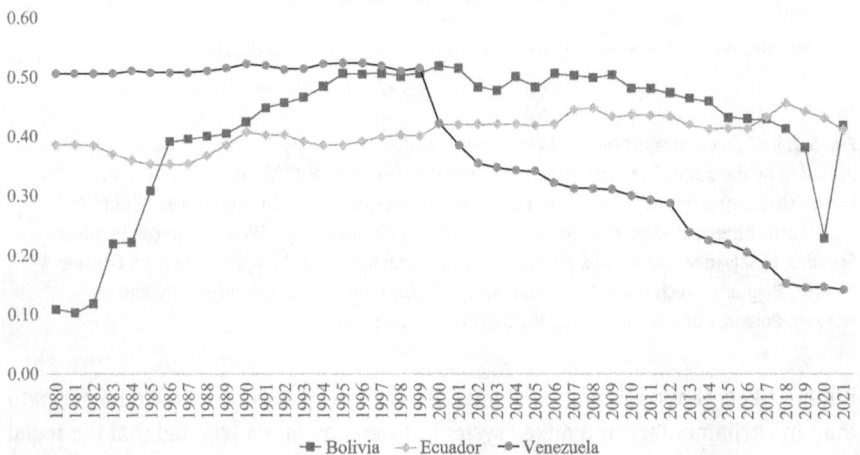

Fig. 5.10: Egalitarian Democracy Index.
SOURCE: Prepared by the author with data from V-Dem, V. 12 (Coppedge et al., 2022b).

(Ansolabehere et al, 2020). In Bolivia, the Bolivarian leader himself broke the rules to which he submitted himself in a constitution he promoted, to pursue an illegitimate re-election with the consequence, among others, of producing negative outcomes for equality, i.e., the essential foundation of rights (Fig. 5.10).

5.3.4 Undue influence

Furthermore, the representation of special interests does have more efficient mechanisms to influence our political regimes. Lobbying in Latin American congresses, the imbalance of power in favor of the executive, the unequal financing of parties and candidates, the translation of the economic power of individuals and groups into political influence and power, are all everyday aspects of politics in the region. The opposite is scarce by definition, namely, greater representativeness, balance of power, efficiency of public policies (especially "social" ones), electoral fairness, and prevalence of the public interest. In addition to the obvious asymmetries of these longtime, ineffable political aspects, the central feature of undue influence is that it resigns citizens to the idea that voting is the only form of civil life -and sometimes the only redoubt of citizenship- and it creates a greater propensity for conflict rather than consensus to be the main figure in the exercise of political will. As a general rule, citizens must wait for a new electoral campaign to include their felt demands, or a new party alternative, or a charismatic leader to appear and turn their gaze towards those excluded from everyday political life. Still another option is to be fed up and join social protest movements -often violent- to change the balance of power in their favor. The continuous interaction between constituents and legislators or authorities does not have the necessary relevance to become a daily routine of public decision making. The state has not included its structure as a political community into this interlocution.

There are indicators to gauge the degree of this inequality of influence that normalizes the disadvantage in the usufruct of government benefits and, consequently, outlines a "public" interest biased towards groups with greater influence. "Power distributed by socioeconomic position" (Fig. 5.1) identifies the degree to which socioeconomic inequality translates into political power. The scale ranges from 0 to 4 where zero indicates that the rich monopolize political power and "average and poor" people have no influence and 4 equals a more or less equal distribution of power among economic groups (Coppedge et al., 2022: 207). In our selection of countries the result is as follows for both regions.

Despite this wide margin for undue influence from the most powerful groups, one of the ways to counteract this inequality is by "diagonal accountability," (Fig. 5.2) which measures the repertoire of options that "citizens, civil society organizations

Tab. 5.1: Power distributed by socioeconomic position.

Power distributed by socioeconomic position			
Country	Average	Country	Average
Sweden	3.3	Bolivia*	3.1
Norway	3.2	Argentina	3
Belarus	3	Uruguay	3
Belgium	3	Brazil	2.4
Czech Republic	3	Ecuador	2.4
Denmark	3	Peru	2.4
France	3	Chile	2.2
Germany	3	Costa Rica	2.2
Greece	3	Dominican Republic	2
Ireland	3	Mexico	2
Italy	3	Panama	2
Poland	3	Paraguay	2
Portugal	3	Colombia	1.8
Spain	3	Guatemala	1.8
Hungary	2.6	El Salvador	1.6
Russia	1.4		
Ukraine	0.8		
Average	**2.8**	**Average**	**2.3**

*Bolivia stands out with less inequality of influence of economic power over other groups due to the impact of left-wing government policies, although this does not contradict the high inequality previously mentioned.
Source: Prepared by the author with data from V-dem version 12 (Coppedge et al., 2022b). Scale 0–4. The higher the values, the lower the power inequality.
SCALE: "0: Wealthy people enjoy a virtual monopoly on political power. Average and poorer people have almost no influence. 1: Wealthy people enjoy a dominant hold on political power. People of average income have little say. Poorer people have essentially no influence. 2: Wealthy people have a very strong hold on political power. People of average or poorer income have some degree of influence but only on issues that matter less for wealthy people. 3: Wealthy people have more political power than others. But people of average income have almost as much influence and poor people also have a significant degree of political power. 4: Wealthy people have no more political power than those whose economic status is average or poor. Political power is more or less equally distributed across economic groups." (Coppedge et al., 2022a, p. 207)

Tab. 5.2: Diagonal Accountability Index.

Diagonal accountability index			
1990–2021			
Country	Average	Country	Average
Denmark	2.1	Costa Rica	1.9
Sweden	2	Uruguay	1.7
Norway	1.9	Argentina	1.5
Germany	1.8	Brazil	1.5
Czech Republic	1.7	Chile	1.5
France	1.7	Dominican Republic	1.1
Greece	1.7	Panama	1.1
Ireland	1.7	Bolivia	1
Italy	1.7	Ecuador	0.9
Spain	1.7	Peru	0.9
Belgium	1.6	El Salvador	0.8
Portugal	1.6	Paraguay	0.8
Poland	1.4	Colombia	0.7
Hungary	1.1	Guatemala	0.7
Ukraine	0.8	Mexico	0.7
Russia	0.3		
Average	**1.4**	**Average**	**1.1**

Source: Prepared by the author with data from V-dem version 12.
(Coppedge et al., 2022b). Scale 0–4, 4 the highest score.

(CSOs), and an independent media can use to hold the government accountable."
(Coppedge et al., 2022a, p. 290). The distribution by country is as shown in Fig. 5.2.

In Chapter 3, we showed the importance of this form of *accountability* and in the factor analysis we revisited it in a different way from the indicator created by V-Dem. The results of this factor in our analysis are consistent with those found with the indicator taken separately, and show the low capacity in the region to control power. Both elements indicate a widespread *undue influence* in most of the countries and confirm the existing gap between most of the countries, and those that excel in both ratings, i.e. those that, like Uruguay and Costa Rica, control the power and excess of power between social classes and between the state and society as a whole. Again, here we encounter the problem of the state.

5.3.5 Stagnant rights and prostrated justice

The human rights gap represents a measurable indicator of the difficulty with which the demands for protection made by society to Latin American states make headway (Ansolabehere et al., 2015; Ansolabehere et al., 2020). In this case there is an international legal system that many countries have adopted through the subscription of treaties and conventions. Including human rights into a country's domestic legal order compels the state to protect them. But this obligation is often not fulfilled. During the 1990s, Latin American governments were enthusiastic signers of agreements and treaties. On the world map, Latin America and the European Union are the two regions that have most protected human rights. Most Latin American countries have signed between 15 and 20 human rights treaties and conventions.[81] and a second group has signed between 10 and 14. Only Cuba lags with 8 recognized treaties.

The slow progress of human rights is essentially related to institutional and ideological obstacles. Despite many countries' adherence to this legal system in the region, institutionalization and compliance have achieved less progress that could be misleadingly inferred from a mapping of treaty signatures. In research conducted between 2010 and 2020,[82] we found relevant factors that help us understand the compliance gap. The institutionalization *form*, i.e., the role human rights play in political activity (their politicization) is a determinant factor before and after their acceptance by a state. Before, because they represent an aspiration and after, because they need to be implemented for the full enjoyment of the freedoms that these rights imply. However, state arrangements are determinant in the equation. When the set of actors defining public policies on human rights is favorable to their actual implementation, institutionalization counts. Moreover, formal institutionalization may be secondary if the political community that defines the agreements in the state has incorporated them "naturally", as in Uruguay, an atypical case because of its low formal institutionalization and high level of effective compliance. The opposite is true in the case of Ecuador, which has been very active in inscribing rights into legislation and has created institutions to implement them. Yet, the degree to which people enjoy those rights remained low due to the absence of state agreement for their effective implementation (Ansolabehere et al., 2020, pp. 9–48, 173–196).

---

81 https://indicators.ohchr.org/ Data for 1996–2014.
82 This refers to the research project "Institucionalización y disfrute de los derechos humanos en las democracias latinoamericanas 1990–2010" [Institutionalization and enjoyment of human rights in Latin American democracies 1990–2010] (Conacyt, Basic Science Fund) (Ansolabehere et al.,2015; Ansolabehere et al., 2020).

Furthermore, some of the governments led by the radical left or by left and right-wing populists have alleged that human rights are an invention of neoliberal capitalism and/or foreign interests. The governments of Venezuela (Chávez-Maduro), Nicaragua (Ortega-Murillo), and Mexico (López Obrador) have been the most prominent in this assertion. Consequently, they have combated local and international human rights defenders' organizations that have systematically reported constant violations. They have done so to varying degrees. Venezuela and Nicaragua have repressed these organizations the most and are the biggest violators. Mexico has maintained considerable ambiguity by allocating resources for the protection of certain victims and allowing the armed forces to violate rights on a daily basis. Other leftist or progressive governments have distinguished themselves by defending and promoting human rights, exemplified by Uruguay, Costa Rica, Chile, and Brazil. There are ideological strongholds on the left and on the right that view human rights as threats to values that they consider superior to the principle of human dignity that the human-rights legal system protects. Across the political spectrum, however, these regressive forces exist alongside others that uphold the defense of human rights as a topmost public priority.

To take a fresh look at this problem, we return to the gap between constitutional compliance with *de jure* and *de facto* rights (measurement methodology developed by Gutman et al. 2022a).[83] What factors explain the gap? For our purposes, Gutman et al. proposed mainly two tentative answers: "Constitutions that allow for the dismissal of the head of state or government for violating the constitution achieve higher compliance levels" (Gutmann et al., 2022a, p. 1), and "Where constitutions are transplanted from foreign constitutional models, compliance is less likely" (Gutmann et al., 2022a, p. 18). The authors' observations refer to a set of 168 countries in their sample, but they can be adjusted to two chronic problems in Latin America. We have referred to the fact that the political regime sends insufficient signals of democratic transformation to the state. The presidential system is one of the obstacles to efforts that would convert citizens' opinion into state will, irrespective of the differences in the ways this occurs in each country, from the strongest that are elected by relative majority and with broad powers to exercise power with low legislative participation and little judicial oversight, to those that have adopted semi-parliamentary regimes – such as Peru. In addition, the different

---

[83] This measure comprises "(1) property rights and the rule of law (encompassing indicators for property rights, judicial independence, equality before the law, and rule of law); (2) political rights (freedom of association, freedom of assembly, and the right to form parties); (3) civil rights (free media, free speech, free movement, and religious freedom); and (4) basic human rights (the right to life, freedom from slavery, and protection from torture)." Gutmann et al. (2022a, p.3). See *supra* chapter 3.

Tab. 5.3: De jure/De facto enforcement gap.

Political rights						
Countries	**Periods**		**Countries**	**Periods**		
	1950–1979	**1980–2020**		**1950–1979**	**1980–2020**	
Paraguay	0.371	0.761	Poland	0.251	0.607	
Honduras	0.327	0.656	Greece	0.407	0.761	
Panama	0.371	0.666	Portugal	0.426	0.761	
Dominican Republic	0.324	0.616	Hungary	0.243	0.543	
Peru	0.405	0.651	Spain	0.575	0.761	
El Salvador	0.243	0.488	Italy	0.575	0.757	
Bolivia	0.309	0.539	Russia	0.371	0.411	
Chile	0.44	0.639	Germany	0.761	0.761	
Guatemala	0.313	0.51	Ireland	0.761	0.761	
Mexico	0.371	0.553	Sweden	0.761	0.761	
Ecuador	0.342	0.503	Denmark	0.575	0.575	
Nicaragua	0.371	0.498	Belgium	0.761	0.757	
Argentina	0.639	0.756	Czech Republic	–	0.761	
Colombia	0.371	0.436	Norway	–	0.761	
Costa Rica	0.761	0.761	Ukraine	–	0.532	
Venezuela	0.532	0.461	France	–	–	
Uruguay	–	0.735				
Brazil	–	0.71				
Averages	**0.405**	**0.608**	**Averages**	0.581	0.685	

Source: Prepared by the author with data from Gutmann et al. (2022b).

hybrid versions that have appeared on the democratic stage continue having this handicap (Negretto, 2018).

Table 5.3 shows that the countries that most closed the gap in *de jure/de facto* compliance with political rights between the two periods were Paraguay, Honduras, Panama, the Dominican Republic, Peru, El Salvador, and Bolivia. Paraguay made notable progress, reaching the same level as Costa Rica (which remained at the same level). The figures for Uruguay and Brazil for the first period are not available. However, the compliance levels of both countries are high. The countries located in the middle and low part of the scale (between .0 and .599) are Guatemala, Mexico, Ecuador, Nicaragua, Colombia and Venezuela. Venezuela regressed, dropping almost one point between the two periods. The final average for these countries is 0.6 and the average overall reduction is 0.2 points.

By way of comparison, in our selection of European countries there is a higher average of 0.77 in the most recent period and a proportionally smaller closing of the gap than in Latin America (fig. 5.4), but having started from higher

Tab. 5.4: De jure/De facto compliance gap with basic human rights.

Basic rights

Countries	Periods		Countries	Periods	
	1950–1979	1980–2020		1950–1979	1980–2020
Paraguay	0.221	0.639	Hungary	0.357	0.595
Bolivia	0.221	0.604	Poland	0.423	0.639
Nicaragua	0.221	0.565	Portugal	0.454	0.639
Dominican Republic	0.289	0.633	Greece	0.491	0.639
El Salvador	0.221	0.509	Germany	0.639	0.639
Honduras	0.221	0.438	Italy	0.639	0.639
Guatemala	0.206	0.354	Spain	0.639	0.639
Brazil	0.335	0.468	Sweden	0.639	0.639
Argentina	0.507	0.639	Russia	0.567	0.298
Ecuador	0.535	0.592	Belgium	–	0.639
Panama	0.553	0.587	Czech Republic	–	0.639
Costa Rica	0.639	0.639	Ireland	–	0.639
Mexico	0.437	0.437	Norway	–	0.639
Venezuela	0.594	0.579	Ukraine	–	0.465
Chile	0.592	0.537	Denmark	–	–
Peru	0.56	0.409	France	–	–
Colombia	0.567	0.41			
Uruguay	–	–			
Average	**0.407**	**0.532**	**Average**	**0.581**	**0.596**

Source: Prepared by the author with data from Gutmann et al. (2022b).
*Note: We used the database found in the paper "The comparative constitutional compliance database". We employed the indicators cc_p and cc_b. Note: Indicators cc_p (political rights) and cc_b (basic rights) were used. These aggregated indicators (as a full base) have a minimum value of (−1.54) and a maximum of (1.57) for political rights (cc_p) and (−2.11) to (0.84) for basic rights (cc_b), respectively. The definitions are explained in detail in Gutman et al. 2022a.

The data were already standardized in the database, i.e., the mean was 0, the standard deviation was 1, and the range of values could be between −3 and 3. Therefore, the averages were positive and negative for each period/country. To facilitate the reader's appreciation of this presentation, the data were normalized so that their values are between 0 and 1, and averages are also between 0 and 1, without altering their shape. The values still have the same relative distance from each other. The difference indicates the change between the two time periods.

levels (0.135 above LA), as shown in the column for the period 1950–1979, Poland, Greece, Portugal, and Hungary reduced the gap the most.

In basic human rights (right to life, no slavery, no torture), Paraguay, Bolivia, Nicaragua, and the Dominican Republic have closed the gap the most, but their overall scores, as well as the average for the region, are a pitiful 0.5. Europe scores better with an average of almost 0.6, and the countries that have notably

Tab. 5.5: Civil justice and criminal justice. (Factor average).

World Justice Project. Civil Justice (7) and Criminal Justice (8).[84]

Latin America	Factor 7: Civil Justice	Factor 8: Criminal Justice	Europe	Factor 7: Civil Justice	Factor 8: Criminal Justice
ARG	0.56	0.42	BEL	0.73	0.71
BOL	0.34	0.23	CZE	0.69	0.71
BRA	0.53	0.37	DNK	0.84	0.83
CHL	0.63	0.57	FRA	0.7	0.64
COL	0.49	0.35	DEU	0.84	0.77
CRI	0.62	0.56	GRC	0.59	0.5
ECU	0.45	0.36	HUN	0.49	0.51
LUN.	0.46	0.37	IRL	0.74	0.72
SLV	0.5	0.3	ITA	0.57	0.64
GTM	0.36	0.31	NOR	0.85	0.83
HND	0.42	0.25	POL	0.63	0.65
MEX	0.4	0.29	PRT	0.66	0.62
PAN	0.48	0.34	RUS	0.51	0.34
PRY	0.43	0.28	ESP	0.65	0.65
PER	0.43	0.35	SWE	0.81	0.8
URY	0.73	0.54			
VEN	0.31	0.15			
Region	**0.48**	**0.35**	**Region**	**0.69**	**0.66**

Source: Prepared by the author with data from WJP (2021).
Note for Latin America: Scale 0–1. Country averages were generated for the years available. The base has from 2012–2013 to 2022, there are, however, countries that have fewer records.
*Costa Rica as of 2016
**Honduras as of 2015
***Paraguay as of 2021
The other countries have 9 records.
The base is from 2012 to 2022. However, the years 2012–2013 go together, as do 2017–2018.
Note for Europe: Scale 0–1. Country averages were generated for the years available. The base has from 2012–2013 to 2022; there are, however, countries that have fewer records.
For the selected European countries, the following have less records:
*Ireland as of 2021
The base is from 2012 to 2022. However the years 2012–2013 go together, as do 2017–2018.

---

84 The Civil Justice factor measures this variables: 7.1 People can access and afford civil justice, 7.2 Civil justice is free of discrimination, 7.3 Civil justice is free of corruption, 7.4 Civil justice is free of improper government influence; 7.5 Civil justice is not subject to unreasonable delay, 7.6 Civil justice is effectively enforced, 7.7 Alternative dispute resolution mechanisms are accessible, impartial, and effective. WJP (2021). The Criminal Justice factor measures this variables: 8.1 Criminal investigative system is effective, 8.2 Criminal adjudication system is timely and effective, 8.3

improved are Hungary, Poland, Portugal, and Greece, i.e., two countries that belonged to the communist bloc and two that recently transitioned. Further, Russia's score drops significantly, revealing extremely high levels of rights violations. Despite some improvements in both regions, for rights as basic as those listed above, the scores are well below the constitutional compliance that would be expected of democracies.

Table 5.5 complements the panorama with measurements provided by the World Justice Project, which ascertains the performance of countries in terms of civil and criminal justice. Latin America stands out for its poorer outcome in enforcing civil justice over criminal justice, while in Europe it is the other way around. Civil justice receives better treatment than criminal justice. In terms of regional averages, Latin America falls below the middle of the scale, while the European countries stand out for their proximity to 0.7 with the exception of some countries that coincide with other low performance scores.

5.4 Conclusion

If democracy is a diarchy that separates the sovereign from the representative, presidentialism retains the remnants of the tradition of a monarchical power that refuses to die, of a resistance to place the sovereign of last resort up above the public servant who forms the government. This is a characteristic of the state. The history of Latin America is a living testimony to the incompleteness of this separation. This flaw is best observed in dictatorships and populism. It is not the presidential system itself, despite all its structural drawbacks, but the secular *presidentialism* that overwhelms the system and epitomizes this obstacle, regardless of the fact that presidential systems *per se* tend to lose the capacity to incorporate average preferences, especially in societies that are highly polarized. Of all the difficulties that can arise in presidential systems (Linz 1994: 69 and *passim*), obstacles that hinder the promotion of rights (human or otherwise) are one of them. The concern of Linz, the great Spanish political scientist, was which regime was more conducive to governing democracy. Almost half a century after the beginning of the third wave and its influence in Latin America, it is in the area of rights, i.e., in the inclusive results of democracy, where progress and deficiencies

---

Correctional system is effective in reducing criminal behavior, 8.4 Criminal justice is impartial, 8.5 Criminal justice is free of corruption, 8.6 Criminal justice is free of improper government influence, 8.7 Due process of the law and rights of the accused. WJP (2021).

are best observed. Most of the cases we analyzed, with the exceptions already mentioned, are polarized societies in which the presidential system encourages the executive branch to take sides and skews its policies to favor privileged groups. An approximation to this change is developed in Chapter 2 by showing the contrast between the deficient commitment to the rule of law and the greater satisfaction of the regulatory role that favors the private sector. Perhaps Brazil during the Lula administration and Bolivia during the first stage of the Morales administration, in which the need to make broad alliances to govern and de facto "parliamentarize" the regime, partially broke this vicious circle.[85]

We ought not overlook that the *quality* of citizenship, an issue that we have only indirectly addressed in this book, is a fundamental aspect shaping the type of political regime that is eventually elected; further, the demands for presidential regime change have not been prominent in demands articulated by civil society and political parties.[86]

Can there be a crisis of representation where democratic representation has been deficient or even non-existent? The answer is yes. Crises do not only affect pre-existing practices; they also have an impact on the imaging of future alternatives, i.e., the "paradigmatic fictions" that arise in the "surplus of politics" (Urbinati) that is produced in democratization. This crisis is characterized by the intertwining of democratic and authoritarian forces in the functioning of democracy, the citizenry, the regime, and the state, the main effect of which is to prevent citizen opinion from reaching the confines of the state in order to transform itself into the free will of self-government.

In reference to elite representativeness, in their pioneering study Luna and Zechsmaister (2005, p. 413) concluded that in party systems with greater tradition and strength (mainly Chile and Uruguay), the relationship between representatives and their constituents adheres more to the formal rules of the citizenship relationship, while in less developed ones, which include countries with larger populations and greater inequality, the relationship tends to be more personal, that is, it fosters clientelist links in the exchange between elites and constituents.

Despite favorable reforms at all levels of democracy, the effects of these reforms remain mostly confined to the regime. Electoral reforms to improve electoral quality and the addition of excluded sectors and groups, to expand the fields of direct democracy (Altman, 2010), to improve access to justice, to shape the presidential institution and the balance of power, among others, demonstrate that ad-

---

85 Leaving aside the cases of Costa Rica and Uruguay for the reasons already explained.
86 Negretto (2018) offers a timely account of the reforms of the presidential system in Latin America and some clues to guide research in that direction.

vances are often considerable but, at the same time, neutralized or significantly hindered to prevent them from reaching their final destination: the transformation of the nature of the political community, i.e. the state, in a democratic sense.

In economic and other public policies, in the enforcement of the law, in the behavior of the mass and social media, in civil society, in political parties, in civic culture -which includes the parameters of acquiescence with the *status quo*-, the standoff between forces that seek to transform and those that hinder democratic change has become naturalized. The fact that this stalemate remains is an indicator of crises from which society tends to emerge and head either towards delegative democracy or oligarchic forms of domination. As Mazzuca and Munck (2020, p. 63) observed, "In Latin America, the state-democracy interaction has not generated a virtuous cycle. Rather, it has generated a self-perpetuating arrangement that provides micro-foundations to the region's middle-quality institutional trap." Most Latin American countries are in this trap. The difference between this study and the approach of other authors lies in the fact that, from our point of view, a good part of state "failures" is due to the absence of transformations that should take place therein, given the nature of representative democracy, namely, the continuous intercourse between the two factors of the democratic diarchy: public judgment and political will.

Chapter 6
What's next for democracy in Latin America?

Latin American state has historically evinced, and continues evincing, poor scores in [. . .] the scarce powers that those states -and their governments- have for further democratizing their societies and, indeed, themselves.
Guillermo O'Donnell

My answer to the question in the title may seem obvious: we face either further democratization of the state or authoritarian regression, although the internal threats that work against and oppose democratization in many ways and at different levels will not disappear. But it is necessary to dwell on the question carefully to see its different angles and difficulties. This chapter addresses the problem taking into account what has been revealed in previous chapters, attempting to give an overall answer for Latin American democracies and for those countries that have already experienced serious authoritarian setbacks.

A first warning regarding the suspicions that the reader who has reached this point may harbor, i.e., that democratization is being equated with socialization and, consequently, democracy with socialism. This is not the case for a simple reason that I will not go into in depth because I hope to clarify it in detail elsewhere. And this reason is that free entry into impersonal political institutions, as it should be in democracy, leads to public deliberation of values, preferences, histories, and desires for the future that are formed in public reason. It is obvious that all ideologies would make their appearance by choosing such an entry, but they would never have the legitimate authority to monopolize public decision and power. All participating actors should have to accept the condition of being part of a collective and equitable negotiation of how the legitimate order should be structured. Some actors would maintain their reservations or disagree, but they would always maintain their rights to intervene in the public sphere and take part in decisions. It is a continuous process in which there is no end; the horizon is permanently uncertain and requires the actors' commitment. To complete this idea, I quote Nadia Urbinati, who summarizes it as follows:

> *the way in which will is imposed matters a lot*, as differences between direct and representative democracy show. Because of its indirect form (citizens authorize lawmakers to decide in their names), modern democracy marks the end of yes-no politics and transforms politics in an open arena of contestable opinions and ever-revisable decisions. Thus [. . .] *the indirect power of opinion characterizes modern democracy no less than suffrage* and does so in a plurality of ways that we do not immediately apprehend if we focus only on one component of the diarchy . . . (Urbinati, 2014, p. 25 Emphasis added).

https://doi.org/10.1515/9783110773675-007

As a political community, the state is the monopoly of public force and administration. But it is also the synthesis of the political personality of a society. Although the democratic state organizes a regime to process conflict fairly (and peacefully), whether this regime is democratic depends on whether the state so decides, because it is in the state that the decision and custody of the values and procedures that give life to and establish the limits and capacities of the regime ultimately reside. As the source of legitimate violence and public administration, the state routinizes what has been admitted as fundamental norms. Each individual and group adopts them singularly and in the course of their customary conduct they guide themselves according to the decisions/norms that the state harbors and which authorize it to act; otherwise, they are subject to the corrective action of justice. The strength of the institutions that emanate from the state derives from the strength of the citizens' decision that encourages it and the determination that they place in its custody. This is, in turn, the product of histories of individuals, groups, and societies that struggle for rights whose intrinsic meaning lies in the appropriation of a part of a sovereign political decision whose realization is embodied in constitutional law. Given the presence and characteristics of this appropriation, we can contend that the state is or is not democratic and distinguish it from the democratic attributes of the political regime, which refer to the daily processing of conflict and cooperation in the public sphere. The state is or is not democratic because the political community ultimately defines the acceptance of precepts, principles, and decisions that are inclusive or exclusive, egalitarian or discriminatory; because it admits or rejects individuals and groups that can participate in public, common, and collective decisions. The regime is the space where political conflict between different visions of the direction of the public sphere is processed and the acceptance or rejection of interests or preferences in public decision-making is determined.

6.1 The metarule and the "surplus of politics"

Systematic empirical observation of the relationship between representatives and their constituencies can be drawn directly or indirectly from a variety of sources.[87] Democratic representation is not usually explored as a continuous relationship that includes the vote that elects and the opinion that judges, complains, censures, proposes, and demands. Based on the available literature and evidence,

---

87 In this book, I have favored indirect observation. Of course, direct observation is possible through field research and case studies.

I have discussed the profiles of this relationship in Latin America in order to delve deeper into the notion that the largest failure of representation is not in the political regime, however deficient it may be, but in the lack of *production of a democratic state* and that the most important obstacle to it is the difficult "balance" between forces that seek to change it in favor of the rights of individuals and collectives and those that try to preserve it. It is a problem -or a political economy conundrum- faced by every nation at different stages of its historical development. There is no pre-established script. The felt and expressed need -especially the latter- signals the passage from dissatisfaction with the prevailing social and institutional arrangements to conflict in the form of demands for citizenship rights (political, economic, social, and cultural), in some cases even approaching the canon of the human rights legal system. The originality of Latin America lies, as Octavio Paz said, in being "an offshoot of the West" in the same way that every cultural continuum is a child of its past. I would add that Latin America is a "melting pot" in which different civilizations converge. Hence, it has a political personality in which demands have left a deep imprint that in democratic times have been reflected in certain levels of inclusion, especially of recognition and resources (Kapiscewski, et al., 2021), although scarcely in access to state power. Of course, the debts owed by Latin American states to their citizens are not limited to excluded groups, but to society as a whole and its projection in the contemporary world.

In general terms, the path followed by the construction of rights in Latin America runs *pari pasu* with democratization.[88] The forms of democracy reflect this dynamic and cannot escape it. The low quality of state performance and representation that we have studied in the preceding chapters is a combination of advances and obstacles to the democratization of the political community that gives specificity to the state. We do not have sufficient ethnologies of Latin American political communities, understood as the elite groups that shape how state decisions are made. Perhaps one day the fields of sociology and anthropology will provide them, but in the meantime we must reconstruct them from the "facts" they produce.

The first of these derives from the political economy. The establishment of an economic policy model such as the one that took shape beginning in the 1980s occurred when the restoration or emergence of democracies determined what limits the actors had for movement. Accepting democracy went hand in hand

---

[88] This is not so true of their enforcement. Even in democratic regimes, rights recede if the state does not protect them or directly attacks them, thanks to the presence of authoritarian forces that lurk therein.

with accepting the inevitable restrictions arising from these policies, yet there was substantial economic growth and the middle class grew in size. Some countries surprisingly reduced poverty and inequality, as we show with figures in Chapter 2, but even so, elites' resistance to redistribution had two apparent dimensions. On the one hand, the enormous concentration of wealth in the highest decile (and in the top one percent of ten percent), and on the other hand, state support of this concentration by avoiding affecting the richest sectors with above-average tax rates and institutional designs that legitimize social inequality and hinder political equality of citizens in the public square. If we were to gather both -the richest and the rest of the citizenry- in that imaginary square, they would not mingle, they would not talk to each other, but perhaps they would gather in groups at each corner to conspire against each other. In fact, this image faithfully describes the prevailing attitudes in Latin American social life and the public sphere.

Representative democracy cannot survive without a considerable degree of socioeconomic integration that can offer prospects of real improvement to most of the population. Ideally this integration could be progressive, but history teaches us that the incorporation of groups previously excluded or less advantaged than others occurs through conflict and political negotiation. At this point we ought to pause and examine how concrete evidence situates us before the normative challenge of democratic theory.

Although there are storm clouds on the horizon, Latin America has navigated the third democratic wave with good fortune. At least in the sense that, although few electoral democracies have moved towards the category of liberal democracies (the most developed, according to V-Dem), there has not been a general tendency to regress to electoral or closed autocracies. This expansion of democracy, mainly electoral as previously seen, has placed at the center of the Latin American drama the classic constitutional conflict in the history of the modern state. This conflict is nurtured by combining the expansion of rights, the institutionalization of contention in the political regime, and the state's low capability to respond to both. Civil society has managed to insert itself in the political regime through political parties, movements, and organizations. In doing so, it has contributed to building a citizenry that is more attentive to public affairs. It has succeeded in inscribing its rights in the letter of the constitutions, but it has yet to succeed in bringing its aspiration to a different legitimate order, i.e., an order whose constituent elements are democratic at the heart of the political community and in the repertoires available for social choice. In fact, this indicates citizens' weakness and the fragility with which the value of equality for political action is rooted in people's mentalities.

In the vast majority of its provisions and acts, the state continues to act as if rights were a dispensable externality, admissible in small cells of a giant mesh, interpretable at the whim of the ruling groups or attainable only if a charismatic leader comes to power. This permissiveness (*de facto* authorization) granted by the citizenry to power is the result of a bedazzlement; something similar or akin to miracle and revelation. Until the moment the chosen one arrives, oligarchies have the necessary space to exercise power to their benefit and, when the charismatic figure arrives, it displaces the place of those oligarchies, but its driving force usually preserves or encourages the uses and customs of the representation gaps characteristic of the old order and frequently does so in their name. We face a recurring archetype: *de jure* rights in abundance and rationed *de facto* compliance. Plentiful imaginary bread in territories starved of justice. With the exception of fewer countries than the fingers of one hand, Ibero-America is condemned to be trapped by a promise without a guarantee of fulfillment. The preceding chapters merely provide an updated picture of this problem and several of its most salient political and policy nuances.

State agreements for the democratization of Latin America focused more on modifying the rules of access to power than on those having to do with its exercise. They increased the categories of individual and collective rights, but not the institutional *procedures* for fulfilling them. Although there are notable differences in some countries' outcomes in constitutional compliance before and after 1980, the best exercises have been unable to affect the inequitable distribution of power that divides the citizenry with deep inequality gaps in all areas: economic, social, educational, ethnic, and cultural. It is a distribution -perhaps with different proportions but with the same behavioral pattern- that continues to be structured around a moderately transformed matrix of oligarchic and authoritarian origin.[89] Moreover, with the importance placed on good regulatory outcomes (See Fig. 2.10), it is evident that the interests of companies and international economic agencies, such as the World Bank and the International Monetary Fund, have priority in the state. These institutions demanded respect for property rights and economic competition as a prerequisite for investment in Latin American markets and the granting of loans to governments. However, the outstanding capacity shown by the state in regulatory matters was not applied in the same way to other areas where it could have been reflected had the political will to do so existed.[90] The particular emphasis of these international organizations on property relations and competition was not an obstacle in building the rule of law and efficient governments to

---

[89] Progress has been fostered by economic globalization and political openness. The latter originates from external and internal stimuli to find new power arrangements.

[90] In fact, many international organizations and other international bodies such as the UN and the European Union have urged developing countries to strengthen the rule of law and the protection of human rights without obtaining similar results as compared to the procurement of regulation and economic competition.

protect rights, produce public goods, control corruption, and improve accountability. To be addressed, these problems required the will of Latin American societies, particularly of progressive political forces and subordinate groups. It is often claimed that these external institutions were to blame for the vacuum of endogenous will for the democratic transformation of the state, but the data show that there were -and there are- important margins of freedom to develop the political conditions necessary for this purpose. That these conditions are not seen and adequately exploited by social and political actors is an ideological problem, or one of a set of epistemological obstacles to democratic political action in addition to other types of limitations.

With democratization, new political regimes were created, but no new states. Only old states with modernizing patches that have not, so far, been sufficient to bring forth the degree of political inclusion required by representative democracy. In order to distinguish a new state from an old and obsolete one, one only need view the difference in the political community that dominates it and directs the administration of the government. Latin American political elites have not remained unchanged. On the contrary, they have changed significantly, but that change has met with resistance from ruling classes reluctant to alter their place in the legitimate order, and democratic and progressive groups have not had the strength and leadership necessary to assert their power in new state configurations. Although it is possible to observe a more plural spectrum of political parties and civil organizations, vast swathes of the demos have no place in that community through the action of their representatives. Nevertheless, democratization is tangible in many areas of political life and has produced relevant differences. Not only does Latin America differ from the dynamics that predominated in its political systems before the third wave of democracy (dictatorships, isolation among nation-states and between the region and the rest of the world, populations captive to local sources of legitimacy, etc.), but the processes of democratization have transformed important areas of public life, for example, legal systems, international relations, public opinion, and political parties. Citizens have also undergone major transformations. The entrenchment of the right to vote, the struggle against inequality, individual and group autonomy, the dismantling of the old corporative forms brought about by changes in the economic structure, etc., have unleashed changes in collective mentalities over more than two generations since dictatorships and authoritarianisms were displaced by democratization. The panorama outlined in the preceding chapters is that of histories in which democratization removed forms of authoritarianism from vast fields of social and political life. However, the resulting picture is mixed, if not downright gray. What hindered progress in the formation of robust systems of law, accountability, and control of corruption? Why do the roots of inequality spread further despite the adoption of egalitarian charters by almost all states? Is this a repetition of the past or a new, unprecedented situation that, despite its defects and problems, offers opportunities for change? Will the region's polyarchies endure or will they be absorbed by the tendencies of autocratization that are emerging from within?

6.2 The insurmountable bulwarks

Democracy makes a substantial difference for inclusion as long as the rules embedded in the political regime open the way to affect the character of the state. This means having an impact on the dominant political community in order to integrate into representation, understood as we developed it in chapter three, all members of the *demos* -or, at least, of the citizenry- equally and without "undue influence" or with as little as possible through control over this type of influence. However, the bridges and processes for getting there in democratic systems differentiate states from one another by the variants in democratic quality. In a classic book, Charles Tilly (2007, p. 188) synthesized in two arguments the meaning of democratization and de-democratization processes of the resulting systems of government:

> Democratization: "1. Integration of trust networks, insulation of public politics from categorical inequality, and reduction of autonomous power centers combine to cause democratization, which does not occur in their absence".[91]

> De-democratization: "2. Reversal of any or all of these processes de-democratizes regimes."

The actual development of these conditions indicated by Tilly in the first point is achieved when the capacities that best serve the public interest have been institutionalized in the state. This institutionalization is the result of the modification of the principles that make up political representation. Plurality, breadth, deliberative and negotiating capacity, and innovative interaction agreements between elites and majorities are key factors for reaching this stage of political development. Referring to France in the 18th and 19th centuries and to Venezuela in the 20th century, Tilly puts it this way:

> expanding state activity drew more citizens into state-coordinated efforts, which enlarged public politics. Inevitably, state-coordinated activities favored some organized interests over others -for example, merchants over landlords- which almost as inevitably incited conflicts among them and drew those conflicts into public politics, thus further enlarging public politics. Enlargement of public politics then made regimes more susceptible to broadening,

---

91 "Autonomous power centers are those powers that operate above the political regime and the constitutional order, e.g., organized crime, influential groups, strong economic powers, etc.

equalizing, protecting, and rendering more definitive whatever mutually binding consultation was occurring – as well as to reversals of each of these changes. Reversals could still
occur to the extent that elites shielded their trust networks from complete integration into
public politics, acquired control over their own segments of the state, and/or retained bases
of coercive power lying outside of public politics [. . .] Conversely, to the extent that elites
came to depend on the state and public politics for their own programs of self-reproduction
and self-aggrandizement, their capacity to precipitate de-democratization through withdrawal from public politics declined [. . .] Thus, regime by regime, both democratization
and de-democratization became possible as never before. (Tilly, 2007, pp. 194–195)

Tilly's observation describes a pattern of behavior that occurs differently but recurrently in each country. This pattern brings together the fundamental characteristics of cycles of democratization and *"de-democratization"* and is reflected in
the quality of political representation.[92] My argument is that, once these factors
that form democratic representation have been achieved, their stability and durability depend on their solid presence as central norms of the state, on which, in
turn, both the regime and the margins of freedom for political action of the governed depend. This is deployed in movements and coalitions that are included in
the regime and determine the results of the process in terms of negotiation of legislative and informal rules of the legitimate order. We return, then, to the problem posed in chapter one: How to distinguish the three spheres -citizenship,
regime, and state- and how to identify their intersections? More importantly, how
can we identify the degree to which democracy is present in each sphere? Satisfactory answers to these questions require future research. However, based on
the research we have undertaken, some observations merit further development.
In my view, the key lies in the two central elements that are components of democracy: the principle of *equality* of all members of the demos and *majority* decision making imprinted in the underpinnings of institutions (Beetham, 1999, p. 153
and *passim*), as well as in the nature and functioning of each of them in accordance with those principles. Presence permits degrees and does not always have
the same intensity. Hence the essential differences. The citizen sphere reflects
them in the political culture, in the density of the active organization of interests
and in its capacity to mobilize power resources. The political regime determines
them in the procedures of access to and negotiation of conflict, from political parties and the media to electoral and non-electoral competition for state decision-
making power. The state depicts them in organic protection, in the construction
of rules and metarules and in the feedback between the two.

---

92 Equality of opinion in the formation of the will, deliberation in the public sphere, accountability and party maturity.

The nature of the rules operating in each type is different. Following Weber, Reinhard Bendix offered a basis for validating the threefold distinction:

> The shared conception of a legitimate order and the persons in formal organizations who help to maintain that order through the exercise of authority constitute a network of social relations which differs qualitatively from the social relationships arising out of a 'coalescence of interests'. In this way *actions may arise from the 'legitimate order' and affect the pursuit of interests in the society*, just as the latter have multiple effects upon the exercise of authority (Bendix, 1977, p. 20 Emphasis added).

The actions that arise from that legitimate order have a defined rationality that is considered typical, to use Weber's expression. Like having a monopoly of legitimate violence, the bureaucratic organization and the legal system operate for the benefit of the group that is governed in that order (O'Donnell, 2010, p. 54). The fact that it benefits the whole does not mean that it is equitable. This depends on the type of order accepted as legitimate.[93] Within the group, a network of links is established, tied together by the meaning produced by the combination of these subsystems: (legitimate) violence, bureaucracy, and law. Each state is a variant of the general type that explains them, and its inner workings acquire an identity distinct from others. Authority is exercised by individuals who are legitimized in that order in the sense of "the probability that action will in fact conform to it, often to a very considerable degree" to adapt to an order "upheld on a purely customary basis through the fact that the corresponding behavior has become habitual" (Weber, 2013, p. 31).

The "state capabilities" displayed by the most advanced democracies are the result of concrete histories of legitimate order building and are part of it, as are the low state capabilities of less developed democracies (Mazzuca and Munck, 2020).[94] The state capabilities characteristic of "good governance" (Rosanvallon, 2018, pp. 261–268) are developments and institutional arrangements achieved by civil society through the political regime -and by other purely civil or civilizational means- that are embodied in a state that protects them through those capabilities that political elites cannot fail to exercise without creating conflict and breaching the legitimate order. Conversely, when these capacities are low, as is the case in most of the Latin American countries we have examined, this is because there is social acceptance of this state of affairs as a legitimate order, even when it is sub-

---

93 I understand "benefit" in the sense that payoffs are positive for all actors with the power to disrupt. Groups for whom this order is unsatisfactory only matter if they can compete for its transformation.

94 And it is possible to identify some developed democracies with low state capacities (the health system in the USA) and vice versa (regulatory power in some Latin American countries).

ject to considerable questioning. The shift towards transformation is intricate and complex. As Weber points out "the transitions between orientation to an order from motives of tradition or expediency to the case where a belief in its legitimacy is involved are empirically gradual." (Weber, 2013, pp. 31). Although Weber's observation refers to the transition between large historical periods in the functioning of the state, this transition can be observed in the micropolitical processes (micro in comparison to long periods) of democratic transitions.

Political instability and the high levels of "deliberation" found in various indicator systems (WGI and V-DEM, supra, Ch. 2–4) show that when democratic conditions are in place, there is a growing tendency toward nonconformity with the *status quo*. Under conditions of more or less equitable political competition, there has been an increase in the alternation of power between parties and a greater political mobilization and growth of the representative demand to obtain states -in the double sense of state and situation- capable of satisfying egalitarian demands through greater access to political power in order to obtain greater welfare. Under democratic conditions the Latin American order is accepted or challenged by its citizens whose "coalitions of interest" may or may not, respectively, advance that arrangement. During its longest democratic period, Latin America has predominantly legitimized political systems that shelter citizens claiming rights, political regimes in which the processing of those demands leads to the inscription of bills of rights that make generous concessions, but without drastically modifying the verticality of power that rations out and, at the end of the day, prevents the full realization of those rights due to the way in which the exercise of power is organized. This situation requires a change in the democratic development agenda, from emphasizing mainly electoral dimensions to focusing on reforming the exercise of state power (Rosanvallon, 2018, pp. 1–19).

Similarly, Roberto Gargarella notes the double contradictory movement that occurs in Latin American constitutionalism at the end of dictatorships and authoritarianisms. "In general terms, the new constitutions strengthened the social commitments of the former ones. At the same time, they left the traditional vertical organization of power almost untouched" (Gargarella, 2013, p. 158). On the one hand, reforms are carried out to empower actors who implement government policies (carried out by the executive branch) inspired by market fundamentalism, and on the other hand, reforms are carried out for social and political rights that help alleviate the effects of economic crises and the ravages of the suppression of political freedoms and human rights violations. Less state, more market; more social and political rights, but also more personal power to the presidential institution and its environment, which are the origin and destination of the tradition of patrimonial exercise of political power. The conflation of presidential strengthening and neoliberal reforms, on the one hand, and the expansion of political and social rights, on the other, is natural and it is only a matter of time before it turns into protest and political radicalization. After market reforms, the reinstatement of civil and political rights, as well as the introduction of human rights -including strong state commitments and pressure from the international community- Latin American countries have established a new political arena with rules of the game that differ from those in the past. Citizens have recovered or obtained rights they could not enjoy and have expanded them; political systems have been populated by parties and movements that promote inclusion in a landscape of widespread exclusion, and distributive demands are put before power more frankly and freely than in the past, placing the vertical structure of the exercise of power under tension. Electoral access is extended, new generations enter the political class, and there is a succession of alternating parties in government. In short, there is a tangible democratization of broad areas of public life that leads to greater demands for inclusion directed at governments dominated by a powerful central power figure that is subject to the dual demands of neoliberal reforms and democratic expansion. The horizontal expansion of citizen power is confronted with the constraints imposed by elite power. Although this tension is manifested in diverse, multifaceted, and even idiosyncratic ways, it has, in any event, the same root cause.

Now, in theory, representative democracy must be capable of capturing the "surplus of politics" that emerges from public opinion in order to convert it into some form of will that is positively implanted within the political community, i.e., in the state. Ideally, it is the liberal rule of law and its extension as a social state that is the tool that allows justice to reach all corners of society. The better and more widespread it is, the greater the opportunities for individuals and groups to protect their rights and enforce them in practice. Kapiszewski et al. (2021) concluded that, of the three types of inclusion of previously excluded groups through legal reforms and public policies, in Latin American democracies resources come first, recognition second, and access far behind them. Although the proportions vary from country to country, the net result gives rise to this sequence. See graphs in Kapiszewski et al. (2021, pp. 11 and 52–55).

This order is not accidental, but reflects the hierarchy of forms of inclusion under the constraints of the environment. As the authors of this volume make clear, resource distribution through direct transfers is the most common tool used by governments to alleviate poverty. This is followed by the "recognition" of marginalized groups (indigenous peoples, women, sexual or ethnic minorities), and finally comes access. "Access" is defined as "the creation of new institutional channels to influence political decision-making or policy making" (p. 5) and is the scarcest of the three. There is no appropriation of public power because there is a low capacity to legitimize the presence of excluded groups in the *exercise of power*. If political modernity emerges from the juridical equality of individual property, in Latin America it comes about as a concession, not as a legitimate appropriation of the fruit of one's own effort. Locke's influence did not displace that of Hobbes. And this is not a mere figure of speech. The Iberian influence in the colonial and postcolonial world in Latin America was premised on the property rights of the Crown and the delegative nature that it possessed to grant rights to individuals or corporations. As such, patrimonialism has a solid predecessor that also extended to individual rights as granted rights and not as natural rights. It seems that the cultural influence of this original imprint translates into a mentality (a "rationality" or a *sense*) regarding the political as foreign and external. A "delegated" activity to use O'Donnell's expression. The effect on the construction of citizenship is pernicious: to be fully authorized, rights have to be granted by an authority that creates them and can withdraw them. What lies beneath this marked tendency towards "delegative democracies"?

In answering this question in a contemporary sense, we can start from one observation: citizens have not succeeded in molding the political community to direct coercion against the use of public and government goods for private benefit in such a way that the public interest is guaranteed. Rather they accept "empty" spaces, black holes in which the legitimate order sanctions this private benefit and extends considerable permissiveness to individuals to carry out the same practice within certain margins whose thresholds are diffuse and constitute a fringe of arbitrariness.[95] This black hole neutralizes the capacities of procedural formality which, in an order of legitimacy centered on equity, would be the repertoire of action to satisfy interests within the predominance of the common interest and, at the end of the day, to build a "legitimate order" that has it as a fundamental value and norm of compliance. This "failure" forces actors to strategically calculate with respect to legal and social norms, inasmuch as their natural application is not that of a rule of law in which reciprocity is fully contained in the legal norm and its enforcement apparatus. Hence, this calculation gives rise to the *constitutional conflict* in which the actors move within that diffuse space in which at least two systems of legitimization coexist: that of rights and the law, on the one hand, and that of arbitrary shortcuts that require the violation or disregard of the law to satisfy particular ends that become part of the universe of what is illegal, but permissible by "necessity" or custom. The spurious interpenetration of legitimate order and coalitions of interest (Bendix, 1977, p. 20 and *passim*) becomes a component of legitimacy itself which, however, begins to lose validity in situations where the value of democracy as a procedure for social empowerment has already been experienced. The concept of

---

95 These fringes are added to the "grey zones" that so disturbed Guillermo O'Donnell (2010, pp. 93–113).

"corruption" is insufficient to explain this logic of individual and collective action. *Law* and *rights* do not run parallel. The recognition of rights is present in the law, but often forms of privilege protection that do not correspond to the formal legitimate order but have some level of social acceptance are also interwoven. Tolerance of corrupt politicians is sometimes one of the shields that protect these privileges. This characteristic of the legitimate order (formal and informal) has been increasingly questioned in the democratizing process and it is possible that the questioning represents a collective movement towards the greater validity of the rule of law and the social state. But this same optimistic view of this widespread demand reveals a tension between social and political agency and the prevailing juridical-political structure.

6.3 Strategy and conflict

Latin America has been a field of constitutional experimentation throughout the democratization period. According to the Timeline of Constitutions of the Comparative Constitutional Project,[96] between 1980 and 2022, 21 new constitutions have been ratified and almost all of them, old or new, have been reformed in substantive aspects to include rights, new forms of regime, and changes in state power. These processes have activated all politically relevant actors to influence the remodeling of the three spheres. The process has had intense conflict in order to modify, to encourage or prevent inclusion in the constitutional text of certain norms disputed among politically relevant actors.[97]

Constitutional conflict is a strategic disposition of the actors with respect to the norms that define the components of the fundamental pact defined in the political constitution of a state. If we accept that this pact constitutes a stable arrangement under certain conditions, more or less recurrent conflict within it implies a crisis in the stability of the arrangement, given the irruption of forces that claim legitimacy to alter the rules and terms of the constitutional pact itself. When events of this type occur, a crisis of equilibrium exists in which the active forces seek conditions and strategies to create a new equilibrium.[98] If the conflict implies an instability of the arrangement, it is because there are significant agents who, when reflecting on how they belong or are ascribed to the social or political

---

96 https://comparativeconstitutionsproject.org/chronology/.
97 A detailed description of the internal tensions and contradictions of this process can be found in Roberto Gargarella (2013, pp. 148–195).
98 This is a reworked version of the original definition of constitutional conflict found in Valdés-Ugalde and Ansolabehere (2012).

group under that arrangement, have reservations about accepting it in whole or in part. This should not be surprising; we start out based on the idea that there is no constitutionality without conflict, but qualified with another: the nature of the conflict varies according to the circumstances. This is a manifestation of the "surplus of politics" to which we have already referred (*supra* chap. 1 and 2) and which signals a need to adjust the mechanisms of representation and the contents of the fundamental pact.[99]

A stable and even long-lasting arrangement may allow a reasonable level of conflict in which disputes about the fairness of the constitutionality of laws and their application would take place. We could call this the zero degree of constitutionality. But at the opposite extreme, we could acknowledge cases of national states that have failed once or several times in establishing a fundamental rule that allows their ways of processing conflict to be governable and produce a *governance* characterized by political integration (Valdés-Ugalde, 2008). Hence, it is possible to think of a scale of conflict in constitutional arrangements based on the measurement of the factors involved in their determination. Three of them are particularly relevant: The first is the definition of the rights and powers that derive from the norms. the second is the ownership of the rights, and the third is the procedures followed to realize the rights. The specification of rights includes defining them with conceptual relevance, disseminating them in the public sphere, defining them through deliberation, debate, and even confrontation between different conceptions, from those that deny their validity or viability to those that maintain the opposite. The definition is linked to the ways they are "inscribed" in the legal text and in the prevailing mentalities. The ownership of rights is related to the specification of who and under what circumstances they are subjects of rights. Finally, we ought to define how they exercise or fulfill them, that is, what procedures produce effective rights and how they are enforced when they are violated or unfulfilled. In the framework of a constitution (dogmatic part and organic part according to the typical legal classification), its articles correspond to a codification of values, the decisions that the law protects (rights) in its holders, and the form and procedures through which they are put into practice, as well as the forms of coercion that correspond to their non-compliance.

Constitutions matter because they contain both rules for the distribution of public and private goods, and for making other rules that regulate the distribution of public goods. In other words, they are rules and metarules that define the

---

99 Of course, the surplus of politics does not refer only to the constitution or constitutional aspects. It may refer to laws or provisions that require change. What unifies their meaning is that in all cases they imply changes or innovations that representative democracy needs to process in order to become updated and respond to new situations.

allocation of resources, both material and power, and therefore affect the procedures for collective decision-making (Valdés-Ugalde, 2010, pp. 19–48). Norms understood as institutions almost never form a coherent, logical and frictionless
framework. On the contrary, insofar as the legislative process and the needs, demands, and pressures to which the framework is subject, they are dynamic over
time and susceptible to deliberation and controversy. Thus, its nature as the ultimate reference of political legitimacy admits conflict.

There are two main types of constitutional conflict: one related to constitutional change and the other linked to constitutional interpretation.[100] The first is
exogenous, the second endogenous with respect to the text of the constitution and
the institutions surrounding it forming a "constitutionality". Some constitutions define procedures to process conflicts concerning the change of one constitution for
another and other mechanisms to modify their content. In the first case, we are
dealing with a metarule that the most advanced democratic constitutions provide
for the moments when an entire constitution can be replaced by a new one. In
the second, we are confronted with procedures for amending the constitution itself.
When individuals or groups within a community, usually domestic, perceive that
they are "entitled to . . ." certain goods[101] of hierarchically superior importance,
and which therefore have the greatest significance for life in society, they seek to
include them in the state constitution. This is the history of the modern state, i.e.,
without conflict there is no politics, without politics there is no equilibrium, and
without the need to establish an equilibrium there is no constitution. The expres-
sions of conflicting balances are embodied in the constitution.

The essential rationale of the increase in constitutional conflict lies in that
the growing strategic disposition with respect to constitutional norms is due to
the fact that the opportunity cost of acquiescing to such norms decreases in comparison to the cost of defying them. Voigt (1999, pp. 107–111) refers to this problem
as a constitutional political *economy* inspired by North (1981), but focuses on the
problem of *bargaining*. However, bargaining implies, first, detecting a *conflict* of
interest. That is why here I call it constitutional conflict, more along the lines of a
constitutional *political* economy, although in essence there is no variation. Voigt
says, "Constitutional change [implies] a (re-) distribution of the net benefits of
order [that] can be explained by conceptualizing it as the outcome of bargaining
processes [. . .] bargaining will be attempted if an opposition believes its own relevance to have increased" (Voigt, 1999, pp. 111).

---

100 This includes judicial review and public deliberation -which are necessarily linked.
101 By goods we mean here the "bundle" that a society considers necessary to include in a set of
constitutional "rights", whether or not they are "fundamental", according to different classifications.

It follows from the above that opportunity cost is not limited exclusively to the conflict over economic distribution interests, but also extends to the distribution of other related aspects whose *political economy is* not reduced to the relationship between the taxes extracted by the ruler and the relative benefits received by the governed through the use of public goods provided with those taxes. Rights are more extensive and include those collective goods of varied scope. Some constitutions contain more rights than others and conceive rights differently, and some fulfill them satisfactorily and others do not. An example of this is the way constitutions incorporate human rights. In each one, the rank conferred on them varies according to the hierarchy between compliance with human rights and other constitutional provisions, as well as acceptance of the jurisdiction of international commissions and courts in each country through which human rights are ultimately governed. Another recent example is that of cultural and ethnic rights. In most of Latin America, indigenous peoples' rights had been left out of constitutional arrangements. The liberal principle of equality did not consider them relevant for inclusion in most constitutions. In the last two decades, various struggles and movements have brought to light an opposition to this omission that is considered significant and perceives that it is less costly to unleash a conflict to include them in constitutional arrangements than to maintain the status quo.

From the internal point of view, constitutional conflict is associated with the clarity and consistency with which rights are specified, the personality of their legitimate holders, and the relevance of the procedures for enforcing them within a constitutional domain (i.e. a state). This conflict involves the constitutional text itself, the implicit constitutional factors (such as customs or tacit agreements), the rights holders or those deprived of rights, and the institutions (and the persons in charge) created to enforce them. A vast territory lies before us, which has been explored from different perspectives. One of them, judicial review, has provided important tools to determine whether legislative, executive, or administrative acts comply with the constitution.

Given that they are the highest level of authority, constitutional courts or tribunals perform the role of interpreting whether laws or acts of authority derived from them are consistent with superior norms. Moreover, in some cases they have the power to indicate whether certain changes to the constitution are constitutional or not, either *ex officio* or to resolve conflicts of interpretation. The meta-regulatory function of the constitution has in the courts of constitutionality an agent that establishes the limits to which conflicts over the constitutionality of the law, controversies, or constitutional provisions can reach.

Yet, the executive and legislative branches can also reach constitutional limits and become spaces of conflict creation or processing. For example, when a constitutional principle contradicts others. Often a fundamental right, for example due process, is violated in exceptions established by the constitution itself. Two examples come to mind. The Mexican Constitution establishes due process in Article 16, but Article 33 establishes an exception: the power of the Executive "to make any foreigner whose stay it deems inconvenient leave the national territory, immediately and without the need for prior trial."[102]

There is another source of conflict in the constitutional powers of the Legislative Branch in systems that allow the congress or national assembly to amend the constitution. In this case, when a legislature, under the conditions specified in the constitution, undertakes a reform or amendment therein, it may incorporate new provisions that are controversial because of their potential contradiction with other provisions. This conflict is between meta-rules and constitutional rules. The legislative branch is designed to formulate the laws that govern behaviors and relationships in society, but not always to change the rules established in the supreme norms. The methods devised to draft new constitutions or to reform current ones invariably lead to the question of who and under what conditions is legally empowered to do so. Legislating ordinary social behavior (civil, criminal, administrative, family law, etc.) is not the same as legislating who and how can legislate on how the power of that first legislation is organized, i.e. the metarules.

Several recent examples shed light on the problem. During the 1990s in Colombia and Venezuela, a political crisis of trustworthiness in political parties had been brewing, leading to instability and profound disagreements on the relevance of sustaining the respective states in force. In short, these were constitutional crises that led to the formation of new constitutions and new states, respectively. The Colombian process led to a renewal of representative democracy, while the Venezuelan process led to its destruction. In Colombia, there was a general recognition of the need for a new agreement with a broad consensus in favor of a con-

---

[102] In recent years this constitutional provision has been challenged for contravening human rights treaties and conventions to which the country is signatory, but has not been modified despite demands to do so. Another conflict involves the status of international treaties signed by Mexico vis-à-vis the Constitution. Article 133 states that "this Constitution, the laws that emanate from the national Congress and all Treaties that are in agreement with it, agreed to and entered into by the President of the Republic, with the approval of the Senate, shall be the Supreme Law of the entire Union." However, in the nineties particularly, a conflict of interpretation arose and a ruling of the Supreme Court of Justice (1475/98) concluded that "international treaties are at a second level immediately below the fundamental law and above federal and local law." More recently, the Court ruled that should there be a contradiction between human rights in force in Mexico (which includes almost all rights), the judicial authority must apply the *pro persona* principle and therefore the legal provision that most favors the subject to be protected. This is a semantic conflict, but also a political one. If we accept that human rights are part of the Constitution, then this conflict is endogenous to the Constitution.

stituent process without radical rupture among the fundamental players. In Venezuela, however, during the first presidency of Hugo Chávez (1999–2001), the national congress was relegated since the new constitution was approved by the constituent assembly of 1999. Like the Colombian constitution, the constitution then in force in Venezuela did not have sufficiently explicit provisions for changing the constitution. In both countries (Colombia in 1990 and Venezuela in 1998) the Supreme Court of the Nation was called upon to render an opinion. On the basis of these opinions (clear and specific from the Colombian Court; ambiguous and timid from the Venezuelan Court) constituent processes were carried out. The fundamental difference between the two was that the new Colombian constitution was drafted by consensus within the previously constituted state organs, in order to create a renewed representative democracy. In contrast, Venezuela broke with the previously elected congress and disrupted the previous order in order to introduce "direct democracy" instead of a representative one. While Colombia's new constitution was based on improving the procedures that define the organs of the state and the balances between them, in Venezuela it sought to replace representative democracy with one that would establish "socialism of the 21st century" by explicitly detaching itself from "bourgeois representative democracy", as it was described by Chavism (Negretto, 2013; Brewer-Carías, 2010, 2011).

One of the differences between the two processes is that while in Colombia the emphasis on the procedural nature of democracy led the judicial organs to expand the enforcement of human rights, in Venezuela a large number of human rights were introduced into the constitution, but at the same time power was concentrated in the executive, which coopted the judiciary while attacking and crushing the political opposition. Venezuela was one of the first recent cases -and perhaps the one that most alarmed democrats around the world- in which the argument was made that the people, the sovereign, can be placed above an existing constitution without building a broad political consensus beforehand. It is obvious that the sovereign can make this decision, what is not so obvious is that such decision is democratic. In the case of Chavism, the "people" are nothing more than the will of the charismatic president with wide recognition who places himself above the law. The standing ruler, elected under the rules of a constitution, decides to dictate a new constitution through his followers gathered in a constituent assembly. This non-democratic formula for establishing constitutions is of long standing in Latin America and was not inaugurated in Venezuela, but the Chavist experiment has been the most prominent and influential in the continent to legitimize constituent processes by non-democratic and anti-constitutional means at a time when democracy was predominating in Latin America. In Ecuador (2007), Honduras (2009) -which aborted- and Bolivia (2017), reform to allow the indefinite reelection of the president was repeated in different ways. This differed from Chile, where naming delegates to the Constituent Assembly was carried out respecting the Constitution, after broad national debate and agreements among political actors. In fact, the Chilean constituent project will have to be repeated because it was rejected in the 2022 referendum. What these populist experiments have in common is the rift with the legislative branch and/or the constitutional courts by convening constituent assemblies by means of a crude interpretation of the majority sovereign law (Brewer-Carías, 2010, pp. 7–68). The difference with the Colombian and Chilean situations is that representative democracy, despite its current limitations, is preferred by all the key players for bringing about constitutional change.

Finally, it is worth noting a dimension of constitutional conflict related to long historical periods. The selective process of constitutions over time has been referred to in the literature as "constitutional competition" (Voigt, 1999, pp. 181–207). Constitutions are "systems of rules specifying the allocation of resources used for the provision of public goods". The selective mechanism of constitutional competition is that "the process of constitutional competition would function in analogy to the process of institutional competition", i.e., "if a society's constitution is a relevant variable in determining its per capita income and an increase in per capita income is generally striven for, then one should expect the competitive process to weed out those collective choice mechanisms that prevent the adoption of welfare-enhancing institutions" (Voigt, 1999, pp. 191–192). Here, in the same sense as before, we must understand "per capita income" in a broad sense, as a basket of preferences that, from the exogenous and endogenous constitutional perspective, is expressed in rights and in political pressure for the legal order to be updated and to correspond to those preferences. In Latin America, by democratic or authoritarian means, this process of constitutional change is taking place precisely when greater freedoms and openness to the world have become a reality throughout the region.

Thus, not every constitutional order is democratic and not every way of changing the constitution is democratic, but given this trend of change towards the reformulation of the state as a generator of public goods,[103] we ought to consider how we can have constitutions that democratically regulate their own forms of change. In other words, how can we establish rules for access to and exit from power through fair and transparent elections that protect citizens' secret vote; that have a division of powers, checks and balances, systems of accountability, and rules for exercising power that allow it to be challenged in the interest of the public good through democratic mechanisms. It is evident that changes in key

---

103 Whether certain tasks are provided for by the state to be carried out by the government or by other agents, such as privatized public services, all imply responsibilities that must be publicly accounted for.

actors' preferences imply changes in the social composition of the community of these actors and their predominant preferences with respect to what the state should protect, which here would be an opening to institutional and constitutional change in accordance with shifts in the needs for public goods. The problem of constitutional change in a democratic state can be linked to the political regime by defining how, by whom and under what conditions, the sovereign right to "fundamental decision" can be exercised. We can see that it is a matter of establishing and guaranteeing how procedures for change work in accordance with values and norms. Thus, once democracy has been established as a regime within the constitution -something that most Latin American countries have achieved- the problem of the legitimacy of its global mutations and partial internal or external changes remains. In the rationale of constitutional conflict, a common feature can be distinguished: It grows in intensity and scope as the political regime processes conflicts unsatisfactorily because the operating rules that structure it (included in the constitutionality of the State) suffer from low representativeness due to deficiencies in the authorization, promotion, or impediment of the agreements resulting from the processing of the conflict to be translated into statehood. This problem is as old as political thought. How can it be addressed in a democratic way?

6.4 Rules to govern the making of rules

Jean Hampton (1994, pp. 13–44)[104] formulated an alternative to this problem by analyzing and trying to overcome Hobbes's "regressive argument"[105] based on the great legal theorist L.A.H. Hart (1998) and Alfred Tarski's logical method.[106] Without going into the philosophical analysis in detail, which can be reviewed in her work (Hampton, 1986, 1994, 1998), in solving the seemingly infinite problem of the regressive argument, Hampton distinguishes three types of rules that govern three different levels of the constitutional political order: 1) the primary rules

---

104 Hampton, an extraordinary contractual political philosopher, died two years after the publication of this short text. After her early death in 1996, "Political Philosophy" (1998) appeared, a text in which she continues to develop her main argument (Chapter 3 Consent and Democracy, pp. 70–120).

105 The argument that defines how authority needs a legitimization from another higher authority and so on (Cfr. Hampton, 1986). The need for a higher authority to legitimize the authority of a lower one led inexorably to a choice between monarchy (the ultimate instance of authority vested by God) or democracy which designates the sovereign as the ultimate source of authorization.

106 Cfr. Tarski (1983, pp. 152–278).

that emanate from a body that has been authorized to formulate them and, thus, are obligatory; 2) Secondary rules that determine who makes up that body authorized to make laws or act on its behalf and that describe how the primary rules that body issues are to be formulated; and 3) Third-order or tertiary rules that stipulate who, under what circumstances, and by what procedures can modify the system of secondary rules, i.e., the structure of the political regime itself *from the highest level of state authority*.[107] Hampton refers to these three layers of political legality considering that the first, the primary rules, are an "object language" that refers to the concrete actions of the governed and the rulers in their ordinary affairs. The legitimacy of these rules, however, is not spontaneous but is obtained thanks to the presence of the second level of rules or "secondary rules" that "identify what is count as the law in the object *political regime* [. . .] these rules operate by defining offices that perform legislative, executive, and judicial functions, offices that, taken together, generate the primary laws in this society". To this layer of secondary rules, related to the functioning of the regime, a third type is added that I call the rules of constitution of the state (from where the regime is created) that establish.

> How it is that people control and/or change the operation of the political regime [. . .] in two ways. First [. . .] how the people install or replace those who hold the offices defined by the structural type of rule just discussed, through either direct or indirect voting procedures. Second, these rules set out the procedures for changing the rules that define these offices and the procedures for filling them (Hampton, 1994, pp. 35–36. Emphasis added).

The democratic state is founded on this tertiary normativity (but not exclusively) that determines who the constitution authorizes to change the political regime and how it should be done. What distinguishes democratic states from non-democratic ones "is that the way one engages in third-tier activities is now governed by rules" (Hampton, 1994, pp. 36). The depth and extension of the representative nature of democracy could reach this level. Thus, the old concept of popular sovereignty can be constitutionally updated to solve the old dilemma of how difficult constitutional change is due to the absence of clear and sufficient rules that authorize people to

---

107 It is true that this activity takes place within the political regime itself, but in doing so it is resorting to the meta-rules specified (or to be specified) in order to bring about a new structure, a new way of being, as we exemplified with the cases of Venezuela and Colombia. At this level, the regime acts as a political community in which the sovereign has the last word. Carl Schmitt defined the sovereign as the power to establish a state of exception, a radical change for the authority of last instance, but he does not distinguish between the legitimacy of an exception produced by means of a violent disruption, such as a coup d'état or the tyranny of the majority, and the democratic decision to change one constitution for another. If the latter is what is sought, the problem to be solved is ultimately how to transform the legitimate order *democratically*.

carry it out, especially when changes do not involve minor revisions, but rather seek to change political regimes. In specialized discussions on this matter, it is common to find how difficult it is to effectuate changes in constitutions. Constitutions are proverbially characterized as "rules of unanimity" or quasi-unanimity (Buchanan and Tullock, 1965), insofar as they require qualified majorities for their approval or change that act *as if* their decision were unanimous. In this sense, constitutions specify agreements established at a moment in time but are projected beyond the lifetime of their creators who enact them to last indefinitely, as long as "nothing else happens". If we assume that whoever the political actors are, rulers or ruled, the institutionalization of rules beyond their lifetimes seeks to maintain a lasting intergenerational link; the question is how to give that link a democratic character. Although it may seem paradoxical, the only way to do so is by including in the constitution a well-defined procedure to amend or replace it. Otherwise we would have -as we do indeed have- constitutional rules that cannot be changed and that base this limitation on disallowing the inevitable strategic actions to modify them.[108]

Yet this claim to longevity contrasts with the actual duration of constitutions. The vast majority of modern constitutions (1789–1993) have lasted only between one and two decades (Lane, 1996:198), with few exceptions such as the United States. Constitutional changes have accelerated with the global expansion of democratization.[109] Leaving aside the statistical problems concerning the characteristics and correlations between constitutions and political regimes (Lane, 1996, pp. 197–212), the crucial issue is that if the validity of a constitution is implicitly diluted or explicitly disputed, or the legitimacy of the institutions that bring it to life, or the relationship established between these institutions and the political and social agents, i.e., the ultimate holders of the rights and procedures established therein, conflict ensues, which consists precisely of a *strategic disposition* that challenges the validity of its norms. For this reason, the connection between the written text and its enforcement, the political culture, and the institutions in which it materializes in daily life is a crucial aspect for its stability. When this connection does not exist or is quite deficient (as in most Latin American constitutions), the codification of procedures and actors empowered to participate in its change becomes an issue that can make the difference between political violence and the peaceful processing of the conflict. Considering the previously discussed distance between representatives and represented and the crisis of representative democracy which seems to trigger protest by sectors marginalized from access to power, then the

---

108 So we can say that there are rigid constitutions and flexible constitutions, according to the degree of difficulty involved in modifying them.

109 For a comprehensive and up-to-date discussion of constitutional change, Negretto and Sanchez-Talanquer (2021) and Dixon and Ginsburg (2017) are helpful.

state as a political community has not accepted representative democracy in its entirety, just as the 19th century political community also ignored this aspect when it was introduced into Latin American constitutions, leading to a different development path from that of the sources from which it came.

The conceptual problem of sovereignty goes back to the theories that defined the constitution of the state as an act of the will and not as a procedural order. True, for all practical purposes, the presence of political wills is indispensable. However, the procedures through which a democratic state is built, that is, a rule of recognition (tertiary according to Hampton) of a body authorized to establish meta-rules that constitute the institutions for the creation of object or primary rules to regulate ordinary behaviors that are binding on all members of society.

Representative democracy in Latin America suffers from a recurrent symptom that is embodied in its constitutional history and its recent incursions towards populism. The cyclical dissatisfaction with institutions and political elites has led to the need for democratic constitutional change, but in most cases no satisfactory formula has been adopted. On one hand, most countries have adopted the creed of constitutional democracy, but on the other, they have faced problems regarding the democratic procedures for implementing state reforms. The recently cited experiences and that of Mexico in recent years (2018–2023) have highlighted the insufficiency of resorting to the principle of simple majority sovereignty as a legitimizing principle of a new political order. I therefore return to Hampton's argument which is, in my opinion, one of the most lucid solutions to the problem of democratic constitutional change, which is none other than that of accommodating and providing an outlet for the "surplus of politics" that wants to exceed the status quo and, at the same time, advance representative democracy instead of trashing it. This solution is none other than the unequivocal definition of the exercise of sovereign rights to constitutional change through democratic procedures. To a greater or a lesser extent, Latin American countries lack this system of rules of recognition that has not been obtained either through historical experience or by express decision.

6.5 An ideological detour

If the advent of democracy was coeval with the introduction of neoliberalism, the latter contains many of the limitations of the former. Let us examine this aspect carefully in order to understand the above statement. First, the introduction does not involve neoclassical economic policy applied by a government derived from a democratic decision. Nor is it classical Smithian liberalism. It is a neoliberalism transformed into market fundamentalism as the organizing principle of society and imposed by force of arms in its first and most famous experiment: Chile starting in 1973. The application of market reforms in Latin America went hand in hand with a foundational event, the military dictatorship, which had repercussions throughout the region. The Chilean junta implemented a policy that was presumed worldwide to be a successful experiment under laboratory conditions. A society forcibly subjected to the dictates of a single rationality, the dictator's, who surrounded himself with followers of Milton Friedman and imposed a market-centered economic policy.[110] The main consequence of the dictatorship is the repression of politics. "In this conception, the market ceases to be just a form of organization of the economy and becomes the basic principle of social regulation" (Pinto and Flisfisch, 2011, p. 42), which is equivalent to the imposition of a way of life. In addition to the conditions of exclusion we described in Chapter 2, the "suppression" of politics was added. The phenomenon did not occur only under military dictatorships, but spread widely as a cultural phenomenon, as a generalized mood in which talking about the state or the importance of politics became anathema. The demonization of politics and the state even extended to public policies: it was frowned upon to speak of industrialization, redistribution of wealth or economic intervention by the state, topics, among others, that were banned from public debate. An economic doctrine appropriated the monopoly of public reason and established its boundaries. Political legitimacy was culturally restricted to the confines of the market (whatever that means); political freedom, which was in the process of being structured in the democratic transitions, came under strong pressure to avoid questioning the legitimacy of this order with universal pretensions. In the ideological horizon of market fundamentalism, democracy would cease to be a risk to its essential principles as long as forces and currents of different socioeconomic thought, capable of competing politically on the same level and with the same rights in forming public opinion, were excluded. Democratization was also a long process of struggle and debate, which only 30 years later managed to assert itself in the public arena. To understand this better, we must take a short detour.

The violent irruption of the military boot on the government of Salvador Allende in Chile,[111] as well as the suppression of peaceful and violent dissidence in other democratic countries such as Argentina and Uruguay, meant that it became

---

110 *El Ladrillo (The Brick)* is the collection of texts that summarizes what inspired the "Chicago boys". It was completed shortly before the military coup and was a guide for Augusto Pinochet's government. It was not publicly known until 1992 when it was published by the Centro de Estudios Públicos (https://www.memoriachilena.gob.cl/602/w3-article-98021.html).

111 A government that made serious strategic mistakes by moving away from representative democracy that was then -and re-emerged 18 years later in its transition away from authoritarianism- the central value of Chilean political society.

impossible to unify under a single banner a social-democratic project -an ersatz name for a motley democratic left that never put together a solid and independent identity-, together with a revolutionary venture of a Castroist or Maoist nature. Such a nonstarter implied that parties and currents on the left had to begin a reorganization that continues to this day. Its two main currents are the democratic left that broke with Marxist-Leninist dogmatism and the radical left whose pretension is to overcome capitalism at all costs and for which democracy is an old, junky tool that can be instrumental to achieve that goal. The first current views political democracy as a substantive component, a value in itself that is inalienable in the process of progressive change; the latter current conceives it as an accessory, at least as long as it is not an exclusive correlate of the all-embracing "popular will", or at least some tropical placebo of the "dictatorship of the proletariat."

Despite the implementation of neoliberal policies, the social and political demands of subordinate and marginalized groups always remained on the political scene. Left-wing parties became closely representative of these demands despite pressure from the dominant pole of market fundamentalism to avoid this linkage. Luna and Zechmeister (2005) found solid evidence of three important factors in the quality of political representation of the popular sectors: 1) left-wing parties tend to have greater direct links with their grassroots; 2) in countries with a greater tradition of political competition and socioeconomic development – which implies experiences of redistribution – democratic representation tends to consolidate; and 3) politicians representing the poorest and most disorganized groups tend more to "cultivate a personal nonprogrammatic link with constituents, independent of the formal electoral rules" (Luna and Zechmeister, 2005, p. 413). It is no coincidence that it is precisely in countries where poor and disorganized groups are more numerous that the left has been more prone to drift into populist formulas. Venezuela, Nicaragua, Ecuador, Bolivia, Brazil, and Mexico -and the longstanding case of Argentina- are examples of using the fertile ground of a huge population as cannon fodder to develop a strong popular representation with political elites willing to transgress the formal rules of the democratic system and, along with them, the political rights of the citizenry. The fact that one or several political parties or leaders are more popular does not mean that democracy is more representative. The charismatic leaderships that often seduce the poor and marginalized and sometimes the authoritarian left are, as previously observed, deformations of representative democracy. To some extent, oligarchic or populist disfigurements of democracy (Urbinati 2014) do not depart entirely from democracy. "Populism in power is a transmutation of democratic principles, though not (yet) an exit from democracy" (Urbinati, 2019b, p. 118). However, Latin America has experienced the extremes of populisms and oligarchies that lead to dictatorships or, using V-Dem's classification, to closed autocracies.

Latin America's half century of democracy shows signs of fatigue and circularity that point to a risk for this system of government if it does not overcome the dilemmas it faces. In my opinion, the main challenge consists in legitimizing the authority of the citizenry to have access to the exercise of political power and to carry out policies oriented towards socioeconomic equality through the provision of the public goods that are indispensable to achieve it. These goods are contained in the legal canon of human rights, but their effective implementation comes after the establishment of democratic procedures to guide political power in a socially meaningful way without forgoing liberal democracy. A vision of a state that looks to the democratic future must acknowledge that the political agenda should give priority to the democratization of the state in a way that we have emphasized: equalizing access of social groups to decision-making power in order to institute habits of public deliberation that foment legitimized (and, therefore, obeyed) distributive changes by the relevant political and economic agents. Moreover, these changes can be made from the inside and the outside. Our analysis posits that the structure of inequality and the deficient democratic representation have their main origin within. Not in "dependency", "colonialism" or "imperialism", but in the internal structure which, in spite of everything, has shown to be susceptible to change. Democratization is proof that such endogenous change is possible and its main risk is de-democratization.

According to normative political theory, representative democracy does not necessarily result in good state performance, but it should favor it.[112] However, in the quality of representative democracy may lie one of the endogenous keys that make the difference in that relationship. Not just any opinion transformed into will necessarily makes for a better match with the way in which states conduct themselves with respect to their societies. The advent of electoral democracy as the fundamental floor of most political systems (except Cuba, Haiti, Nicaragua, and Venezuela) has not led to a general democratic consensus. If the regular holding of elections is accepted as part of the legitimate order, the acceptance of the legitimacy of rivals is not, and this is a major cause of instability and a failure of the constituent value of the "inclusion of the other" (Habermas, 1999). It is generally recognized that elections are the means to reach power and that exercising power means political pluralism must be respected, but time and again groups

---

[112] As I have already mentioned, better institutional performance is associated with greater access to political power by the "average citizen" (Colomer, 2001) and in systems where the removal of the executive is more accessible, as is the case of parliamentary systems (Gutman et al., 2022a).

and forces appear that to a greater or lesser extent propose violating this essential principle. The most notorious cases are those of Chávez in Venezuela, Uribe in Colombia, Fujimori in Peru, Bolsonaro in Brazil, Morales in Bolivia, Correa in Ecuador, López Obrador in Mexico, and Ortega in Nicaragua. Venezuela and Nicaragua closed the paths to alternation; Fujimori and Morales tried to take things to that extreme, but failed in the attempt; and AMLO seeks to do so by creating a scenario whose prognosis is uncertain. On the contrary, Chile, Uruguay, Costa Rica, Dominican Republic, Honduras, and Panama seem to have learned that democracy, if it is to work for a good government, is a guarantee that no political force has an assured majority, thus driving a continuous conversation beyond elections. This is a key problem. When relevant actors question the legitimacy of other actors who compete for power or participate in it, the former provoke situations in which common ground established by the rule of recognition ceases to be common, becomes fictitious, and is replaced by intolerance. When it comes to political confrontation, destruction of the adversary, if possible, is the guideline followed by actors in countries that are most polarized. This is the story in Peru with the continuous and abrupt removals of its presidents; in Brazil the populist ultra-right and a radicalized sector of the left aspire to destroy their respective antipodes. Latin American democracy will not make a qualitative leap towards stability and the development of its power structures as long as "the inclusion of the other" is not voluntarily and fundamentally recognized within the constitutionality of its states.[113] The countries of the northern triangle of Central America (Guatemala, Honduras, and El Salvador) are typical examples of this illness. Unfortunately, the contagion has spread to many other countries (United States, France, Italy, Russia, Poland, Hungary, and Turkey, among others), creating a hostile environment for representative democracy and propitious for greater autocratization. This means that the regions that had advanced in democratization during the third wave are now heading toward authoritarian regression.

6.6 The new world (dis)order

The present moment has both difficulties and opportunities, and perhaps more of the latter than is usually imagined. At the end of the Cold War, Latin America emerged, at least temporarily, from the crossfire between two great rival power

---

113 Such inclusion implies the reduction of extremes, and the obligation of all actors to agree to the rules of the game that include the legitimacy of the presence of the other and that must be part of the rule of recognition.

blocs. The United States' gaze south of its border changed significantly once the specter of communism ceased to be the main threat to Western democracies; today the region has plunged into a "new solitude" (Lagos et al., 2022). The United States' global hegemony remained in place between the fall of the Soviet Union and the great crisis produced by the terrorist attacks on the Twin Towers in New York. After this act and others, mainly in Western Europe, China, and, to a lesser extent, Russia emerged as actors demanding a role in the global power game. Before Russia's invasion of Ukraine and the U.S.-China trade war, the main antagonisms had shifted to the periphery, but now they are finding their way back to center stage. The new global distribution of power is very different today than what existed when the Berlin Wall fell and the Soviet Union was dismantled. Latin America today has relations with each of the blocs in an environment of greater competition and freedom of decision to establish them. Moreover, the pressure to align themselves with the North Atlantic countries diminished and several countries increased their relations with Asia and Russia. The third wave of democratization developed in the final stage of the bipolar world characteristic of the Cold War. The displacement of the paradigms that underpinned it allowed democracy to have better internal and external conditions for institutionalization. With the unpredictable change in the global order -which remains global-[114] and the low strength of representative democracy, we are likely to see Latin America realigning with different trading partners and mimicking aspects of their political systems.[115] The result could be multiple isolations that would lead to confirming the image that Latin America cannot be a unity beyond entelechies and deliriums of 19th century origins.[116]

Jürgen Habermas has lucidly set out the central parameters of the new world order. Since the collapse of actually existing socialism, the main centers of power have failed to reach a consensus on three factors that strongly influence the reorganization of the global order. First, the "defeated party," i.e., Soviet communism and its surviving defenders have not acknowledged having dogmatically identified the socialist project as "the design -and violent implementation- of a concrete form of life." At the other pole, capitalism "lacks the energy to drive ahead with

---

114 I have discussed this in Valdés-Ugalde (2023), Chapters 4 and 5.

115 In political circles in various countries, polarization abounds regarding the possibilities of development and internal reform, aligning with an emerging second power (China), or strengthening ties with North America and Europe. The Russian invasion of Ukraine has further accentuated this polarization.

116 Carlos Granés has masterfully traced the influence of "delirium" in Latin American politics and shown the pernicious influence of unrealizable utopias and sterile radicalisms in our historical personality (Granés, 2022, pp. 337–517).

the task of imposing social and ecological restraints [on itself] at the breathtaking level of global society." (Habermas, 1998, p. xli) The conflict over the foundations on which the world order should rest is at an impasse, a stalemate that could be broken by drafting an updated vision of the 1948 human rights accords and its following treaties and covenants, but now with a recognition of democracy as the only possible regime to accommodate all "members of the demos." China intends to open the way for the export of its model of political economy, market socialism with political authoritarianism. It has vigorously expanded into Africa and in Asia it has begun its "long march" in the construction of a Silk Road 2.0. Europe - and Canada- are optimistic of economic development given the vigorous market that China offers. However, the United States has begun to relocate its production facilities in an effort to disengage from China in order to shorten production chains. This state of affairs offers valuable opportunities for Latin America. However, when we observe the political leadership landscape, both right and left, it is a mixture of confusion and ignorance of the fundamental challenges. China has increasingly influenced Latin America. It exerts increasing influence in various forums and appears ever more frequently in the economic landscape of Latin America. Although its investment levels are not yet competitive with those of Europe or the United States, its influence grows. At some point Latin American countries will have to decide how to position themselves in the face of China's growth and its authoritarian model of social and political development and the North Atlantic alliance to which they have belonged and which could be strengthened by their active presence.[117]

Given the evidence, we must be pessimistic for several reasons. First, leftist governments have not generated (except for Brazil in the first Lula government and Bolivia in the first stage of Evo Morales, and perhaps Chile and Colombia at present) a model of internal social reforms sustained over time, in order to appear before the world as a region capable of modifying three of its greatest vices: crony capitalism, extreme social inequalities, and the radical polarization of left and right. Regarding the Chinese option, apparently a passive attitude prevails that hopes that the influence of the Asian giant will help to bring order to their economies albeit through a dependent relationship. In the case of the Atlantic alliance, although this attitude may also be present, there is another way out, which paradoxically proposes a reinvention of the welfare state as the means to achieve broad social reform policies that will foment a dynamic economic model -oriented towards high technology and all its upstream and downstream links in industry and

---

117 This dilemma and the way in which each country resolves it will be all the more acute should the confrontation between the United States and China become militarily complicated.

agriculture- based on a type of representative democracy that establishes the human rights system as the foundation for public action. Expanding human rights could be the lever for the development of dynamic capitalism. As Ishay pointed out, the progressive way out of the current global (dis)order is to prioritize "the indivisibility and inalienability of security, political, social, economic, and cultural human rights objectives in all efforts" (Ishay, 2008, p. xii).[118] This perspective requires two main tasks: to move towards a truly applied rule of law and towards a consensus on the basic duties of the political community in order to focus on human dignity. In Latin America, the main obstacles are found simultaneously at the polar opposites of politics: a radical right that wants to preserve an order that is impossible to justify under conditions of political democracy, and a left, also radical, that seeks to "overcome capitalism" -and "colonialism"- at all costs by offering alternatives that can only be attractive in political ventures as authoritarian as those of its counterpart. As pundits from Latin America frequently point out, migrants do not choose the promised paradises of Venezuela, Cuba or Nicaragua, but rather move away as soon as possible, saturating the Mexico-U.S. border, Europe, or other Latin American countries by the thousands. There is sizable emigration from Venezuelan and Peruvian to Chile, Mexico, Brazil, and Argentina. Thus, crony capitalism, extreme social inequalities, and the radical polarization are hindrances to consolidating a path that offers development with social reform and representative democracy. In order to reverse the pessimism, internal will and projects would have to appear to make it possible to achieve a place of our own in the fragile world order that is being reshaped. However, this "will" cannot be justified merely by beginning to have a new international voice; that voice must be accompanied by the growing legitimacy of socioeconomic and political reforms centered on compliance with the legal and political regime of human rights. This is precisely what a reform of the state looks like, beyond the solipsism of political reforms situated exclusively within the political regime and which only change parties, electoral systems, and other peripheral institutions of the political state.

6.7 The need to think concretely

The journey we have made shows us that representative democracy in Latin America faces an ambiguous panorama, to say the least. On the one hand, substantial progress has been made in implementing democratic political systems and mainstreaming the conviction that stripping previously acquired rights is an explosive,

---

118 See also (Ch. 6. Pp. 215–355).

if not impossible, route. On the other hand, these democracies drag along throwbacks from past eras that can be summed up as endemic backwardness in implementing modern social institutions of equality, understood as the appropriate combination of impersonality given the rules of power and free access to opportunities derived from state-protected or produced goods. More recent evolution has brought three types of democratic systems: a) those that maintain a stable democracy with an appreciable improvement in social equality (Uruguay, Chile, Panama, Costa Rica, Dominican Republic); b) those that have democratic systems with serious problems of stability (Brazil, Guatemala, Colombia, Bolivia, Ecuador); and c) those that have drifted towards forms of political Caesarism (Nicaragua, Venezuela, El Salvador, and Mexico) and away from liberal democracy, arguing that the latter is not capable of solving the problems of the majority. We ponder whether the future of the most advanced representative democracy depends on the capacity and lucidness of the fundamental actors to confront obstacles that stand in the way of alternatives for building social states. Any route that should emerge in this direction will have no effect if it eschews adjustments that would bring fundamental changes to state institutions (Lijphardt, 1999; Colomer, 2001). The extension of democracy in most Latin American countries is an ideal scenario, favorable to the development of new options to create mixed (proportional) forms of regime and government and social negotiation. Such a scenario would give greater ductility to incorporating social diversity in the formation of policies and may consequently have a greater impact on progressive income distribution. The core of any democratic solution would involve reducing the inequality gap without suppressing freedoms; without reviving individual or party populisms that turn citizens into mere voters, or mere cannon fodder for adventurous hegemonies. This is the key to public responsibility of all social sectors and mostly government and social leaders.

The most pressing problem in Latin America today is reorganizing how collective action can achieve social welfare while respecting and deepening the democratic systems that have managed to gain a precarious foothold in the region. There is a "surplus of politics" that political systems are unable to collect. This is happening in Peru and Brazil, in Chile and Mexico, in El Salvador and Ecuador. For this surplus to be channeled as added value, it needs new structures to be processed. These structures require political innovation, something that goes against the grain of the chronic revisiting of patrimonial and authoritarian characteristics of the past. This repetition has led countries to vacillate between the dominance of local oligarchies and their alliances with developed countries, on the one hand, and populist Caesarism, on the other. The keys to understanding these oscillations are the ebb and flow of "the majorities" and their political organizations, sometimes pulverized or oppressed by military dictatorships, sometimes brought to power by caudillos, strongmen, or populist condottieri, but rarely by the personal and collective empowerment of citizens.

Conceptualizing democracy under the broad idea of democratic governance, and not just as immediate governance, implies, as Axel Hadenius (1992, p. 9) pointed out, that "public policy is to be governed by the freely expressed will of the people whereby all individuals are to be treated as equals". Making this possible in very heterogeneous societies where democracy is precarious and inequality high implies recognizing the need to introduce mixed forms of political representation and open widely receptive channels of collective decision making. The mixed forms of political representation have been discussed in the literature for more than sixty years (Downs, 1957), and the debate around it continues. However, with few exceptions, misunderstanding of the underlying problem predominates in the paradigms of politics, in the programs of political parties, in legislators and magistrates, and not infrequently in academia. There are two opposing tendencies that lead to equally counterproductive extremes. On the one hand, there are the minimalist visions of democracy. Those who subscribe to them believe that democracy begins and ends with the act of electing rulers; that the electoral aspect of democracy is its essential referent and that issues related to the effects and quality of governance should be treated separately because they correspond to a different type of analysis. This view has often been justified on the grounds of "unburdening" democracy of excessive responsibilities, such as the solution of problems of social welfare, income distribution, and others. It is often pointed out that giving democracy the task of solving "all" problems is an excess; rather, the concept needs to be restricted to the idea of free and periodic elections of rulers. The theoretical and political problem that leaves this stance unsolved is that it can easily be contradicted by its opposite. For example, there are those who, inspired by the idea of direct action and government "of the people and for the people", also concomitant with the democratic tradition, would object, alleging that minimalism leads to an aporia, since the inability of the political system to "take charge" of social problems sterilizes it and, worse still, ends up paving the way for "special interests", or the capture of the state, or citizen disaffection with respect to the political system. The maximalism that stems from the latter tends to fall into the excess of making democracy everything and nothing at the same time, which we referred to in chapter 1.

From the theoretical point of view, both perspectives come from different contributions to democratic theory. On the one hand, there are those who, like Montesquieu, have defended the aristocratic notion of democracy in which the containment of the exercise of power (equilibrium) takes precedence over the exercise of sovereignty. Then there are those who, in the tradition of Rousseau (and Marx) (Della Volpe, 1963), propose that, unless democracy leads to the transformation of the class structure, whether in a socialist or similar tradition, it becomes a mere instrument that can be discarded in order to achieve socialism, or, once socialism has been achieved, the democratic system and political representation become dispensable.

The flaw evidenced by this polarization is the lack of conceptualizing of the problems of representative democracy. Maintaining the false dilemma (although no less pernicious when it becomes ideological) between democracy as an elected aristocracy and democracy as one more form of social oppression leads to the tragic result that Robert Dahl refers to: the transition from democracy to oligarchy when "most members of the demos [. . .] fail to undertake the political actions that would be necessary in order to protect and preserve those rights from infringements imposed by political leaders who possess greater resources for gaining their own political ends." (Dahl, 2006, p. 18). The ideological expression of this problem in Latin America can be stated as follows: If democracy does not solve people's problems, there is only one of two alternatives; either it is hegemonized through a Caesarist leadership (the aristocracy of shabby charisma), or it is discarded as an undesirable political system. Or if democracy facilitates the channeling of demands that are unacceptable to the power elites, then it is necessary for them to limit it by building a retaining wall. Commenting on Aristotle's observation that ancient democracies used to impose heavy punishments on the rich and insignificant punishments on the poor for not participating in the assembly, Jon Elster observes, "If one set of individuals can enhance their power by limiting their own freedom, they can also *reduce the power of others by expanding their freedom*" (2000, p. 94 Emphasis in the original).

Evidence suggests that the deep flaw lies in the absence of a robust and mature citizenry and in a structural framework of institutions that act effectively as a vehicle to represent their interests. This problem deserves greater attention that it has so far garnered (Urbinati, 2006). Newly defined democratic representation is the most consistent and realistic way to build and consolidate democracy as a system in which citizens can be involved both through voting and active participation in the public sphere (*supra* Chapter 3). The idea of a political system in which there are only voters, parties, and government becomes somewhat a work of fiction when it ignores the diversity of citizens' public action. Through organizations, movements, opinions, and other methods, citizens have a presence that (more or less) influences (for better or worse) public decisions, and the vital core of this influence is the *ongoing* relationship between representatives and constituents.

What we need to deal with are forms of mediation. Yet representative mediations can be designed and expanded; they admit expansion and innovation. Accountability by representatives to those they represent can be modified by means of appropriate legislation. The influence of citizens on legislative action can be increased without the need for enlightened leaders who avoid accountability and ultimately provoke calamities. All this implies not restricting democratic representation to mere elections, which would lead citizens to withdraw into "private" life between elections. The most developed forms of democratic representation are directly related to an increase in political equality and the extension of rights by binding legal procedures. If citizens can equally approach the polity and have close and frequent relations, and receive greater attention from their representatives (an obligation, based on binding norms), the quality of representation can lead to greater political equality and better conditions for the organization of social life.

Given the heterogeneity of social preferences, an improvement in the quality of representation must also mean a greater mix of public policies and the decision-making variations on which they are based. The literature is highly suggestive in this regard. Mixed political regimes, i.e., those that combine different representative institutions and, among them, those that come closest to pure proportional representation tend to be a melting pot in which the diversity of social preferences is fused, the probability of imposing oligarchic preferences tends to be lower, and public policy is the result of aggregating social preferences in a more complex and cohesive way than in other regimes. The opposite case are simple majority regimes and, especially, presidential systems. The basic reason is that the former produces "multiple winners" (Linz, 1985; 1994; Colomer, 2001, pp. 230–237; Lijphart, 1999, pp. 275–300), while the latter usually accompanies the "winner-take-all" outcome derived from majority rule.

Naturally, the strategic vision of socio-political development as progressive inclusion in representation and democratic action leads to the question of needed fiscal resources and robust structures of representation and public decision-making. Hence, a tax collection policy that strengthens the state and treats citizens as economic equals must obtain the necessary resources, which, at present, implies the establishment of high collection rates, proportional to those of countries that raise market income through distribution, such as Ireland or Greece (see Figure 2.4). Yet, a tax collection policy only makes developmental sense if the resources are actually applied to objectives of gaining universal and quality health and education, among other public goods. Without them, there can be no real options for individual development that convincingly relates "freedom-achievements" of individuals and "welfare-achievements" of the collectivity, a relationship that depends on policies of equality of people in all areas (Sen, 2017, pp. 337–364).

Unfortunately, it is difficult to be optimistic. Public policies aimed at improving social condition in the realms of health to education or science and technology have had little encouraging progress. Fiscal imbalances, the savage capitalism that has been foisted onto international economic policy and, above all, the inability of political elites to set a serious agenda for building a decent future, reveal a lack of adequate guidelines for establishing institutions that can both harbor and encourage the transformation of "low intensity" (O'Donnell) citizens into "high intensity" citizens. Without such institutions dedicated to providing education, culture, and effective procedures to enforce civil and social rights within political frameworks of freedom, neither sustainable economic and social development nor a viable democracy will be possible. In short, these institutions are a basic component of the basket of goods contained in the idea of democratic development or, perhaps, a democratic "income".

We have seen that a democratic and representative regime, as it is today, is unable to impact the state's structural framework. This backwardness means that, despite the existence of basic freedoms and the periodic election of rulers, the representative system is blocked from making broad distributive changes involving fundamental decisions regarding how important public policies are decided (fiscal, educational, labor, or health). So, power relations of the "legitimate order" remain unchanged or armored against democratic politics. It would be wrong to believe that such a vision needs to be approached exclusively from a left-wing perspective. Initially, it probably has that origin, but history demonstrates that this is not necessarily the case.[119] The issue of political development is strategic and can therefore be a reason for political forces with different ideologies to converge, and yet may agree that this factor is a *sine qua non* of the public sphere for "coming to grips with the need to include all people in the process of social decision-making." This is the basic challenge of democracy at the crossroads of the local and global order (Sen, 2017, p. 269), as we noted previously. This alternative depends, however, on the ability of political parties and leaders to understand that the strategic thrust of combining democracy and development, democracy and equality, does not necessarily run parallel to the left-right ideological spectrum. This has been clearly shown by the evolution of advanced capitalist countries and by the historical failure of Caesarism and of totalitarianism, whether from the left or the right.

Thus, the left-right spectrum does not represent the fundamental normative dilemma. The challenge lies in overcoming minimalist reductionism in conceiving democracy and its projections on practical politics, which leads to its limitation by the powers that benefit from its precariousness and, *per contra*, to strengthening it with effective systems of law and inclusive policies while avoiding populism, which is authoritarian by necessity. Within representative democracy, it is a matter of making a real break with the obstacles set up to block its natural tendency to include all citizens in social decision-making.

---

119 Tilly (2007) and Przeworski (2009), among others, analyze democratizing changes in the state that originate in different social groups. Another example of the advancement of social rights are the labor laws in England in the 19th and early 20th centuries that ended with a consensus on accepting a welfare state by all significant economic and political actors.

When representative democracy comes up against a structural obstacle or, better said, collides with the fork that bifurcates it into two paths (oligarchy or populism), we are faced with the obstruction of institutionalizing within the state the agreements that emerge from resolving fundamental conflicts in the regime. This is the gap between the negotiation and resolution of conflicts in the regime and the constitutional norms of the state that do not wholly integrate legitimate demands and enforceable rights. The fork is formed by the invisible barriers of the untouchable, i.e., what no one or almost no one dares name or modify because it must be protected by the elites' implicit and explicit agreements that make democracy a matter of the few (whether oligarchic or populist in nature), and prevent the doors of *inclusion in the exercise of power* from opening, given the weight of political equality. The fork also appears in the cultural rules that reinforce the obstacles to equality. Thanks to this fork in the road, left-wing populisms and radicalisms find fertile ground to plant the seeds of regressive transformations that share the tendency to monopolize power and dismantle or destroy precarious democratic arrangements that are erroneously blamed for economic and social unfairness. The barrier created by this wedge only becomes visible when it acquires full public presence, and the fate of representative democracy is at stake in its demolition. Whatever its versions, representative democracy is the most pliable for achieving equality.

6.8 Summarizing. Democracy as procedure, constitution, and statehood. A theory that is pending

A descriptive theory of the democratization (and de-democratization) of the state and a normative theory of the democratic state are needed. Both would help to distinguish the state more clearly from other forms of domination. The democratic representativeness found in states may be greater than in the past, but not necessarily better regarding the balance between *doxa* and *episteme* or between majority and equality. Citizens have become more involved in the game of power in the political regime, but this has not made the state more democratic or better. In addition to the opinion of the "people" we ought to add other normative requirements to judge (evaluate, assess) the character of the state. This is a work in progress in political science and normative theory although we can find its rudiments in different contributions that have been developed in the third wave of democratization.[120]

---

120 The foundations of this proposal can be found in the work of authors such as Norberto Bobbio, Jürgen Habermas, Charles Tilly, Nadia Urbinati, John Rawls, John Keane and others.

Nevertheless, we can summarize some of the observations that emerge from our analyses.

Democracy is essentially procedural or it is not. In chapter one we alluded to this characteristic of representative democracy. At the close of this book I want to elaborate on this idea because the condition of democratic development lies in the conviction that the unity between what is substantial and what is formal is the product of obtaining substantive benefits by means of procedures. If this is true, the debate about the need for "substantial democracy" rather than "formal democracy" is a false debate. Let me give a simple example: due process. The basic idea is that what we know today as routine legal procedures were originally "substantive" claims. The right to due process is one of the oldest precedents of state obligations (the crown being the origin in this case) to its subjects (starting with the groups with more bargaining power, such as the nobility). Legal history dates the beginnings of due process to the Magna Carta of England (1215–1225), which was one of the first attempts to limit feudalism. Holt records the painful and long trajectory that the "due process of law" underwent between 1215 and 1363, an interval in which internal strife and warfare gave way in 1363 to Parliament transforming the phrase "the law of the land" to "'lawful judgement of peers'" in order to include trial by peers and therefore trial by jury, a process which existed only in embryo in 1215" into "the law of the land". Furthermore, "'law of the land' was defined in terms of yet another potent and durable phrase, 'due process of law', which meant procedure by original writ or by an indicating jury" (Holt, 1965, p. 9 and *passim*). Thus "free men" were protected from being tried by special courts or unauthorized bodies. The concept of the protected subject referred to in "free men" also changed during this period. Originally, the expression "free man" did not refer to all men, but to special categories recognized by law under the system of estates. It was not until 1254 that this principle became inclusive by stipulating that "no free man of whatever estate or condition he may be" would be deprived of due process.

The concrete history of this right arises from the events in which the arbitrariness of the monarchical authority to condemn an individual at will becomes morally inadmissible. As it became a constitutionally accepted norm, it was transformed into a procedure that, once its value had been widely accepted, became a routine application that every authority must comply with and that every moderately informed subject can demand as a right that must be respected under penalty of sanction imposed on the transgressor. We can imagine the documented bloody struggles and the long time that had to pass before the principle was accepted and its value recognized as part of the natural "legitimate order". History repeats itself in other latitudes and processes. Current violations of rights in general, and notably of human rights, are far from being eliminated. They are the world's bread and butter and Latin America stands out as one of the regions in which there is a worrying decline. The demand for "substantial democracy" has arisen above all in people's claims for social, economic, and cultural rights, which require the provision of goods for their enjoyment and not just the state's abstention from providing them, as market fundamentalism demands.

The difference between abstention and provision as actions of the state is not of nature but historical. Abstention arose from the limitation of the ruler's power -as is the case of due process- and the provision of public goods -which implies state action. This is also a limitation of the distributive power of the political community in favor of a standard of equality that some states have achieved by demonstrating that other states can do the same. In a well-developed democratic state, abstention and provision are part of the same procedural repertoire in which the individual or groups of individuals endowed with rights can avail themselves of the constitutional and legal resources at their disposal to avoid the aggressions of power, while obtaining the necessary satisfactions (according to the prevailing notion of a legitimate order) to develop their lives freely and satisfactorily. Unlike the ideological sources to which populism draws upon, democracy understood as a procedure is the idea that respects the democratic diarchy of *judgment and will*, without turning the citizen into a subject under the fictitious unity of "all the people" guided by a leader. Populism is nurtured by the idea of democracy as a search for truth or a hegemonic unity of the people through a charismatic leader who gives, grants, and validates according to his will. In Latin America this drift is the result of an overload of politics on the regime that is indigestible because it is powerless to translate it into statehood and is overtaken, if not swept away, by this overload. This is the same overload that neoliberalism identified in the welfare state and in its defective imitations in developing countries. To counteract it, neoliberalism imposed restrictions in such a way as to make politics impervious to it, leaving it in the hands of the market. Habermas interpreted this process as follows: "The sheer quantity of politics ends up overburdening the legal medium *only if the political process violates the procedural conditions of legitimate lawmaking that are spelled out by constitutional principles; ultimately, this is to violate the democratic procedure for a politically autonomous elaboration of the system of rights.*" (Habermas, 1998, p. 428, emphasis added). If we adapt this formula that stipulates that power be subordinated to law, we can see that when the constitutional system pretends to restrict the legality of politics below the leeway admitted by rights, the result will be the repression of the right in the name of the law.

Constitutionality requires creating and activating procedures that allow the construction of a system of rights demanded by politics and realized democratically. This is necessary to make it possible for representative democracy to acquire the character of statehood, understood as the capacity to update the procedures demanded and created by the *demos* when it is included in *kratia*, in political decision. "The state *is* constitution, in other words, an actually present condition, a *status* of unity and order" states Carl Schmitt in *Constitutional Theory* (2008, p. 60). His static view of constitutional order as "unity" allowed him to assert that constitutions are like "the song or musical piece of a choir [that] *remains the same* if the people singing or performing change or if the place where they perform changes. The unity and order reside in the song and in the score, just as the unity and order of the state reside in its constitution" (Schmitt, 2008, p. 60 emphasis added). In opposition to this totalizing vision, in which populisms and totalitarianisms feed, democracies seek to include members of the demos. The inevitable transformations of the choir and the places of performance of the song call for its modification, for the appearance of a new statehood, a new constitutionality that procedurally guarantees the system of rights without undermining freedom.

References

Achen, C. H. (1978). Measuring representation. *American Journal of Political Science*, 475–510.

Alonso, S., Keane, J., and Merkel, W. (Eds.). (2011). *The future of representative democracy*. Cambridge University Press.

Altman, D. (2010). *Direct Democracy Worldwide*. Cambridge University Press.

Alvarez, M., Cheibub, J. A., Limongi, F., and Przeworski, A. (1996). Classifying political regimes. *Studies in Comparative International Development, 31*, 3–36.

Annino, A., and Guerra, F. X. (2003). *Inventando la nación: Iberoamérica siglo XIX*. Fondo de Cultura Económica.

Ansolabehere, S., Snyder Jr, J. M., and Stewart III, C. (2001). Candidate positioning in US House elections. *American Journal of Political Science*, 136–159.

Ansolabehere, K., Valdés-Ugalde, F. and Vázquez D. (2015). *Entre el Pesimismo y la Esperanza. Los Derechos Humanos en América Latina, Metodología para su Estudio y Medición*. FLACSO México.

Ansolabehere, K., Valdés-Ugalde, F., and Vázquez, D. (2020). *El Estado y los derechos humanos: México, Ecuador y Uruguay*. FLACSO Mexico.

Arat, Z. F. (1991). Democracy and human rights in developing countries. Lynne Rienner Publishers.

Arrow, K. (1970). *Social Choice and Individual Values*. Cowles Foundation Monographs Series.

Axtmann, R. (2004). The state of the state: The model of the modern state and its contemporary transformation. *International Political Science Review, 25*(3), 259–279.

Bafumi, J., and Herron, M. C. (2010). Leapfrog representation and extremism: A study of American voters and their members in Congress. *American Political Science Review, 104*(3), 519–542.

Bartels, L. M. (1991). Constituency opinion and congressional policy making: The Reagan defense buildup. *American Political Science Review, 85*(2), 457–474.

Beetham, D. (1999). *Democracy and human rights*. Polity Press.

Bendix, R. (1977). *Nation-building and citizenship: studies of our changing social order*. New Enlarged Edition. University of California Press.

Berlin, I. (1990). *Four Essays on Liberty*. Oxford.

Bertelsmann Foundation. (2022). Bertelsmann Transformation Index. https://bti-project.org/en/index/political-transformation

Block, F., and Somers, M. R. (2014). *The power of market fundamentalism: Karl Polanyi's critique*. Harvard University Press.

Bobbio, N. (1992). *La Democracia en América Latina*. FCE.

Boix, C., Miller, M. and Rosato S. (2013). A Complete Dataset of Political Regimes, 1800–2007. *Comparative Political Studies*, 46(12), 1523–1554.

Bollen, K. A. (1980). Issues in the comparative measurement of political democracy. *American Sociological Review*, 370–390.

Bollen, K. A. (2001). Indicator: Methodology. In N.J. Smelser and P. B. Baltes (Eds.), *International Encyclopedia of the Social and Behavioral Sciences* (pp. 7282–7287). Elsevier Science.

Brewer-Carias, A. R. (2010). *Dismantling democracy in Venezuela: The Chávez authoritarian experiment*. Cambridge University Press.

Brewer-Carías, A. R. (2011, May 12–14). El Proceso Constituyente y la Constitución Colombiana de 1991 como antecedentes directos del Proceso Constituyente y de Algunas previsiones de la Constitución Venezolana de 1999 [Conference session]. Congreso Internacional de Derecho Constitucional (20 Años de la Constitución de Colombia de 1991). Pontifica Universidad Javeriana, Bogotá, Colombia. https://allanbrewercarias.com/wp-content/uploads/2011/05/1086.-1033.-

https://doi.org/10.1515/9783110773675-008

Brewer.-LA-CONSTITUCION-COLOMBIANA-de-1991-Y-LA-CONSTITUCI%C3%93N-VENEZOLANA-de-1999.-Bogot%C3%A1-Javeriana.pdf

Brinks, D. M., Levitsky, S., and Murillo, M. V. (Eds.). (2020). *The politics of institutional weakness in Latin America*. Cambridge University Press.

Buchanan, J. M., and Tullock, G. (1965). *The calculus of consent: Logical foundations of constitutional democracy* (Vol. 100). University of Michigan Press.

Centro de Estudios Públicos. (1992). *El Ladrillo. Bases de la política económica del gobierno militar chileno*. Santiago.

Cheibub, J. A., Gandhi, J., and Vreeland, J. R. (2010). Democracy and dictatorship revisited. *Public choice, 143*(1–2), 67–101.

Cheibub, J. A., and Limongi, F. (2002). Democratic institutions and regime survival: Parliamentary and presidential democracies reconsidered. *Annual review of political science, 5*(1), 151–179.

Comisión Económica para América Latina y el Caribe (CEPAL). (2019). *Panorama Social de América Latina*, (LC/PUB.2019/22-P/Re v.1). UN.

Comisión Económica para América Latina y el Caribe (CEPAL) (2021). Anuario estadístico de América Latina y el Caribe, 2020.

Comisión Económica para América Latina y el Caribe (CEPAL) (2022, August 1). Total population. https://statistics.cepal.org/portal/cepalstat/index.html

Coatsworth, J. H. (1978). Obstacles to economic growth in nineteenth-century Mexico. *The American Historical Review, 83*(1), 80–100.

Coatsworth, J. H. (1990). *Los orígenes del atraso: nueve ensayos de historia económica de México en los siglos XVIII y XIX*. Alianza Editorial Mexicana.

Collier, D., and Adcock, R. (1999). Democracy and dichotomies: A pragmatic approach to choices about concepts. *Annual review of political science, 2*(1), 537–565.

Collier, R. B., and Collier, D. (1991). *Shaping the Political Arena: Critical Junctures, the Labor Movement, and Regime Dynamics in Latin America*. Princeton University Press.

Colomer, J. M. (2001). *Instituciones Políticas*. Editorial Ariel.

Colomer, J. M., and Negretto, G. L. (2005). Can Presidentialism Work Like Parliamentarism?1. *Government and Opposition, 40*(1), 60–89. https://doi.org/10.1111/j.1477-7053.2005.00143.x

Converse, P. E., and Pierce, R. (1986). *Political representation in France*. Harvard University Press.

Coppedge, M., and Reinicke, W. H. (1990). Measuring polyarchy. *Studies in Comparative International Development, 25*, 51–72.

Coppedge, M., Gerring, J., Altman, D., Bernhard, M., Fish, S., Hicken, A. Hicken, Kroening, M., Lindberg S.I., McMann, K., Paxton, P., Semetko, H. A., Skaaning, S., Staton, J., and Teorell, J. (2011). Conceptualizing and measuring democracy: A new approach. *Perspectives on Politics, 9*(2), 247–267.

Coppedge, M., Gerring, J., Glynn, A., Knutsen, C. H., Lindberg, S. I., Pemstein, D., Seim, B., Skaaning, S., Teorell, J. (2020). *Varieties of Democracy: measuring two centuries of political change*. Cambridge University Press.

Coppedge, M., Gerring J., Knutsen, C.H., Lindberg, S.I., Teorell J., Altman, D., Bernhard, M., Cornell, A., Fish, M. S., Gastaldi, L., Gjerløw, H., Glynn, A., Grahn, S., Hicken, A., Kinzelbach, K., Marquardt, K. L., McMann, K., Mechkova, V., Paxton, P., Pemstein, D., von Römer, J., Seim, B., Sigman, R., Skaaning, S., Staton, J., Tzelgov, E., Uberti, L., Wang, Y., Wig, T., and Ziblatt, D. (2022a). *V-Dem Codebook v12*. Varieties of Democracy (V-Dem) Project.

Coppedge, M., Gerring J., Knutsen, C.H., Lindberg, S.I., Teorell J., Alizada, N., Altman, D., Bernhard, M., Cornell, A., Fish, M. S., Gastaldi, L., Gjerløw, H., Glynn, A., Grahn, S., Hicken, Hindle, G., Ilchenko, N., A., Kinzelbach, Krusel, J., K., Marquardt, K. L., McMann, K., Mechkova, V.,

Medzihorsky, J., Paxton, P., Pemstein, Pernes, J., Rydén, O., D., von Römer, J., Seim, B., Sigman, R., Skaaning, S., Staton, J., Sundström, A., Tzelgov, E., Uberti, L., Wang, Y., Wig, T., and Ziblatt, D. (2022b). V- Dem [Country–Year/Country–Date] Dataset v12 [Data set]. Varieties of Democracy (V-Dem) Project. https://doi.org/10.23696/vdemds22.

Corporación Latinobarometro (2020). Latinobarometro. [Data set]. https://www.latinobarometro.org/latContents.jsp

Crozier, M. J., Huntington, S. P., and Watanuki, J. (1975). The Crisis of Democracy. Report on the Governability of democracies to the Trilateral Commission. *Sociología histórica*. New York University Press.

Cunningham, F. (2002). *Theories of democracy: A critical introduction*. Psychology Press.

Dahl, R. A. (1971). *La Poliarquía*. REI.

Dahl, R. A. (1998). *On Democracy*. Yale University Press.

Dahl, R. A. (2006). *On Political Equality*. Yale University Press.

Dalton, R. J. (1985). Political parties and political representation: Party supporters and party elites in nine nations. *Comparative political studies, 18*(3), 267–299.

De Ferranti, D., Perry, G., Ferreira, F., Walton, M., and Coday, D. (2003). Desigualdad en América Latina y el Caribe: ¿Ruptura con la historia? *Washington DC: Banco Mundial*, 3–40.

Della Volpe, G. (1963). *Rousseau y Marx y otros ensayos de crítica materialista*. Platina.

Diamond, L. (1999). Developing Democracy: Toward Consolidation. Baltimore, MD: Johns Hopkins University Press.

Dixon, R., and Ginsburg, T. (2017). Comparative constitutional law in Latin America: an introduction. In R. Dixon and Ginsburg (Eds.), *Comparative Constitutional Law in Latin America (pp. 11–26)*. Edward Elgar Publishing.

Downs, A. (1957). *An Economic Theory of Democracy*. Harper and Row.

Drake, P. (2009). *Between tyranny and anarchy: A history of democracy in Latin America, 1800–2006*. Stanford University Press.

Dunn, J. (2019). *Setting the People Free*. Princeton University Press.

Elkins, Z. (2000). Gradations of democracy? Empirical tests of alternative conceptualizations. *American Journal of Political Science*, 293–300.

Elkins, Z. (2021). Gradations of democracy? Empirical tests of alternative conceptualizations. *American Journal of Political Science*, 293–300.

Elster, J. (2000). *Ulysses Unbound*. Cambridge University Press.

Engler, S., Leemann L., Abou-Chadi, T., Giebler, H., Bousbah, K., Bochsler, D., Bühlmann, M., Hänni, M., Heyne, L., Juon, A., Merkel, W., Müller, L., Ruth, S., and Wessels, B. (2020). Democracy Barometer. Codebook. Version 7. [Data set]. Aarau: Zentrum der Demokratie. https://democracybarometer.org/data-and-documentation/

Ferrajoli, L. (2014). *La democracia a través de los derechos. El constitucionalismo garantista como modelo teórico y proyecto político*. Trotta.

Flisfisch, Á. (2014). *Ciudadanía Política. Voz y Participación Ciudadana en América Latina*. Siglo XXI, AECID, PNUD.

Freidenberg, F. and Gilas, K. (2022). Conclusiones: las reglas cambian, pero la política sigue igual. In F. Freidenberg (Ed.). *Las reformas a la representación política en América Latina* (1st ed., pp. 503–516). UNAM, Instituto de Investigaciones Jurídicas.

Fukuyama, F. (2008). *Falling Behind: Explaining the Development Gap Between Latin America and the United States*. Reprint edition. Oxford University Press.

Fukuyama, F. (2014). *Political order and political decay: From the industrial revolution to the globalization of democracy*. Farrar, Strauss and Giroux.

Gargarella, R. (2013). *Latin American Constitutionalism 1810–2010. The Engine Room of the Constitution*. Oxford.

Gerber, E. R., and Lewis, J. B. (2004). Beyond the median: Voter preferences, district heterogeneity, and political representation. *Journal of Political Economy, 112*(6), 1364–1383.

Gilas, K. (2022). La personalización del voto y la calidad de la representación política en américa latina. In F. Freidenberg (Ed.), *Las reformas a la representación política en América* Latina (pp.129–158). UNAM, Instituto de Investigaciones Jurídicas.

Gilens, M., and Page, B. I. (2014). Testing theories of American politics: Elites, interest groups, and average citizens. *Perspectives on politics, 12*(3), 564–581.

Granés, C. (2022). *Delirio americano. Una historia cultural y política de América Latina*. Taurus, Penguin Random House Grupo Editorial España.

Guerra, F. X. (Ed.). (1995). *Las revoluciones hispánicas: independencias americanas y liberalismo español* . (Vol. 93). Editorial Complutense.

Gutmann, J., Metelska-Szaniawska, K. and Voigt, S. (2022a). The Comparative Constitutional Compliance Database. *ILE Working Paper Series*, No. 57, University of Hamburg, Institute of Law and Economics (ILE). Hamburg. www.jerg-gutmann.de/data

Gutmann, J., Metelska-Szaniawska, K., Voigt, S. (2022b), The comparative constitutional compliance database [Data set]. https://sites.google.com/site/jerggutmann/data

Habermas, J. (1998). *Between Facts and Norms: Contributions to a Discourse Theory of Law and Democracy (Studies in Contemporary German Social Thought)*. MIT Press.

Habermas, J. (1999). *Inclusion of the Other*. Polity Press.

Hadenius, A. (1992). *Democracy and development*. Cambridge University Press.

Hadenius, A., and Teorell, J. (2005). Cultural and economic prerequisites of democracy: Reassessing recent evidence. *Studies in comparative international development, 39*(4), 87–106.

Hampton, J. (1986). *Hobbes and the Social Contract Tradition*. Cambridge University Press.

Hampton, J. (1994). Democracy and the Rule of Law. In Shapiro (ed.): *The Rule of Law*. New York University Press.

Hampton, J. (1998). *Political Philosophy*. West View Press.

Hart, H. L. A. (1998). *The Concept of Law*. Oxford University Press.

Held, D. (2006). *Models of democracy*. Stanford University Press.

Holt, J. C. (1965). *Magna Carta*. Cambridge University Press.

Htun, M. (2016). *Inclusion without Representation in Latin America: Gender Quotas and Ethnic Reservations*. Cambridge University Press.

Human Rights Watch (2008). *World Report. HRW*. https://www.hrw.org/sites/default/files/reports/wr2k8_web.pdf

Huntington, S. P. (1993). *The third wave: Democratization in the late twentieth century* . (Vol. 4). University of Oklahoma Press.

Inglehart, R., Haerpfer, C., Moreno, A., Welzel, C., Kizilova, K., Diez-Medrano, J, Lagos, M., Norris, P., Ponarin, E. and Puranen, B. (eds.). (2014). World Values Survey: Round Six –[Data set]. www.worldvaluessurvey.org/WVSDocumentationWV6.jsp.

International Institute for Democracy and Electoral Assistance (IDEA). (2017). *The Global State of Democracy: Exploring Democracy's Resilience*. International IDEA.

Ishay, M. (2008). *The History of Human Rights*. University of California Press.

Iversen, T. (1994a). Political leadership and representation in West European democracies: A test of three models of voting. *American Journal of Political Science*, 45–74.

Iversen, T. (1994b). The logics of electoral politics: Spatial, directional, and mobilizational effects. *Comparative Political Studies, 27*(2), 155–189.

Judt, T. (2006). *Postwar. A History of Europe Since 1945*. Penguin.

Kapiszewski, D., Levitsky, S., and Yashar, D. J. (Eds.). (2021). *The inclusionary turn in Latin American democracies*. Cambridge University Press.

Kaufmann, D., Kraay, A. and Mastruzzi, M. (2010). *The Worldwide Governance Indicators. Methodology and Analytical Issues* (World Bank Policy Research Working Paper 5430). http://hdl.handle.net/10986/3913

Kaufmann, D., Kraay, A. and Mastruzzi, M. (2022). *The Worldwide Governance Indicators*. [Data set]. https://info.worldbank.org/governance/wgi/Home/Reports

Keane, J. (2009). *The Life and Death of Democracy*. Simon and Schuster.

Knutsen, C. H. (2010). Measuring effective democracy. International Political Science Review, 31(2), 109–128.

Lagos, R., Castañeda J., and Aguilar H. (2022). *La nueva Soledad de América Latina. Una Conversación*. Debate, Penguin Random House.

Lane, J. E. (1996). *Constitutions and Political Theory*. Manchester University Press.

Lax, J. R., and Phillips, J. H. (2009). Gay rights in the states: Public opinion and policy responsiveness. *American Political Science Review, 103*(3), 367–386.

Lefort, C. (1991). *Democracy and Political Theory*. Wiley.

Lijphart, A. (1999). *Patterns of Democracy. Government Forms and Performance in Thirty-Six Countries*. Yale University Press.

Lindberg, S. I., Coppedge, M., Gerring, J., and Teorell, J. (2014). V-Dem: A new way to measure democracy. *Journal of Democracy, 25*(3), 159–169.

Linz, J. J. (1985). Democracy: Presidential or Parliamentary. Does it Make a Difference? Manuscript. Retrieved from https://davelevy.info/wiki/wp-content/uploads/2016/08/Linz-Presidentialism-sansserif.pdf

Linz, J. J. (1985). Democracy: Presidential or Parliamentary. Does it Make a Difference?" Manuscript. Paper prepared for the project, "The Role of Political Parties in the Return to Democracy in the Southern Cone," sponsored by the Latin American Program of the Woodrow Wilson International Center for Scholars, and the World Peace Foundation.

Linz, J. J. (1994). Democracy: Presidential or parliamentary democracy: Does it make a difference?" in Linz, Juan and Arturo Valenzuela (Eds.) 1994. *The Failure of Presidential Democracy. The Case of Latin América*. Volume 2. The Johns Hopkins University Press.

Linz, J. J., Linz, J. J., and Stepan, A. (1996). *Problems of democratic transition and consolidation: Southern Europe, South America, and post-communist Europe*. Johns Hopkins University Press.

Linz, J. J., and Valenzuela, A. (Eds.). (1994). *The failure of presidential democracy . The Case of Latin América* (Vol. 2). The Johns Hopkins University Press.

Looney, R. E. (Ed.). (2018). *Handbook of International Trade Agreements: Country, regional and global approaches*. Routledge.

Lührmann, A., and Lindberg, S. I. (2019). A third wave of autocratization is here: what is new about it? *Democratization, 26*(7), 1095–1113.

Lührmann, A., Lindberg, S. I., and Tannenberg, M. (May, 2017). *Regimes in the world (RIW): A robust regime type measure based on V-Dem*. (V-Dem Working Paper, 47). https://papers.ssrn.com/sol3/papers.cfm?abstract_id=2971869

Lührmann, A., Maerz, S. F., Grahn, S., Alizada, N., Gastaldi, L., Hellmeier, S., Hindle, G. and Lindberg, S.I. (2020). Autocratization Surges – Resistance Grows. Democracy Report 2020. Varieties of Democracy Institute (V-Dem). https://www.v-dem.net/documents/14/dr_2020_dqumD5e.pdf

Luna, J. P., and Zechmeister, E. J. (2005). Political representation in Latin America: a study of elite-mass congruence in nine countries. *Comparative political studies, 38*(4), 388–416.

Mainwaring, S., and Pérez-Liñán, A. (2013). *Democracies and dictatorships in Latin America: emergence, survival, and fall*. Cambridge University Press.

Manin, B. (1997). The Principles of Representative Government. Cambridge University Press.

Mansbridge, J. (2003). Rethinking representation. *American political science review, 97*(4), 515–528.

Marshall, T. H. (1950). *Citizenship and Social Class and Other Essays*. Cambridge university Press.

Marshall, T. H., and Bottomore, T. B. (1992). Citizenship and social class (Vol. 2). Pluto Press.

Marván, M. (2022). Hay reformas electorales que no perfeccionan la democracia. In F. Freidenberg (Ed.), *Las reformas a la representación política en América Latina*. UNAM, Instituto de Investigaciones Jurídicas.

Mattoo, A., Rocha, N., and Ruta, M. (Eds.). (2020). Handbook of deep trade agreements. World Bank Publications.

Mazzuca, S. L. (2010). Access to power versus exercise of power reconceptualizing the quality of democracy in Latin America. *Studies in Comparative International Development, 45*, 334–357.

Mazzuca, S. L., and Munck, G. L. (2014). State or democracy first? Alternative perspectives on the state-democracy nexus. *Democratization, 21*(7), 1221–1243.

Mazzuca, S. L., and Munck, G. L. (2020). *A Middle-Quality Institutional Trap: Democracy and State Capacity in Latin America*. Cambridge University Press.

Mazzuca, S. L. (2021) *Latecomer State Formation: Political Geography and Capacity Failure in Latin America*. Yale University Press.

Milanovic, B. (2019). Capitalism, alone. Harvard University Press.

Moller, J., and Skaaning, S. E. (2013). *Democracy and Democratization in Comparative Perspective: Conceptions, Conjunctures, Causes, and Consequences*. Routledge.

Munck, G. L. (2011). La medición de la democracia: enmarcando un debate necesario. *Revista Latinoamericana de Política Comparada. 1*(4), 11–21.

Munck, G. L. (2016). What is democracy? A reconceptualization of the quality of democracy. *Democratization, 23*(1), 1–26.

Munck, G. L., and Verkuilen, J. (2002). Conceptualizing and measuring democracy: Evaluating alternative indices. *Comparative political studies, 35*(1), 5–34.

Narva, Á. (2020). Nadia Urbinati 'Me the people: how populism transforms democracy', Harvard University Press, Massachusetts, Cambridge, 2019. 272 páginas. ISBN: 9780674240889. *Foro interno, 20*, 93.

Negretto, G. L. (2013). *Making constitutions: presidents, parties, and institutional choice in Latin America*. Cambridge University Press.

Negretto, G. L. (2018). La reforma del presidencialismo en América Latina hacia un modelo híbrido. *Revista Uruguaya de Ciencia Política, 27*(1), 131–151.

Negretto, G. L., and Sánchez-Talanquer, M. (2021). Constitutional origins and liberal democracy: a global analysis, 1900–2015. *American Political Science Review, 115*(2), 522–536.

North, D. C. (1981). *Structure and Change in Economic History*. Norton.

North, D. C. (1982). *Structure and Change in Economic History*. W.W. Norton And Company.

North, D. C., and Thomas, R. P. (1973). *The rise of the western world: A new economic history*. Cambridge University Press.

North, D. C., Wallis, J. J., and Weingast, B. R. (2009). *Violence and social orders: A conceptual framework for interpreting recorded human history*. Cambridge University Press.

O'Donnell, G., Schmitter, P.C., Witehead, L. (1986). *Transitions from Authoritarian Rule*. Johns Hopkins University Press.

O'Donnell, G. (1993). On the state, democratization and some conceptual problems: A Latin American view with glances at some postcommunist countries. *World Development, 21*(8), 1355–1369.

O'Donnell, G. (1994). Delegative democracy. *Journal of democracy, 5*(1), 55–69.

O'Donnell, G. (2010). *Democracy, agency, and the state: theory with comparative intent.* Oxford University Press.

O'Donnell, G., Cullell, J. V., and Iazzetta, O. M. (Eds.) (2004). The Quality of Democracy: Theory and Applications. University of Notre Dame Press.

Organización para la Cooperación y el Desarrollo Económicos (OECD) (2016). Income Distribution Database. https://stats.oecd.org/Index.aspx?DataSetCode=IDD

Organización para la Cooperación y el Desarrollo Económicos (OECD) (2018). Tax revenue share gdp. https://ourworldindata.org/grapher/tax-revenue-share-gdp-oecd-grsd?tab=table&country=Latin+America+and+the+Caribbean~Africa~OECD+-+Average

Organización para la Cooperación y el Desarrollo Económicos (OECD) (2022). Social Expenditure Databse (SOCX). [Data set]. https://www.oecd.org/social/expenditure.htm

Our World in Data (OWID) and Herre, B. (2023). Regimes of the world. Based on the criteria of the classification by Lührmann et al. (2018) and the assessment by V-Dem's Experts. [Data set]. https://ourworldindata.org/grapher/political-regime

Page, B., and Shapiro, R. (1983). Effects of Public Opinion on Policy. *The American Political Science Review, 77*(1), 175–190. doi:10.2307/1956018.

Pemstein, D., Meserve, S. A., and Melton, J. (2010). Democratic compromise: A latent variable analysis of ten measures of regime type. *Political Analysis, 18*(4), 426–449.

Pinto, Á., and Flisfisch, Á. (2011). *El Estado de Ciudadanía: transformaciones, logros y desafíos del Estado en América Latina en el siglo XXI.* Sudamericana.

Pitkin, H. F. (1967). *The concept of representation* (Vol. 75). University of California Press.

Programa de las Naciones Unidas para el Desarrollo (PNUD) (2004). *La democracia en América Latina. Hacia una democracia de ciudadanas y ciudadanos.* Aguilar, Altea, Taurus, Alfaguara, S.A.

Programa de las Naciones Unidas para el Desarrollo (PNUD) (2010). *Nuestra Democracia.* Fondo de Cultura Económica.

Polanyi, K. (1957 [1944]). *The Great Transformation. The Political and Economic Origins of our Time.* Deacon Press.

Powell, G. B. (1982). *Contemporary democracies.* Harvard University Press.

Powell, C. T. (1989). *Reform versus ruptura in Spain's transition to democracy* (Doctoral dissertation, University of Oxford). https://ethos.bl.uk/OrderDetails.do?uin=uk.bl.ethos.303588

Przeworski, A. (2009). Conquered or granted? A history of suffrage extensions. *British Journal of Political Science, 39*(2), 291–321.

Przeworski, A. (2019). *Crises of Democracy.* Cambridge University Press.

Przeworski, A., Alvarez, M., Cheibub, J. A., and Limongi, F. (1996). What makes democracies endure? *Journal of democracy, 7*(1).

Przeworski, A., Alvarez, R. M., Alvarez, M. E., Cheibub, J. A., and Limongi, F. (2000). *Democracy and development: Political institutions and well-being in the world, 1950–1990* (Vol. 3). Cambridge University Press.

Przeworski, A., Stokes, S. C., and Manin, B. (Eds.). (1999). *Democracy, accountability, and representation* (Vol. 2). Cambridge University Press.

Ranney, A. (1962). *Essays on the behavioral study of politics.* University of Illinois Press.

Roberts, K. M. (2021). The Inclusionary Turn and Its Political Limitations. In D. Kapiszewski, Levitsky, S., Yashar, D. J. *The Inclusionary Turn in Latin American Democracies.* Cambridge University Press.

Rosanvallon, P. (2018). *Good Government. Democracy Beyond Elections.* Harvard University Press.

Roser, M. and Ortiz-Ospina, E. (2022, November 23) – "Income Inequality". https://ourworldindata.org/income-inequality

Saavedra, C. (2022). Reformas electorales y democracia en américa latina (1977–2019). In F. Freidenberg (Ed.), *Las reformas a la representación política en América Latina* (pp. *35–58).* UNAM, Instituto de Investigaciones Jurídicas.

Salmorán, G. (2022). Las consultas populares en manos de las presidencias en la américa latina del siglo XXI. In F. Freidenberg (Ed.), *Las reformas a la representación política en América Latina* (pp.93–126). UNAM, Instituto de Investigaciones Jurídicas.

Sartori, G. (1987). *The theory of democracy revisited* (Vol. 1). Chatham House Pub.

Sartori, G. (1994). *Constitutional comparative Engineering. An Inquiry into Structures, Incentives and Outcomes.* New York University Press.

Sartori, G. (1999). En defensa de la representación política. *Claves de razón práctica, 91,* 2–6.

Sartori, G. (2005). *Parties and Party Systems. A Framework for Analysis.* Oxford, European Consortium of Political Research.

Saward, M. (1994). Democratic theory and indices of democratization. Sage Modern Politics Series, *36,* 6–6.

Saward, M. (2006). The Representative Claim. *Contemporary Political Theory* 5(3): 297–318.

Schmitt, C. (2008). *Constitutional Theory.* Duke University Press.

Schmitt, H. and Thomassen, J. (1999). Issue congruence. *Political representation and legitimacy in the European Union,* 186–208.

Schmitter, P. C., and Karl, T. L. (1991). What democracy is . . . and is not. *Journal of democracy, 2*(3), 75–88.

Schumpeter, J. A. (1992). *Capitalism, Socialism and Democracy.* London and New York: Routledge; first published 1942.

Sen, A. (2017). *Collective choice and social welfare.* Expanded edition. Harvard University Press.

Shapiro, I. (Ed.). (1994). *The Rule of law* (Vol. 23). NYU Press.

Sigman, R., and Lindberg, S. I. (2015). The Index of Egalitarian Democracy and Its Components: V-Dem's Conceptualization and Measurement (*V-Dem Working Paper,22*), . https://v-dem.net/media/publications/v-dem_working_paper_2015_22.pdf

Skaaning, Svend-Erik, John Gerring, and Henrikas Bartusevičius. (2015). A Lexical Index of Electoral Democracy. *Comparative Political Studies,* 48(12), 1491–1525.

Soifer, H. D. (2015) *State building in Latin America.* Cambridge University Press.

National Consortium for the Study of Terrorism and Responses to Terrorism (START) (2022). Global Terrorism Database [Data set]. National Consortium for the Study of Terrorism and Responses to Terrorism (START). https://ourworldindata.org/grapher/terrorist-incidents?country=South+America~North+America~Central+America+%26+Caribbean

Center of Distributive, Labor and Social Studies (CEDLAS). (2018). Gini Index. Socio-Economic Database for Latin America and the Caribbean (SEDLAC). [Data set]. https://ourworldindata.org/grapher/income-inequality-in-latin-america

Stiglitz, J. E. (2018). *Globalization and Its Discontents Revisited: Anti-Globalization in the Era of Trump.* W. W. Norton & Company.

Stimson, J. A. (1991). *Public opinion in America: Moods, cycles, and swings, transforming* American politics.

Stimson, J. A., MacKuen, M. B., and Erikson, R. S. (1995). Dynamic representation. *American political science review, 89*(3), 543–565.

Tarski, A. (1983). *Logic, Semantics, Meta-Mathematics.* Hackett Publishing Company.

Tilly, C. (1992). *Coercion, capital, and European states, AD 990–1992* (p. 70). Blackwell.

Tilly, C. (1998). Where Do Rights Come From? Skocpol.

Tilly, C. (2007). *Democracy*. Cambridge University Press.

The Economist. (2009, February 14). A special poll on middle-class attitudes. The Economist. https://www.economist.com/special-report/2009/02/14/what-do-you-think

Urbinati, N. (2006). *Representative democracy: principles and genealogy*. University of Chicago Press.

Urbinati, N. (2011). Representative democracy and its critics. In S. Alonso, J. Keane, and W. Merkel (Eds.) *The Future of Representative Democracy* (pp. 23–50). Cambridge University Press.

Urbinati, N. (2014). *Democracy Disfigured. Opinion, Truth and the People*. Harvard University Press.

Urbinati, N. (2019a). *Me the People. How Populism Transforms Democracy*. Harvard University Press.

Urbinati, N. (2019b). Political theory of populism.*Annual review of political science, 22*, 111–127.

Urbinati, N., and Warren, M. E. (2008). The concept of representation in contemporary democratic theory. *Annual Review Political Science, 11*, 387–412.

Valdés-Ugalde, F. (2008). Gobernanza e instituciones. Propuestas para una agenda de investigación. *Perfiles Latinoamericanos*, 16(31), 95–119.

Valdés-Ugalde, F. (2010). *La regla ausente: democracia y conflicto constitucional en México*. Gedisa, FLACSO México, UNAM.

Valdés-Ugalde, F. (2023). *Ensayo para después del naufragio. Democracia, derechos y Estado en los tiempos de la ira*. México: Debate.

Valdés-Ugalde, F. and Ansolabehere K., (2012). Panorama Político. Conflicto constitucional en América Latina: entre la inclusión y el cinismo. In M. Puchet, M. Rojas, R. Salazar, F. Valdés-Ugalde and G. Valenti (Eds.), *América Latina en los albores del siglo XXI. 2. Aspectos Sociales y Políticos* (pp. 235–259). FLACSO México.

Valdés-Ugalde, F., and Salazar-Elena, R. (2015). Igualdad política. ¿Cómo medirla? Elaboraciones sobre el esquema de Dahl. In K. Ansolabehere, F. Valdés-Ugalde, D. Vázquez (Eds.) *Entre el pesimismo y la esperanza. Los derechos Humanos en América Latina. Metodología para su estudio y medición* (pp. 117–138). FLACSO México.

Vanhanen, T. (1990). *The process of democratization: A comparative study of 147 states, 1980–1988*. Crane-Russak.

Vanhanen, T. (1997). *Prospects of democracy: A study of 172 countries*. Psychology Press.

Vanhanen, T. (2000) The Polyarchy dataset. [Data set]. https://www.prio.org/data/20

Voigt, S. (1999). *Explaining Constitutional Change*. Edward Elgar.

Von Beyme, K. (2011). Representative democracy and the populist temptation. In S. Alonso, J. Keane and W. Merkel (Eds.), *The Future of Representative Democracy* (pp. 50–73*)*. Cambridge University Press.

Weber, M. (2004). *The Vocation Lectures*. Hackett Publishing Co.

Weber, M. (2013). *Economy and Society*. Edited by Guenther Roth and Claus Wittich. University of California.

Welp, Y. (2022). *The Will of the People. Populism and Citizen Participation in Latin America*. De Gruyter.

World Bank. (2022, May 18). Gini Index. https://datos.bancomundial.org/indicador/SI.POV.GINI?end=2020&locations=BR-MX&start=2020&view=bar

World Justice Project (WJP) (2021). *Rule of Law Index 2021*. [Data set]. World Justice Project.

Worlwide Governance Indicators (WGI). (2022, December 23). *Documentation*. https://info.worldbank.org/governance/wgi/Home/Documents

Zakaria, F. (1997). The rise of illiberal democracy. *Foreign Aff., 76*, 22.